To Have
and To Hold

Jenny Cozens is a Chartered Clinical Psychologist and researcher at the University of Leeds. She has columns in *Good Housekeeping* and the *Yorkshire Post*. A regular consultant for national newspapers, radio and television, she has been married for twenty-six years and has two sons.

To Have and To Hold

Men, Sex and Marriage

Jenny Cozens

PAN BOOKS

First published 1995 by Pan Books

an imprint of Macmillan General Books
Cavaye Place London SW10 9PG
and Basingstoke

Associated companies throughout the world

ISBN 0 330 33252 X

1 3 5 7 9 8 6 4 2

A CIP catalogue record for this book is available from
the British Library

Typeset by CentraCet Limited, Cambridge
Printed and bound in Great Britain by
Cox & Wyman Ltd, Reading, Berkshire

To Tony, Rob and Ben

Acknowledgements

Many people have contributed towards the ideas that have been put together in this book. In particular my thanks goes to: friends and colleagues, especially Clare Venables, Laurann Yen, Chris Brewin and Louise Ricklander, for witty and wise conversations; to Dr Bob Hobson for all he taught me in psychotherapy; to my husband for his support; to Catherine Hurley of Macmillan, for the tricky questions she asked; to Joanne Greenhalgh for her trips to the library; and most of all to the men and women whose descriptions of dilemmas and difficulties in marriage provided early on the thoughts that led eventually to this book.

Contents

Preface

This is a book about men and women, and the relationships between them. Love and marriage are as popular as ever, but the growing divorce rate shows that they are not always accompanied by the happiness that we've been taught to expect. This book is concerned primarily with how things go wrong in these relationships, on the premise that understanding the causes of problems puts you half way towards solving them. More than this, an insight into the reasons behind the problems might stop them starting in the first place, whether in ourselves or in our children.

Although I consider both men and women throughout the book, it is the psychology of men and the effects of this on their longterm relationships that is my primary focus. Long aisles in bookshops are filled with works on women, and recently they've been joined by a growing number of books on men, primarily written by men for men. Women want to understand men, too. In fact, apart from the few who totally condemn men, the primary preoccupation of large numbers of women might be seen as a quest to learn what is happening in their partners' minds: 'My wife doesn't understand me', might be true, but it's not for want of trying. So this book focuses on men, but is for both men and women, looking at how they are taught to be masculine and feminine, the psychological events that happen on the way, and how this path affects adult relations between them.

I know it's pretty risky for a woman to talk about men and

their behaviour in such an intimate way, especially as it's bound to feel at times that I am being critical and even biased in my views of the ways they relate to women. I can only say in my defence that my clinical and counselling work has made me realize just how unhappy apparently strong and forceful men can be (and how distressed their wives are too), and that it's this rather than any urge to frown on them that has prompted me to write the book. Although many of the quotes I use describe men who are behaving pretty badly, there are also examples from clinical work about the ways that men are facing their problems and dealing with them with courage. The fact that I have been married for quite a long time and have two adult sons and many male friends helps me to stay very fond of men and simply to wish them well. In addition, I try to point out, wherever it happens, the woman's role in maintaining her husband's behaviour.

The ideas in the book come from various research interests that have developed over the years I've been an academic psychologist, and from applying these in my clinical work with individuals, with couples, and in my advice columns, in order to understand better what goes wrong in marriage. The two areas that have intrigued me most are, first, the ways our early experiences affect how we behave as adults, in particular how we relate to those around us both at home and at work; and, second, the ways we allocate blame for what goes wrong in our lives.

The people's stories and letters that illustrate the book are all real, but changed or sometimes combined to assure anonymity. Using case studies and agony letters inevitably biases my evidence towards unhappy or failing marriages, and that's certainly a main theme within the book. However, it also allows those of you whose marriages are feeling fine to understand what can go wrong and why. No marriage is entirely stable: it reacts to changes in the world around, and to those within the individual man and woman. Each partner brings to the marriage an undercurrent from their early experience which can reappear in new situations, and so even the happiest couple at times can feel like strangers. This can happen whether you are in an old established partnership with more traditional ways of living, or in a young and modern relationship where each partner is determined on equality. Prevention is undoubtedly much better than cure, not just in physical health but in relationship difficulties as well, and understanding the dynamics that both of you have brought to the relationship is the best prophylactic I know.

Because much of the book talks about the development of masculinity – the way the mythic Real Man is created – and how this affects marriage, homosexuality is not within its focus, though inevitably the fear of not being a Real Man is very much linked to homophobia, or a fear of the woman in man.

Finally, I must point out that, although this isn't really an advice book, the implications for couples of how to change what's happening to them are writ suitably large. Gaining insight into the ways that our early experience affects how we act and react as adults is the basis of most psychotherapies, and an important step in stopping destructive patterns of living. Some people find that the 'Aha!' they experience, when they can see at last what is happening and why, is enough in itself to bring about change. In addition to the explanations, the book also contains some exercises to help readers understand more about themselves and their relationships.

And every now and again, being a woman and so trying to keep you attached to me by making things better, I do throw in the odd titbit (and even an occasional chapter) of out-and-out advice.

The Organization of the Book

IN PART ONE of the book I offer a theory, developed from various other theories and from research, and support it using psychological case studies and letters as evidence. It describes why men behave as men, women as women, and what happens when they come together; what goes wrong in marriage, and why. Part two deals with the practice – the myths and collusions of marriage, the madnesses that keep both partners painfully stuck – and what happens when the myths they've lived by finally become transparently false. The last chapter describes various agendas that might help to bring about change in terms of male–female relationships – agendas for men, women, couples and parents.

If you are not too fond of theory or if you want help and understanding now, today, then feel free simply to read the bare bones of part one, which I've set out in the box opposite, and head straight for part two. You can always return to the background explanations of the problems later.

Jenny Cozens
May 1994

The Bare Bones

• The deepest fear with which all of us are born, and only to some extent learn to control, is of abandonment. Women in particular retain this fear all their lives, which makes relationships central to them and might keep them in unhappy marriages longer than perhaps is healthy for them.

• Although men and women are anatomically different, gender – the idea of yourself as a man or as a woman – is learned, starting at birth and reinforced throughout our young lives. An important step in this occurs for boys at about the age of two, when they notice the physical and social differences between men and women and, to a greater or lesser degree, decide to be a male. To do this they have to 'leave' mum and join dad. At this point, but growing over the next two decades, their simple fear of abandonment becomes instead a fear of abandonment for not being male.

• Because of this, the relatively small biological differences between men and women are exaggerated and developed to support the man's image of himself as, above all, not woman. Although research makes it clear that there are much greater differences within each sex than there are between them, these exaggerations of difference are maintained by both men and women and reinforced by society in a number of ways.

• Within marriage, the man's need to prove himself a Real Man beyond all else means he is more likely to continue in stereotypically male behaviours – often ones that hurt both partners – while the woman's fear of abandonment helps to make her stay with her husband and often to take most of the blame, and most of the responsibility for improving things. This stops anything changing for either of them in ways that would help.

Around this central core of a theory other theories are fitted, explaining such characteristics as men's competitiveness, their need for recognition, misogyny, sexual problems, fathering and mothering.

Chapter one of the book sets the scene for why this is crucially relevant now. It describes this as a period in which men are under particular threats which are to do with their definition of themselves as masculine (primarily in terms of being not feminine) – threats caused by the increasing power of women, by the rise in unemployment, and by physiological assaults on their sexuality. The theory is offered to make sense of why these are threats and the strategies men use to deflect them – ones that are often harmful to them and to their partners.

Chapter 1

All Change?

Adam and Lilith [his first wife] never found peace together; for when he wished to lie with her, she took offence at the recumbent posture he demanded.

'Why must I lie beneath you?' she asked. 'I also was made from dust, and am therefore your equal.'

But Adam tried to make her obedient to him by force. And Lilith, in a rage, uttered the magic name of God, rose into the air and left him.

Numera Rabba (ancient Jewish commentary on the scriptures)

MARRIAGE SHOULD be made in heaven, and weddings should be fairytale. Bells will chime, rings encircle, confetti fall, and the cake sits waiting, all frosty and white. Its tiers narrow as they rise towards the top while there on its summit, locked together in eternity, stand the model groom and his bride, safe from all temptation. Travel away from them over the icy landscape and you come to a circle of small silver horseshoes. Horseshoes for luck. Whatever else happens to these two who are now a couple, luck it seems, could be a useful ingredient for a long and happy marriage.

But that's the only hint in the whole affair that anything could possibly go wrong. Fairytales end with the wedding, they say little about what comes next. We're left only with the notion of living happily ever after, but given little advice on how to do it. Nevertheless, the idea of ever-lasting happiness

1

is alluring and so the modern picture of marriage as loving and comfortable has changed very little over the century. Back in the fifties we had adverts of the Ovaltine family showing dad with his pipe and paper and mum in her flowery pinny. They were smiling at each other and you knew they were as one. Today we see the Oxo-cube couple: there's more activity, a little sexual innuendo, and mum is giving quip for quip as good as she gets. But she's still there waiting on hubby, making things nice for everyone. Although dad's kind and fair you know that, in the end, what he says goes. Nostalgia, it seems, is just what it used to be.

And yet this view of marriage and the family is miles away from the experiences that many of us have had, either as children or as adults. We still have a dream of a marriage and a dream of a family, and we still marry in order to fulfil them. Despite predictions about liberalism and mobility causing its inevitable demise, men and women are marrying more than ever. Almost everyone does it at least once: for better or, increasingly frequently, for worse, since almost half are ending in divorce and many more report themselves unhappy but never come to court.

When people go on doing things which logic suggests they might cease, and it continues all over the world, then you get a clue that they are doing it for psychological reasons – because it's a need, something that's felt so strongly at times that it's almost physical. Such a strong need to attach yourself to another, some psychologists would say, is done in order to make up for inadequate attachments in early life: the more inadequate, the more we'll yearn for the dream relationship as adults. Others suggest that unconsciously we choose a partner who will be most likely to help us remedy early difficulties. These reasons and others are discussed throughout the book, clues as to the mystery of why we keep on marrying – despite the widening odds on its being a success, despite the pain, emptiness and confusion it often seems to bring. Such feelings are the stuff of countless novels, Victorian and modern – the way two people seem unable to come together in a relationship, can pass by without knowing how to touch in any sense at all. And it's the theme of many letters I receive. For example:

I don't know what he wants, what he thinks, anything about him – not even after seven years of marriage. He turns a brick wall to me every time we're together, and in bed he just turns away. His replies to my attempts to start conversations are simply grunts. He tells me to initiate sex, but when I do, he says he doesn't want it. I'm still trying, but he makes me so angry – I don't know how long I'll bother.

Nowadays, at least 70 per cent of divorce petitions are brought by women. This statistic might come about because their partners are behaving less well than they did once, or maybe the women are just that much less patient than their men. Certainly it's clear that both partners are rather less tolerant of disappointment than they used to be, helped along by liberal divorce laws which make falling out of love sufficient grounds to leave. The hopes on which second unions are built are even greater than the first time round, and their chances of survival even less. Maybe they expect more, maybe they get less. Perhaps marriage has become an oasis of hope in a desert of modern living, an Elastoplast for the wounds of the world. Whatever the reasons, the luck of the horseshoes is not enough to ward off disappointment. Nor, it seems, is love.

We're told by the pundits that the growing divorce rate is inevitable: it's simply the result of our increasing longevity which has made the length of a single life commitment quite impossibly long. People change drastically over the course of forty to fifty years, so the argument goes, and we cannot think that they will continue to suit each other until death do them part. I find this argument quite illogical. If people can change over a lifetime, then that should be a real benefit to marriage, not a blot on it. If we can change enough to cause problems, then surely this means we should be able to adapt sufficiently to heal them too?

And yet, although this is a century of frightening turmoil, novelty and change – in science, in organizations and reorgan- izations, and through the consequences of mobility and the shrinking of community – men and women, particularly men, have barely changed at all. Men introduce change in their surroundings and in the lives of others, but internally they cannot grasp it for themselves. They introduce it, I suspect, because of their own unhappiness, hoping that altering something external to themselves will make things feel better deep down: if I just have that sort of car, restructure the organization in that sort of way, turn national services topsy-turvy, have a particular sort of sex with this sort of woman, buy that type of desk, mobile phone, motorway, whatever – then my life will be OK. Wonderful even. They tinker with the environment, terrified to tamper with their selves.

Women are part of that environment. They too might not be all that keen on change, but they are infinitely more adaptable because they've had to be. For centuries, and still today, they have contorted their bodies, their minds and their behaviour to fit in with men. It sounds dreadful – to change according to fashion, according to the whims of the current man – but at least it's given them the skill to make themselves different. Over the last thirty years in particular, they've begun to adapt not just for men, but for themselves; not just to be chameleons, but to stand out from the crowd. Part of their wish to divorce must stem from these urges. Yes, legislation has made things easier, but also women are starting to say enough's enough. Not that most of them don't want to try again, they do: but not with the same man, thank you very much.

Of course, this new impatience matches everything else in our society. 'If it doesn't work, throw it away and buy another' has been the message of capitalism for the last fifty years. In a soundbite society, we want it all, now, at once, briefly. We move on when interest starts to wane. We pick away at snacks, rather than constructing and enjoying a good substantial meal. We flick channels to find something that tempts us more. Our concentration span is now so brief, it's hardly surprising that our abilities to last the course of marriage are declining. But more than simple impatience, the door has now been opened, just a chink, for women to glimpse a new way of living. They can see the light, and it shines on a marriage that isn't always the way they'd wanted it. They can see the world outside, and although most of them still want to make their partnerships into the ones they'd dreamed of, and struggle to bring this about, others, like Lilith in the epigraph, are off.

First Prize for the Man in the Grey Suit

I T SEEMS no time ago that men had it all. Even when I was at school we learnt to recite Kipling's poem 'If' and believed with utter certainty his promise that, if you did all the right things, followed to the letter the list of virile activities that he suggested, then you could be sure '. . . you'll be a Man, my son'. It sounded like a prize, something well worth fighting for, and so to some extent it was. But just for boys.

Young people today still appear to have few doubts that the world is fine if you're a man. They are part of the edifice, and so it's understandably difficult for them to see the cracks. I asked my male students what it would be like if they woke up tomorrow and found they were women. Other researchers have asked this, and the answers are often the same: almost every perception about life as a woman was negative. When I asked the female students about being a man, most of what they said was positive. It would seem that women are still a despised lot, throughout every religion, every culture, most countries of the world. The edifice of male domination is almost universal. In India baby girls are murdered because they're thought to be no use; in Moslem countries schools stop for pupils to watch a wife stoned to death for adultery; in Great Britain women are unofficially barred from top layers of the establishment, kept away from having any substantial slice of the cake that is the world despite any apparent advances of the women's movement.

These isolated events and experiences – big and small – are just a few of the reasons why we cling to the view that it's still definitely a man's world. The preference for being male starts · at conception. A survey of brand-new mothers showed that those who had boys felt they had achieved more than those with girls. Now you can choose the sex of your baby, western governments are panicking because even here they know that 75 per cent of parents will choose a boy. You set off a long

5

way behind when you're female. So surely it must be better to be male?

Certainly it was until very recently. If you were a Man, you would have money (varying amounts, but invariably more than your wife); there would be women to care for you and provide you with sex and children; you could count on the clubs and fraternity of other men: the benefits were endless. On the downside, it's true that you could at any stage be asked to be cannon-fodder; you were more likely than women to be the victims of aggression; and, in order to have money, you had to work in what were often dangerous and dreary sur-roundings. But the goodies must have vastly outweighed the difficulties because men have clung to the power for so many thousands of years. Although they might not think they have a choice in any of this, it seems to me that overall being a man must have seemed better than being a woman.

But now, despite the students' perceptions, despite the structures of the world that hold things in place as best they can, this conclusion is getting harder to reach. As the turmoil of the millennium swirls its panic around us in wars and AIDS, murderous children and environmental disasters, there is another source of turbulence within all this that concerns the potential demise of the traditional role of men. Symptoms of this malady are signified by the rising male suicide rate, by the fact that men are dying increasingly earlier than women, and that impotence seems to be rising fast. As we approach the year 2000, I realize that I'm starting to feel grateful I'm a woman.

As women take their first tentative steps towards some-thing different from the last 10,000 years, men are having a difficult time of it. As men's employment depends less and less on physical strength, and more on intellect and skill, then women's capacity for economic equality increases. It's true that if you try to capture statistically the changes that feminism has brought about, you'll find things are not at all impressive even in western countries, let alone throughout the world. Women still earn far less than men, those that have reached the upper echelons of organizations remain a rare and isolated species, a large proportion are still subjected to domestic violence and increasingly to rape. But if you look at the emotional culture of the West and the changes that have happened for women in this century and especially over the last twenty-five years since women really began to make a fuss, women's lot seems to have improved no end. It might not be a dramatic quantitative change, but qualitatively things feel different, and it's this difference that is permeating relationships and making people ask 'Who'd be a man, nowadays?'

The Threats to Mankind

IT'S NOT the gross noisy changes I'm talking about, not the political correctness which ties men and women in knots so that any form of relating seems too fraught to take on in the first place. It's the more subtle kind, those which men have used against women for centuries, which are beginning to undermine men and make them unsure about themselves in all sorts of ways. Just watch the ads on television: see how many are anti-male. Cars used to be sold to men – women just got to choose the colour – but now many of them target women and in very different ways to those which are aimed at men. They show a young woman chucking away the objects that attached her to her man, slipping down the court steps after a divorce with all the joy and exuberance of marriage, slinging her boyfriend's doorkey over the bridge as she drives through the States. Men have never been sold cars by showing their female partners to be stupid or not worth staying with; the message has been much more to do with the car making the man a Man – envied, powerful, rich, with a beautiful woman to stroke the back of his neck and look adoring. She's something he owns, and you wouldn't want to own a mug, would you? But women can, we're being told, at the snap of their fingers abandon their mugs for something more exciting. Other ads show men being made to look stupid and pompous by the female owner of the coffee company; unbelievably boring and unadventurous in the way he plans his life with his exasperated girlfriend; ogled and wolf-whistled by a gang of slick businesswomen. And so on. Men are being publicly pilloried.

You can be sure that advertising agencies wouldn't be making ads like these if they hadn't picked up that the culture was favouring this new way of thinking: one that makes men the joke, the inferior, the unreliable, and utterly leavable. What this means, of course, is that women have money. It may not be spread evenly across the female cake, but it's there in sufficient amounts to make them suddenly a recognizable marketing target. The drip-drip effect of these adverts will undoubtedly be to demoralize men and make them seem as ineffectual as all those music-hall jokes have made women feel over the years: the ones about poor driving, an aversion to sex, illogical thinking and so on, that eventually affect the confidence of the most stalwart of women.

Linked to this new public image of men being better to leave than to marry, we get the constant and disproportionate amount of news concerned with how badly they behave. It concentrates on the few: those who rape women, mug old ladies, abuse boys and girls, and murder indiscriminately. Now, suddenly, it's become almost impossible to find fostering or adopting parents for young boys. Males, it seems, are bad news. Although the vast majority of men never get nearer to violence than snarling at the dog, they tell me that they are starting to feel guilty just for being a man. They feel the accusation coming from each and every woman, and they judge themselves guilty. Guilt is a strange emotion: it makes you feel very uncomfortable and, if you don't decide to change your behaviour, it can make you feel very angry at the person who makes you guilty. And so on.

A Bad Job Too

AND THEN there's unemployment. For centuries, perhaps from the time we stopped being hunters and gatherers, most men have taken on the role of going out to work, of bringing home the bacon, while wives cared for the children, the cooking, the garden, and various other work, such as weaving, which could be done at home. Now globally this is changing. Unemployment is a feature of the modern world and it isn't going to go away. Without all the other threats to men, this alone is enough to bring about huge changes to the power relationships of men and women, to what happens within a marriage. In some parts of Britain, there are already more women working than men; women will not only work for less, but they are used to being adaptable, to working part-time and to changing their tasks without making a fuss. They are used to being exploited and even being grateful. These are not the ladies in the adverts, tripping down the steps of the divorce court and into their convertibles: but the money they earn, little as it is, means something to them just the same. The breadwinner has the power, however ambivalent about it she is, however hard she might try to cover it up.

For those who are still in work, almost all of them report having to work harder and harder, striving towards carrots just that bit further away. For many who became the dual-career couples of the eighties this has come to mean two people working to exhaustion, rarely eating together, at best negotiating nannies and cleaners and gardeners, but maybe instead doing the chores themselves. Small wonder that such marriages are frequently seen to fade away rather than going off with a bang: one partner wakes up one morning to realize that the other must have gone. Couples in these marriages report little or no sexual desire; it drifted away from them like everything else that used to make life vibrant.

Health Warnings

ON TOP of all these sociological threats to man, there are also biological ones. There are the health hazards of suicide and violence I mentioned above – an 80 per cent increase in male suicides over the last ten years is not to be sniffed at, and when you see that female suicides over that period have actually gone down, you begin to realize that the evidence that it might now be better to be female is getting stronger. On average, men die seven years earlier than women: that's really quite a gap. And when you think that back in the twenties (when men quoted Kipling to each other with complete confidence in its veracity) the gap was only one year, again it's apparent that things are getting tougher in some mysterious way for men, or maybe easier for women – or both. If you take depression rates, you find that married women have higher rates than unmarried women and married men – but only when they are in a traditional stay-at-home marriage. If both partners go out to work, then their depression rates are equal. Men's health and happiness, it seems, deteriorates as women's power and confidence begins to surge.

Perhaps the most important threat that men perceive, and one that is discussed in different ways throughout this book, is to their sexual behaviour. Sex – in the shape of an erect and hopefully reasonably large penis, fertile testes and an eye for the girls – is an absolutely essential ingredient in men's definition of what it is to be masculine. These days it may seem that it's almost all they've got, now women are encroaching on every other traditional male preserve. Take kiss-and-tell, for example: that was something only men did, comparing notes and elaborating conquests to enhance their reputations in the Real Man stakes. But now women do it even more brazenly than men, and with no shame at all. As cabinet ministers know, the details of what needs to be done to arouse them can now become front page news. These kiss-and-tell women aren't saying how wonderful the fellows were in bed, as men did of them in their nudge-nudge stories: 'Cor, she was a little cracker!' and all that sort of thing. Instead, they're revealing the little difficulties the men had – the gymslips, football strips and feather dusters of slow arousal. 'Women do not find it difficult nowadays to behave like men,' said Sir Compton Mackenzie. 'But they often find it extremely difficult to behave like gentlemen.'

But doubt men's sexuality and you attack their very essence; they will fight back tooth and claw. Take it away in any sense at all, and they are likely to wither and fade, get depressed, and even kill themselves. And that's just what's happening today: aggression turned outwards against others, and aggression turned inwards against themselves.

Even physiologically something seems to be happening to men that is denting their definitions of themselves as sexual and therefore masculine. There is a large rise in testicular cancer, a 40 per cent increase in the non-descent of testes in small boys, a rise too in the incidence of abnormal penises and hermaphrodites. Although there is debate in Britain about the correctness of its statistical analyses, a Danish study has shown an enormous decrease in sperm counts over the last half century, reduced by around 50 per cent, and this alongside an increase in abnormal sperm. It was thought that the mysterious demasculinization was to do with a rise in oestrogen, perhaps by women's excessive use of the contraceptive pill, but the amount this could produce is completely insufficient to cause such an effect. Scientists, producing tankfuls of hermaphrodite fish, have shown that it is more likely to be the result of man-made chemicals which mimic oestrogen.

Whatever the biochemistry of this attack on male sexuality, whether the chemicals were made by men or not, the emphasis on oestrogen, or oestrogen-like substances, becomes almost a metaphor for the rise of women who are truly ball-crushers, castrators in the eyes of men. In their extreme form there is Mrs Bobbitt, the young American before the courts for alleg-edly hacking off her husband's penis. We mustn't underesti-mate the psychological power of the image of a woman doing this and, almost worse, discarding it on a rubbish heap. But the fear has always been there. It fed the ancient myths of *vagina dentata* – the knife-like teeth that lived behind the hymen ready to injure the penis or even bite it off. Lederer, in his book *The Fear of Women*, describes the way this myth exists even today in various communities around the world. Freud translated these into penis envy, but Mrs Bobbitt has shown that envy may not come into it at all.

Orgasms on Demand

As a young woman, one of my favourite cartoons was of a large aproned lady at the sink, head lowered over the suds, with hubby in an armchair, partly hidden by a news-paper. A child is tugging urgently at her skirt. 'Mummy, Mummy,' she's asking, 'what's an orgasm?' 'I don't know, dear,' mother replies. 'Ask your father.'

11

The modern changes in female sexual behaviour started with the freedom provided for women by efficient contraception, but were quickly fortified by *Cosmopolitan*-fuelled demands from women upon men to be given an orgasm or two or three. This was not unfair: men had been telling women for years that they should say what they wanted, and gradually they began to do so. But when women did this, the reports began flooding in that men had turned right off. Although men *say* they would like women to initiate sex more often, when faced with unfettered female desire, the man frequently backs away. His sexuality, he's been taught, is linked to being in control, not to being told what to do. His whole brittle sense of masculinity revolves around achievement and dominance, symbolized by the phallus, alongside a demonstration of complete incompetence at such feminine activities as getting close or intimate, nurturing children, or expressing emotions.

As the old means to achieve and win and be a Man slip from his fist, we see a rise in rape, an increase in the use of anabolic steroids to puff themselves up artificially, and even a growing demand by men to have their penises lengthened. Of course, this might just be that the techniques and drugs were not around in the good or bad old days, but there's no doubt that there have always been ways to operate on women to achieve whatever was wanted, and so I suspect that, if a strong desire for longer penises was there in previous times, then this relatively simple operation could also have been achieved in some way or other. Just as women suffered terrible damage for the sake of enhancing the prevailing vogue of femininity, so men on anabolic steroids find themselves later with shrunken testes, enlarged breasts, infertile, impotent and sometimes with priapism, a persistent erection which is painful and which in itself can lead to impotence. Much better, perhaps, to be that nine-stone skinny runt from the dumb-bell ads, than a pantomime parody of masculinity gone mad.

Just as important in terms of women's new sexuality was the rise to fame of psychologists and sex gurus Masters and Johnson, back in the sixties and seventies. It was they who let the world know that penetration was not the most effective means to female orgasm; clitoral stimulation was much better. But then do we really, some people wondered, need a man for that? So, alongside the rise in economic redundancy that has now reached the marketing gurus and the world of advertising, the potential of sexual redundancy has also developed. It has been fuelled by cloning, by effective contraception, by female employment and male unemployment, by a whisper that is becoming a roar that women can do without badly behaved men.

And yet despite all this, more than ever, men and women are getting married – once, twice, even three of four times – always trying to meet with love, and frequently failing to meet at all.

Threats and Counter-threats

WE HUMANS are programmed to react to threats in ways that will preserve us. We can do it creatively or destructively – just as we've tackled so much in this chaotic century with its extremes of innovation and damage. Men can react creatively or destructively, too, to the sociological, political, and psychological attacks on their definitions of themselves as masculine, to the possibility that, even if they seem to do everything they should, still someone might not see them as Real Men.

They can, for example, decide that being a Real Man is not so wonderful and that they should do more to understand themselves and change more fundamentally in ways that women are beginning to do. This would involve admitting that something was not as they'd like it, and perhaps that they were at a loss and unhappy, and this isn't an easy thing to do. It might involve embracing the more female side of themselves – not just by a parody of women, kissing half naked on the football pitch, or gossiping endlessly in all-male cliques like locker-rooms or senior management meetings. Instead it might be to develop, as Robert Bly has suggested, their deep, dark, truly male side, discovering the Wild Man, alone in the wilderness. What Wild Man is I'm not clear about (and that's probably the way it should stay), but it has to do not with being macho, but with being strong, and strength here involves

13

not domination, but compassion and resolve. The aim of the new men's movement is to discover true masculinity, not the type that's been thrust upon you.

Alternatively, men might react with depression or impotence or both – going so far as to admit that something is wrong, and that they are deeply unhappy, but perhaps not able to know what they can do about it. Although I do believe that many men are in real pain nowadays, their lessons in how to be a man have not, for most of them, involved learning how to recognize the sources of their pain or how to change things. Terry Kupers, a psychotherapist, says in his book *Revisioning Men's Lives*:

> Men complain that they feel dead, empty inside, lack meaning in their lives, do not know why they should go on living. Or they say they feel depressed, impotent, anxious in the wake of a heart attack, or just plain uneasy. When I ask what they think is wrong, they do not know . . . When I ask what they really desire in life beyond symptom reduction, they are unable to say.

A third strategy, and one that we are seeing as frequently as either of the others, is that men may dig their heels in and enhance still further every aspect of what society has told them about being a Man, my son. The best form of defence, they might conclude, is to attack. 'When the going gets tough, the tough get going,' they told us in the eighties. But Marina Warner has suggested that, 'The girls are getting tough, but the tough are getting tougher.' Attacks on women – physical, sexual, psychological and economic – are the order of the day, and the gloves are off. Here are two letters I've received recently:

> My husband stopped sex with me about two years ago. I thought it was because he worries about having a heart attack like his father, but we've never talked about it. Then last month I went down into our cellar to find something, and came across a pile of hidden magazines, all about vicious attacks on women, beatings and tortures ending in sex. He's a psychiatrist and, when I

confronted him with them, he told me I was repressed and that that was why he couldn't fancy me any more.

Another woman told me:

Since I started work my husband has become the meanest man you could imagine. He checks the black bin bags each night to make sure I haven't thrown out any food that I or the children could eat. He wakes me up in the middle of the night to shout that I have had a biscuit or a pork pie that he wanted. He buys nothing whatsoever for the home so I have to use every single penny I earn in my part-time job paying bills and buying food. He has a good job, a company car, and a mobile phone, and now he wants to have the phone at home removed as he says it's a waste. He tells me I'm irresponsible and that I do not know how to manage my money.

We could see this type of behaviour as pathological in some way, but that wouldn't be very helpful. It's much more to do with the fight that many men feel impelled to have in order to protect themselves from what they fear most – not being thought of as truly male. Most men see themselves as either overtly heterosexual or else homosexual: on the whole they allow themselves very little in between. Moreover, their definitions of masculinity are painfully rigid. Many see the narrow corridor between being a woman and being gay as a dangerous one, lined with potential ambushes.

Sociologist Cooper Thompson considers that homophobia (fearing and hating gay men) and misogyny (hating women) are just two sides of the same coin. The pressure to be different to women is, he says, the ultimate driving force in turning boys into men.

Women, on the other hand, travel in a wider plain. They are allowed to play with sexuality – to be tomboys, to be temporarily attracted to other women without its affecting their essential heterosexuality, and so forth. They are not in the straitjacket of *True Grit* maleness that men force themselves to wear.

The weft and woof of this straitjacket consists of definitions of masculinity that have to do almost purely with a defined form of sexuality on the one hand, and with not being a woman on the other. That is, men describe themselves as men because they have a penis, because it is used effectively in sex with a woman, because it produces babies, and so on. Beyond this they know they are men because they don't act like women: they work in real jobs, they're not emotional light-weights, they're not weak, not ruled by their hormones, not soft. Not anything that could possibly be thought of as female. But then women whom they know sneak into key jobs and spoil this division; then they learn that the guy at the next desk, the one who beats them regularly at squash, is actually gay. The fabric is starting to fray. Men still cling to their knowledge of themselves as men through their insistence on the differences between the sexes. And so do the majority of women. Together they construct these differences, and they organize male-female relationships, especially in marriage, around them. Then they wonder why, when the construction starts to rot, nothing feels right any longer.

Part I

In Theory . . .

_____ *Chapter 2* _____

Vive La Différence!

A man is as old as he feels, and a woman is as old as she looks.

(Proverb)

HALLA BELOFF, a psychologist from Edinburgh University, does an interesting experiment each year with her new students. She asks them to estimate the IQs of their mothers and fathers and their own IQ. What she finds consistently, year after year, is that both men and women produce a lower average score for their mothers than they do for their fathers. What's more the female students estimate their own IQs lower than the male students do. These rather dismal findings from a group of our most educated youngsters (potential psychologists, what's more) are contrary to all the research on IQ, but show the extent to which the old stereotypes of sex differences still remain deeply ingrained. It demonstrates beautifully one of the many myths about sex differences which affect fundamentally the ways we operate as couples. Women are no more and no less intelligent than men, nor has it been proved that they have different spatial skills, or reasoning abilities. We must have some pretty deep-seated need to insist to the contrary as we do. What's more, if men and women go on believing this, even after thirty years of feminism, won't it have some effect upon the quality of their relationships together? Of course it will; sometimes in quite fundamental ways, and sometimes subtly – just taking the icing off what could be a really good cake. One woman told me:

> Each time I had a driving lesson with George he'd start laughing at me. First of all it seemed good humoured and he just had a few digs, but it always ended up with him ripping out his hair and shouting: 'For God's sake, woman!' I gave up. In the end I was frightened of even sitting behind the wheel. I know we're not as good as men at reversing and the mechanical stuff, but I'm sure I didn't deserve all that. I wasn't that bad. Anyway, anything for a quiet life: I decided that enough's enough and I gave up driving and now I take taxis. That'll teach him – hit him in the pocket where it hurts.

Not a disaster, but sad enough: two people using a myth to maintain the status quo and both of them smarting under its strictures. You can see how it might develop as their mutual resentment nudges away at one another. Of course, there's lots more going on when a couple uses this means of making sure the woman doesn't drive (and we'll talk about some of them in chapter nine), but it shows how potentially damaging our beliefs about differences can be. Like so many other myths about men and women and their relationships together, it is the fundamental dishonesty of the belief that makes it so pernicious to relationships.

Beliefs about the differences between the sexes – their abilities, their personalities, their sexual urges, and so on – are widespread and show remarkable similarities right round the world. One study, for example, looked at sexual stereotypes in thirty-two countries and found considerable consistency about the words used to describe men and women. Women were seen as sexy, affectionate and attractive. Words about sexuality were, surprisingly, not used about men, who were described much more in terms of being rational, analytic, assertive, strong, etc. That women are seen as sexy and men are not – despite all the evidence which shows that men are on the whole more sexually active than women – fits into many of our ancient myths about the voraciousness of women, given half a chance; illustrated, for example, by the sirens that

Ulysses came across as he struggled to get home to his long-suffering Penelope; to the mermaids that lured men onto the rocks. Myths like this make things simple: here some women are consumed by lust, ill-will towards men, and downright deviousness, while others, like Penelope, are chaste – though also devious in turning men away from them. The belief in two very different types of women has become almost a defence against sexual failure for men: if women dislike sex (frigid or chaste, in other words), then men can be excused for not managing to seduce them or satisfy them; if on the other hand they are insatiable, then again it's not surprising that sometimes men fail to satisfy them. But more about that later. In fact, women's sex drives are as wide-ranging as men's, and they suffer similar difficulties from lost libido through to premature orgasm.

In another study in the seventies, by Broverman and her colleagues, still a classic in this area, American men and women of all ages were asked to list the various ways that the sexes differed in terms of their behaviours, abilities and character-istics. The vast majority, regardless of age or sex or back-ground, considered that the sexes differed, and, of the forty-one ways they gave, only twelve favoured women (for example, very talkative, very tactful, very aware of feelings of others), while twenty-nine favoured men (for example, not at all emotional, very logical, very dominant, not at all depend-ent, and even very aggressive). From this you can see, first, that people considered the differences as numerous, and, second, they were much more likely to find desirable those attributes they called masculine.

What was worse in terms of how women are treated by both sexes was the finding that when they were asked also to describe the behaviour of mentally healthy people (without saying whether these were men or women) they used adjectives and descriptions which were similar to or even identical with those they used for men. So men were seen as very active, hiding emotions, their feelings not easily hurt, never crying, and so on; and these traits were also seen as indicators of mental health. In other words, women were not only seen as inferior or less nice to have around than men; they also fitted the bill for having psychological disorders, just because they're

21

seen as the opposite of men. And we all know what that means: people who are neurotic, anxious, or depressed need to be looked after and certainly can't be taken seriously.

Worse still, when clinicians were asked to do the same distinguishing task, they hardly differed from the rest in using similar labels for men and for mentally healthy. Recent research still shows differences like this. Small wonder then that women have been prescribed so many more tranquillizers and antidepressants than men have. Poor men – they'd hardly dare to complain of feeling emotional or of acting irrationally; if they do they are not reporting a psychological problem so much as saying they're behaving like a female. No wonder they head for the pub rather than their doctor! No wonder they divert themselves with external things like alcohol and other women rather than declaring themselves depressed.

Stereotyping of the kind illustrated by the Broverman studies and others seems to be an almost inevitable effect of having one group of people in power over another group. Susan Fiske, a distinguished American psychologist, has shown in laboratory settings how those given power notice less about those below them. So bosses notice little about the distinguishing features of their employees, masters about slaves, husbands about wives (at least in the traditional marriage). The unpleasant cliché that 'all blacks look the same to me' comes from this psychological limitation on the part of whites. It also means that those 'below' have to be seen simply rather than appreciated as complex. So when I grew up (which doesn't feel all that long ago) it was thought almost impossible for a pretty girl to be also intelligent. Even Confucius said: 'Only the untalented woman is virtuous', while more recently Nietzsche wrote: 'When a woman inclines to learning there is usually something wrong with her sex apparatus.' Keep it simple – especially if it's a woman!

So, apart from the biological sex differences we can actually see when we lie in the bath (and we know that frequently even these are not as distinctive as we might hope), what evidence is there that men and women differ in any significant ways? Sex differences were big business in psychology during the sixties and seventies. Researchers seemed desperate to show that, despite men's hair flowing past their shoulders just like women's, despite their beads and flowers, really the sexes were fundamentally different because of their biology. They were born different because of the organization of their brains or, especially, because of their hormones. This was the time, for example, when a huge proportion of women were being prescribed minor tranquillizers, like Valium. The variations in their behaviours and in the way society treated them could be easily explained: it was an inevitable result of the fact that they were born different. But evidence for this has been hard to find. Whenever scientists look for a clear distinction they are much more likely to find greater differences within women as a whole, or men as a whole, than they are between the two sexes.

The Problem of Raging Hormones

NONE OF this is to say that men and women actually behave similarly. In very many respects they don't at all, but these variations are learned rather than biological: meaning they have the capability to behave similarly but they are taught not to. What the research has tried to show is that there are biological differences between men and women, such as brain functioning or hormone production, which go on to have fundamental effects upon their behaviours. The two hormonal effects which are thought to produce key differences between men and women are emotionality – seen as higher in women; and aggression – seen as higher in men.

Women have always been seen as more emotional, more unhappy, more neurotic. Now we have better ways of keeping records and of analysing data, we can see that most of the statistics seem to bear out that historic idea. For example, if we compare hospitalizations for psychological disorders we find that women are admitted more than men for depression and anxiety, in particular, but also as much as men for the more severe disorders like schizophrenia and mania. Only when you look at the data for alcoholism and drug abuse and personality disorders (a hotchpotch of difficult or antisocial behaviours that don't fit anywhere else) do men clearly outdo women when it comes to taking a spell inside. Much more dramatic are the differences between the number of men and women going to see their general practitioners – women go far more frequently, are prescribed vastly more mood-altering drugs, and are referred more often for psychological help (well, certainly if they're young and attractive, they are).

Much rests on these statistics. For a start, doctors frequently see women's physical complaints as offshoots of some psychological foundation, something which for the patient can be exasperating or even downright dangerous. But men too can take this 'common knowledge' about women's mental difficulties as a reason for their partners' behaviour. If she is angry about something which seems perfectly reasonable to him, she is being irrational and emotional because she is a woman. If she's depressed it's because she's premenstrual or menopausal – not because her life is actually pretty dire.

This type of stereotyping is practised by both men and women. Even doctors, of both sexes, can succumb. I have sat in ward rounds in psychiatric hospitals where a new female patient has been brought in looking pale and wan, shabby and extremely unhappy. Everyone has sat around discussing her ('probably an early menopause') and her therapy, and then finally brought in the husband to discuss things with him. He's overweight, ill-kempt, generally pugnacious, and angry about her unreasonable behaviour. The psychiatrists explain to him that she's a sick woman, she needs help, drugs, maybe even shock therapy. No one thinks to say that it's not surprising that she's depressed, living with someone like that. Everyone fits the woman into his or her own beliefs that perhaps because of her erratic hormones, perhaps due to a chemical deficiency in her brain, she is behaving irrationally. If it can happen with psychiatrists, then imagine how ingrained it is for the rest of us.

This widely reported sex difference can therefore have quite global effects on the ways men treat women as well as the ways that women understand themselves. Remember the film *Gaslight*, where Charles Boyer encourages his wife Ingrid Bergman to gradually believe she is mad, just so he can get hold of her money? Although I haven't heard of anyone going to such lengths in real life, I get plenty of letters from women whose husbands are hinting at this, even if they're not setting traps to help her on her way.

> Every time I get angry over something my husband says, 'Watch out kids – your mum's got the PMT rants again.' Or if I stall the car (something I swear he does as often as me), he says 'Oops, a bit strong on the oestrogen, dear.'

Whether one has a husband who uses the *Gaslight* technique to actually make you and the world see you as mad, or whether he just acts in a conciliatory fashion and tells you it's PMT, it will still have an effect on your beliefs about yourself and in yourself which can in turn affect your behaviour. For example, as a woman, if I begin to see myself as distressed rather than downright angry, I am less likely to do anything constructive about the causes of my anger. As a man, if you see yourself simply as rational and so never in the wrong about things that require thought, you're likely to get very little help from those around you, especially women. The little man whose wife was depressed is going to stay grumpy and dissatisfied because nothing will change for him while both of them believe that her misery is just to do with her hormones and nothing to do with him or with their lives together.

Because of this we need to look more carefully at those statistics about higher levels of depression, for example, in women than in men, and, if they are found to be true, to see if the biological explanations given have any foundation. I'm not arbitrarily using depression or anxiety to look at sex differences or at men's and women's lives together. They are conditions of humans that are signs – useful ones in my opinion – that things are not going well and that we should change some aspect of our lives. A bit like pain is a sign: if you're sitting uncomfortably or touching something hot, you'll feel pain and move. In that way, both pain and depression are useful to us and, if you're denying feeling unhappy, as men do, then you're going to be in just as bad a position as if every aspect of your life was seen as caused by it in a biological and so unchangeable form.

Miserable Women

THERE IS no doubt that the statistics about female neuroses exaggerate things – not deliberately, I'm sure, but casually, to reinforce our need for differences and male superiority. One underlying bias has been touched on already: women do go to the doctor more than men, and they do report feeling depressed or anxious more than men. But men go to the pub when they are depressed. They know that any expression of emotion is forbidden unless everyone has reached the stage of maudlin drunk, when anything goes. Or they bring home a couple of cans of Special Brew and anaesthetize their emotions that way. The tiny tip of the evidence for this (though you need do no more than count the men and women in your local) is the much higher proportion of male admissions and male deaths from alcoholism.

Moreover, research has shown on a number of occasions that women are much more open about their feelings than men: small wonder then that they go and talk to their doctors more frequently, since their husbands are more likely to be absent, playing sport, at the pub, or at work. This isn't a biological difference – it's one that's learned, but it inevitably affects the number reported as depressed.

And when they do seek help in this way, another bias in the statistics is undoubtedly caused because the doctor is very likely to believe that their problems are psychological, just as the women themselves think this. If I feel miserable or frightened, I am as a woman much more likely to see this as a female biological problem (as the Broverman study showed) and so go for help, and my doctor (subject to the same myth) is likely to agree. Until very recently, when it was challenged, almost every advertisement for anti-depression or anti-anxiety drugs found in medical journals used the photo or drawing of a woman; never a man. This is how we have been taught about differences – everywhere, all the time – and it is why the creeping advance of adverts that show strong women and weak or unreliable men is such a significant cultural change.

As a result of the age-old stereotyping, men are much less

likely to realize that the unhappiness, dissatisfaction or panic that they're experiencing is actually psychological. They are taught over the years to see the same miserable feeling – often described by both sexes as an emptiness – as simply needing a drink, for example, because society, by various means, has always told them that. Men have told me of going to their doctors (usually male, but sometimes female) and being told to take up a sport or have a couple of whiskies, or being given just a physical check-up. Although I still find it strange, I realize that most men I've seen in therapy would far rather be suffering from coronary heart disease than from anxiety; but then none of us, men or women, seem to want men to have psychological problems. Clearly we find the thought disturbing. Here's one man's story:

> My mother died when I was seventeen. I was devastated. She'd just got free of my father the year before and now I felt she could really start to live again. Then she got cancer and died horribly. I wanted to howl like an animal; instead I just spluttered and sobbed. My sister and my brother-in-law were embarrassed. I remember that she was crying but also looking at me like I was a worm or something. Her husband said I should get drunk – that that would blot it all out. I don't remember the funeral. Not at all. Really I drank from then on. Each time any unhappiness came up – failing my medical exams, problems in my marriage, whatever – I drank.

Another way that men cover up or avoid their problems rather than talking about them or seeking help is by overwork. They use the office toil and bulging briefcase as a defence against being overwhelmed by feelings when they stop and do nothing. Matthew described to me how, as a senior person in the ministry of defence, he worked each day from eight in the morning till eight at night. When he got home he would invariably find more papers to read or to write, and after a rushed meal, he'd go to his study till midnight or even later. His wife left him for someone else and his boss suggested that he take a holiday as the whole business seemed to be affecting the quality of his work. It was this week, on his own in a cottage in Scotland, that brought home to him just how unhappy he was. Even alcohol didn't blot out the desperate feelings he had by stopping work and exposing himself to the misery he'd been fighting by his manic behaviour – filling every minute, hardly sleeping, structuring the whole weekend so emptiness could never intrude.

But again, behaviour like Matthew's goes on all the time without it being regarded as disordered unless and until it really reaches a crisis. Far from counting it in our statistics on male psychopathology, the economy of the west is at least partly made prosperous as a result of it. That sort of driven behaviour earns brownie points, gets jobs done, at least in the early years. If things get out of hand there's always more young men to behave in a similar fashion. Nowadays I'm seeing women behave in equally driven ways. The difference is that they are rather more likely to change direction abruptly if Mr Right comes along or, more often, if they have a baby or two. Men who use work as a defence against unhappiness rarely see other options unless they have a coronary or a breakdown.

Death by Silence

ALTHOUGH THE statistics show that non-physical conditions like depression or anxiety appear to be higher in women than in men, there is no doubt that men lead the field when it comes to early death. Women live considerably longer than men do. This is a statistic that we're often told about, a male weakness that it is legitimate to discuss, perhaps because it's seen as poor men toiling away for years to support their wives and families and then dying just as they collect their engraved carriage clocks. However, since the vast majority of women also work, and often just as hard as their partners, as well as still running their homes, this is again a fabrication which maintains the idea of difference.

There is good research evidence which shows that talking or writing about unhappy events actually improves your health. For example, psychologists had one group of students write about a recent event which had troubled or upset them, while the other group wrote about something less personal. They then measured the number of visits both groups made to the student health service over the following year and found that those who had described their distress made far fewer visits than the others. Findings such as this provide a much more obvious reason for the statistics on sex differences in premature death. What they (and related research) suggest is that men and women differ in their abilities to talk about emotional topics, which then results in women being seen as more emotional but men being ultimately more vulnerable to dying before their time. This is not because of any biological differences but because they either repress their feelings of unhappiness or use alcohol or work to numb them. And, as we saw in chapter one, the gap between the average ages of death for the sexes is getting larger all the time.

Where we investigate even apparently well-accepted differences, ultimately we find things are far from clear-cut. Nevertheless, when you take into account all the points I've made above and then use good statistical techniques on the sex differences in psychological disorders, you still find that about twice as many women are depressed as men. This doesn't mean they have higher levels of emotionality, simply that they suffer more frequently from the symptoms of depression.

Looking for Clues

M ANY PEOPLE (mainly male) have suggested that the obvious cause for sex differences in depression is that for much of their lives women are subjected to the undulating influences of their hormones. Let's face it, from the first budding of breasts to patterning of wrinkles and widening of hips, there's the curse of the monthly cycle, the build-up to birth, the postnatal blues, and finally the menopause. Surely the hormonal variations that happen at these times are quite enough to explain why women get depressed? Well, no, actually, they're not.

The research which goes against a physiological explanation shows, for example, that women who adopt babies also have a rise in psychological symptoms right from the traditional baby blues through to full-blown psychosis – just like those whose hormones are actually changing. Even PMS, which most of us find easy to have faith in, has never really been shown to exist when careful research has investigated it without the presumption that it does. As for the change of life, studies show that when Indian women reach the menopause, rather than the incidence of depression increasing, as it does for western women, it actually decreases. This is probably because, contrary to their western sisters, the change marks the beginning of freedom for them. Their culture encourages them to take a much more active role socially, just at a time when women in the west are restricted by the redundancy that our society bequeaths to those with wrinkles and a thickening girth. And if you count all the life events that surround women when they reach around the age of fifty, then the influence of hormones by comparison just fades away to a statistical nothing. Let's face it – this is the age that children leave, that the type of looks favoured by society begin to fade, that parents die, and that husbands all too frequently run off with someone younger. For western women this is the age of loss, and it's that – not the hormones – that helps to account for the differences in their depression scores.

Finally, if the higher depression rates in women are due to hormones, then we should see equal levels across all women. Instead we find that single women have significantly lower rates than married women. Contrary to the message in the film *Fatal Attraction*, marriage can be a health hazard for women. For men, on the other hand, it is a bonus: single men are more depressed than married ones. However, as I described earlier, if you take a marriage where both partners have careers, then the rates are about equal. It seems, therefore, that the situation you're in has pretty strong effects on your emotional state, and many women's situations are simply not that good. Research is beginning to show that joint marital therapy is much more effective in relieving a woman's depression than therapy just for her, suggesting once more that it might be the marriage itself that's the cause rather than anything intrinsically female.

So again, most of the research which looks for biological differences to account for behavioural distinctions between men and women in the end comes up with very little.

The differences in statistics for depression and anxiety are much more logically explained by the fact that women have been shown to have more adverse life events than men, they have less control over their lives because of financial dependency, and they learn (or are taught) to think differently in a way that is likely to lead to depression.

A number of animal studies have shown that, if you give inescapable shocks to animals, they quickly lose their motivation to find a way out and, even if you then give them warning of the shocks, they no longer try to escape. This condition is called learned helplessness and has been seen as a good model for some forms of depression, especially in women. Many women, even those in comfortable middle-class homes, have much less control over their lives than men, especially if they don't work. Even where they do, it's still relatively rare for them to have an independent bank balance. On the whole too, women are more likely than men to suffer violence, physical or mental, from their partners than vice versa; and as children and adults, the rates of sexual abuse appear to be far higher in females than in males. All this sets them up neatly for experiences of learned helplessness – they experience traumas in situations from which there appears to be no escape – and research suggests that this may be one of the reasons why many women stay in extraordinarily poor marriages.

Perhaps equally important is the way men and women learn to give different causes for the negative things that happen in their lives. Although the evidence is not clearcut, it seems that while men in certain situations are more likely to attribute blame to things that are external to themselves ('It's the wife', or 'My boss is hopeless'), women are much more likely to blame themselves when things go wrong ('I'm ugly', 'I'm unlovable', 'I'm mad', for example).

This negative way of thinking is very predictive of depression: blaming yourself constantly for things that go wrong is as good as taking a pill marked misery. The attributions of men, on the other hand – external and controllable –

are much more likely to make them get cracking and do something – leave your wife or job perhaps. We are not born to make negative or positive attributions: we learn them along the way.

Apart from its implications for psychological disorders, the importance of this difference in terms of marriage is that women are much more likely to see themselves as being in the wrong than men are. To make up for this we find them constantly trying to repair themselves – get slimmer, wear nicer clothes, cook better, and so on.

> My husband was made unemployed about nine months ago. He'd been an executive with one of the major banks. It's hit him very hard and I suspect he's depressed. He never does anything and we don't make love any more. He says that it's my fault that he lost his job, because I didn't much like socializing with his bosses from the bank. He says I just didn't try hard enough, and that's probably true. I do feel awful about it, especially as he's clearly been struck so low. Can you tell me what I can do to help him – both in trying to get him back to work, and also some ways of improving my self-confidence and social skills so I can mix better in the future.

As this letter shows, blaming behaviour – whether of yourself or of others – is never very useful, and it's anathema to a healthy marriage. If you always blame people or things outside of yourself then that's not going to give you much of a sense of power, or of being able to actually change things. So while this man blames his wife, he won't get off his butt; and while she takes the blame and thinks that a dose of social skills will make all the difference, again nothing will alter and she is likely to become depressed as well. In this way marriages can get very stuck indeed.

Does Aggression Make the Difference?

THE OTHER belief that is completely part of our culture and so affects the ways we behave is that men differ from women in being significantly more violent, this time due to higher levels of the hormone testosterone. If men are biologically much more violent than women then that means they can't do much about it; any bad behaviour on their part is natural and so can be largely condoned, or channelled into 'useful' forms of aggression, like war.

The nine o'clock news provides nightly evidence that men are more violent than women. It's men who fight the wars, men who rape and abuse and murder, who elbow their way to the top of their organizations. It's women, not men, who write letters about their abusive husbands, fathers, and even sons. If we just look at the numbers in gaol, surely that gives us indisputable evidence that men are biologically the aggressive sex?

Certainly if you compare violent crime in young men and women, then men win hands down. But if this is biological rather than environmentally caused aggression, then the statistics should stay the same, rather than change as culture changes. But the statistics show us that the proportion of young women convicted of violent crimes in Britain has risen from 1.3 per cent in 1950 to over 8 per cent in 1991 and to 23 per cent of those cautioned. This increase is mirrored by the increase in aggressive behaviour in schools: recent research shows that girls are just as likely to be involved in bullying as boys are. You've heard many pundits tut-tut at statistics such as these and point accusing fingers towards the women's movement. But in his book *Men and Women: How Different Are They?*, John Nicholson suggests that before we blame feminism for this rise in female crime, we need to take into account a study of US women, in prison for violence of some sort, which found that they had quite remarkably unliberated attitudes, with the majority strongly in favour of women maintaining their traditional roles. In other words, violent women are by no means feminist in their views or, one presumes, vice versa.

Of course, it depends too on how you define aggression. It might be, for example, that women have learnt subtler forms of attack. Although women can rarely be said to be truly Amazonian in their behaviour, it's still true that many use psychological, if not physical, aggression towards their partners and their children. They may force themselves some areas of power by ill humour, making scenes, or even threats of suicide. Here's one man's description of his wife:

> What of the woman . . . whose normal voice is a near scream, who nags on and on over trivial and often contrived provocations, who cleans the house with a fervent obsession, who hurls verbal abuse and personal insults when she does not get what she wants and becomes physically violent on occasion.

Clearly violence can take many forms, and there is a growing awareness of husband battering which stays largely unrecognized because it goes right against our beliefs about difference, and our need for men to be narrowly defined as Men, strong and in charge. Nevertheless, in this regard the case of the Bobbitts (see page 11) has sent a ripple of concern and a crossing of legs throughout the males of the world.

It's possible that some of the differences in crime statistics might partly be explained by the law being more lenient with women than with men when it comes to reporting and convicting for violent crime. Certainly I remember two incidents which bear this out. In one case that took place in the town where I was growing up, a well-known local beauty, jilted by her man, took a gun and waited for him and his new girlfriend to leave a restaurant where she knew they'd be. She shot him very thoroughly. But the judge and jury at her trial for premeditated murder found her completely innocent. She was let off everything. I found that strangely reassuring as an adolescent – you could be violent as a female and no one would even notice!

Another woman that I met years later when I was training in a psychiatric hospital had stabbed her highly respectable husband in the stomach while he dozed off his Sunday lunch. She was found by the court to have done this while the balance of her mind was disturbed, and sent to this hospital for help. I met her as she was about to be discharged, some months later. Staff told me what a lovely woman she was, how it had just been a tiny moment of madness, limited only to him, and that it was clear she would never do anything like that again. Well, I agree she was charming and I'm sure they were right that it was just her husband she wanted to kill, but I was bewildered at this new diagnosis of 'a tiny moment of madness', believed by court and psychiatric staff alike.

Surely, in both these cases what was happening was that neither the men nor the women could possibly believe that any woman (especially ones that seemed so perfectly feminine in every respect, as these both did) could possibly viciously kill another person, particularly if the victim is a man. In other words, we all want men and women to be different: it lets us believe more faithfully in Real Men. If women are able to act like men and show a fundamental characteristic such as violence, then the differences between the sexes in other things must be slight indeed. And that is disturbing and unacceptable to our ideas of masculinity and feminity. If you look at the men around you rather than those that the news selects, you realize that very few of us know any who are violent, that the vast majority of men, like women, behave in a perfectly harmless way, but that both sexes can be provoked into anger and even real aggression, given sufficient reason.

What's more, to hark back to the previous discussion, many clinicians see depression as being internalized anger – anger directed against oneself rather than at others. I've certainly noticed the clenched fists and tight voices of a number of people who suffer depression, and some psychologists (such as Dr Roger Daldrup from the University of Arizona) work almost entirely on the release of anger as a treatment for depression – and very successfully too.

But we can be more scientific than any of this and test the hypothesis about difference by doing physiological experiments in relatively controlled conditions. Certainly most research carried out in this way suggests that the male hormone testosterone plays a part in human aggression; for example, baby boys who at birth had relatively high levels of testosterone played in rougher ways aged four, while girls with the lowest levels were the most docile in their play. Nevertheless, there was very wide variation in the boys, as there was in the girls, with some of them being more rough-and-tumble than some of the boys. In other words, there was more variety in levels of aggression within each sex than there were differences between the sexes.

There is also evidence from the laboratory that boys are more willing than girls to inflict pain on another person. However, none of these studies (understandably) truly involves giving pain – the boy or girl just *thinks* they are giving a punishment by pressing a button (psychologists haven't got round to letting it really happen) and the differences the experimenters find are really very slight. In at least half of the studies using similar techniques, no distinction has been found at all. If you use adults in this type of experiment, the distinction between the sexes blurs still more. Most of the research shows that women give just as strong electric shocks, for example, as men do, especially if the experimenter convinces them that they will help the victim to learn or to become better at something. Women, it seems, need a socially desirable reason to be cruel: it's easier if they can say 'it's for your own good'.

All that laboratory activity is, however, a long way away from the violence that takes place in the city. If instead we look at the reasons behind more everyday violence, we find that a significant reason for women is that they have been rejected by a lover: hell definitely hath no fury like a woman scorned. For men, on the other hand, it is much more to do with the fact that someone has cast doubt on their virility. In the Clint Eastwood film *The Unforgiven*, a trail of death and despair is created when a prostitute, new to the game, laughs at the size of a client's penis. Most of the male characters can understand perfectly why he felt compelled to cut up her face for such an insult. This violent action is played out less dramatically between boys in the playground – just see the raw rage on a boy's face when he's called a cissy or a poof and is in a position to strike back – by young men in a bar, or even between employees in an organization. The man at work, clear about his lower position in the hierarchy, will manage to transfer the aggression that he feels at the implications this has for his manliness from his boss or colleagues over to subordinates or his wife. She knows he's having a hard time at work, but frequently the hard time is caused simply by his presence in a hierarchy – anywhere but on top. And of course it's made worse by the need of those above to make sure that subordinates understand who's boss. I have run dozens of workshops on occupational stress over the last few years. Almost 90 per cent of male participants state that a sign of stress for them is irritability, and 80 per cent say they take it out at home rather than in the office. I'm not sure that their staff would always agree with this, but it's certainly true that the anger experienced as a result of the workplace spreads far and wide. And anger is never caused by overload – it's always caused by the person who overloads you!

Marie, the wife of a middle-manager in his fifties, told me:

> He bullies me. I realize that now, but it's gone on for years. He humiliates me in public, says I'm stupid or something. He bangs and crashes around the house each evening when he comes home. I know now it's to do with feeling crushed at work: his boss is younger than him and he's taken away most of the staff that were under him.

The only place many men think they will be safe is up above the rest – cock of the class. Of course, very few of them will get there but when they do, they often feel even less secure than they did before. There, it seems, the chance of being seen as not quite the man they thought he was is enough to reduce some of our leaders to jelly. People were surprised when they read about President Johnson being cuddled by his secretary, but the fear he felt is not that unusual. David told me:

> I think all the time that someone will find out about me, that I'm a con and I don't really know if I'm up to the job. I couldn't stand being found out and I wake up

in the morning in a cold sweat. God knows what Sally thinks. And then I go to work and play being boss again.

American psychotherapist Terry Kupers sees this as a theme for all men:

In my clinical work with men ... I have been impressed by the omnipresence of a single theme: Men view themselves, consciously or unconsciously, as at the top or the bottom of some hierarchy – and, if at the top, needing always to remain vigilant lest they fall or be thrown to the bottom. The man on top is successful, powerful, virile, admirable, heroic, lovable, and so on. At the bottom he is weak, humiliated, impotent, shunned, cowardly, and despised – a failure. There is a rigid either/or quality to the theme, the man feeling at times there is no third alternative.

What We Need is a War

COULD THE urge for difference – for men to be men (and preferably for women to be women) – be involved in the grandscale self-destructiveness that might one day wipe us out? Historians have commented that there are times when we almost urge ourselves to war. After the Edwardian days of dandies, during the perceived decadence of the thirties in Germany, during the Californian dream of the sixties, for example. The most striking fashion notes written in any catwalk journalist's column during those periods of history over and over again remarked about the increasing similarity of men and women. A famous *Punch* cartoon from shortly before the First World War, for example, shows a man and woman talking together, both leaning on their sticks, both clad in the same long overcoats, both similarly hatted. The Berlin of Thomas Mann and *Cabaret*, shortly before World War II, is one of lipsticked men and trouser-suited women. And then there was the Unisex period of the sixties and Vietnam: the flowers, the beads, the caftans. And the draft which fixed those long-haired hippies and made Men of them.

People don't like men and women looking similar – they don't like it at all. It makes them feel very uncomfortable not to be able to tell clearly that he's a boy and she's a girl. It's why men still ogle pin-ups in suspenders and stockings: it makes them clear about the difference. It lets them have no doubts that the sex of the person they're fancying is different to their own. Then they feel safe to be aroused.

After the Second World War women, who had dressed in overalls and dungarees for six long years, quickly reverted to big skirts and cinched waists which lasted with little variation right through to the late fifties. After such a disturbing period, where men were absent and women did their work with ease, the differentiation of the sexes was high on society's agenda.

But let's face it, they might tut-tut and ultimately declare that unisex is never acceptable, but they can tolerate it much more easily if women edge towards the masculine rather than men edge towards the feminine. *Vive la différence!* because it's the difference that lets men know they're male. Women may play at being men but men (unless it's a fancy dress, when they'll leap at the opportunity) must never change, never look like women. This is no game for them. Fashion is feminine – it's women who wear stilettos or platforms, hobbled skirts or minis, skinnyribs or halter tops. Men barely alter their clothing from one decade to the next – the suit, the jeans, the shirt. But the 20th century is the first time that this has been so. Up till now men have been as frivolous in their fashions as women. And this is also the first century that women have worn trousers. It makes things difficult: how can men create the difference now without resorting to the crinoline themselves. But now, blatantly for all the world to see, transvestites, transsexuals and some homosexuals come out dressed as women or in feminine ways. Now hunks like Rock Hudson turn out to have been gay all along. People like John Scholtenberg argue that even genital organs are all a continuum between large penises through to tiny penises, on to hermaphrodites, through to small vulva and finally large vulva. All on a scale. No differentiation.

This is a disturbing century for a man, and we shouldn't

underestimate their dislocation. For thousands of years he could rely on the fact that he wore the leggings or the trousers, and women wore the skirts and he was different to her. Now he really can't be half as sure. No wonder the search for sex differences in skills and so forth was a major task of psychology in the sixties. There was by then a desperate need to reverse all that equality granted by the Second World War, not just by hoop petticoats but by demonstrating once and for all, both to women and to men, that the man's virility, his notion of his self, would possibly survive. To do that men and women needed to show that the sexes were very, very different.

Little Battlegrounds

THE URGE to war takes place not just in the world's troublespots, but in marriage too. By believing men are naturally more aggressive, rather than simply taught to be that way, society lets them get away with all kinds of cruel behaviours within the walls of home. Women put any bad or cruel treatment down to male biology and so see it as inevitable. They put their reaction (depression, anxiety, dissatisfaction) to the man's behaviour down to their female biology. And men do the same. It seems that we have, as individuals and as a society, a quite desperate need to see men and women as different; more especially to see men as stereotypically male.

New research shows that babies – boys and girls – are born sociable and pleasant. Like Frankenstein's monster, it's life that teaches them to be different. But the good news is that what can be learned can also be unlearned. The trouble is, if we acknowledge that the effects of any biological variations between the sexes are negligible compared to those within the sexes, then men's claims to be Men – to know for sure that they are not like women – are much more tenuous than many of them feel comfortable with. So as it seems so critical, where does this great urge to be different come from?

Chapter 3

Small Beginnings

By education most have been misled;
So they believe, because they so were bred.
The priest continues what the nurse began,
And thus the child imposes on the man.

John Dryden, *The Hind and the Panther*

WHEN I was a teenager I remember people saying to young men, if you want to pick a good wife look at her mother first. I remember feeling relieved that my mother was still nice to look at, slim, good at cooking and sewing, and skilled at making a home look good on very little money. Nobody suggested that I might look at the fathers of the men I thought about setting up house with, though it might have helped a lot. How those fathers treated their wives and children, how close and affectionate they were able to be, how much they drank, whether they were there at all. All good clues to what I might expect from their sons.

One of the most significant things we have learned this century is the importance of our early experiences, our first relationships, for the way we grow into adults. Some of these experiences are purely developmental, faced to some extent by the majority; for example, learning to feed oneself or use a lavatory. However, even here, the way that these early steps are handled and the roles played by the individual parents at these stages of the child's development can be highly influential in how they behave in certain ways as adults. A friend of mine has a difficult relationship with her adult son:

> He was born in a London teaching hospital where the midwives all had frilly hats and huge elaborate buckles on their belts to show how important they were. I was trying to breastfeed him, and not doing very well, because he kept dropping off to sleep. One of the senior midwives told me I had to flick his big toe hard each time he dropped off. It sounds dreadful today, but this was the sixties and I'd been brought up to do what I was told. Poor little devil. He'd wake up with a scream and I'd push the breast into his mouth! Not surprisingly he was a difficult eater as a child and, what's worse, we've had a very love-hate relationship ever since. I suppose I taught him you can't really trust a woman: just when you're feeling lovely they hurt you and then try to make you feel lovely all over again!

Over the last few years we have begun to see the results of very long psychological studies where babies and small children have been followed up well into their adult lives in order to see what it was at the beginning that predicted how they are as grown-ups. Some of these studies look at very definite adult problems or disorders; for example, they study men who physically abuse their wives and discover that a large proportion of their sons go on to abuse their own wives and children. In other words, this is the way they have learnt to take out their feelings about the world, and the way they have learnt to see and use women.

Other studies have followed up children to see who becomes depressed and who doesn't. For example, one recent piece of research by Block and his colleagues looked at young men and women aged eighteen who were now labelled clinically depressed, and then looked back at their records to see how they behaved aged seven. What they found is relevant to a lot of what I've said in the previous chapter: the girls were self-punishing, over-controlling, and over-socialized – in other words good little girls who blamed themselves and tried to do everything for others – whereas the boys were badly behaved, aggressive, showing off, and so on.

This study is important in understanding much of how men in general behave as adults – and how their female partners treat them. Although there is no doubt that quite a number of adult males show depression in exactly the same way that women do – crying, withdrawing, losing their appetite and seeing nothing good either now or in the future – I suspect that a much greater number handle their unhappiness in the same way they did as children: they act badly towards others in any ways that their culture allows. So some men might use actual violence, whether to wives or others, while others are more likely to use psychological or economic violence. 'Behaving badly' can have a much wider definition than we usually give it. As I showed in the last chapter, the wives are more likely to blame themselves just because they've learnt to do so, but even more likely if they too are depressed (and who wouldn't be with an abusive husband). So both of them fit into the partnership very neatly indeed.

Another fascinating US study, by Frantz and colleagues, has followed up men and women over thirty-six years – from the age of five to forty-one – and has looked at the predictors not of real problems but of ordinary everyday functioning. They called this 'social accomplishment' and it consists of marrying (but only once), having children, being active in a creative way, doing well at work, having friends, and having a good sense of wellbeing (a euphemism for mental health). People who had all or most of these were much more likely, aged five, to have had an affectionate close relationship with one or other parent. In the case of the men, those who as boys had had a cold distant relationship with their dads had done less well in their jobs, married more frequently or not at all, had fewer children, fewer friends and lower mental health. It's not just the Royal family that might learn from this research.

What these studies are showing us is what we all know deep down: children are not as resilient as we want to believe, but are affected in all sorts of ways by their early experiences – not just the major events but the everyday relationships as well. We want to deny it not just because of possible guilt over our own children, but also because it means we ourselves are perhaps hurt in some way too. Men, in particular, find that hurt, weak part inside them hard to bear. They learn to deny it in themselves and attack it in others, rather than recognizing and accepting it which is the only way ultimately that people stop being ruled by old hurts.

It's true then: if you want a good partner, look at the parents, especially the one of the same sex. If they're warm, affectionate, sociable and relaxed, chances are you're onto a good thing in marrying the offspring! This doesn't necessarily mean that if we come from a less-than-perfect family we won't be a loving partner. As I shall be showing in the rest of the book, we all have an opportunity to overcome the less positive aspects of our emotional heritage.

Family Stories

ONE WAY to think about how your early experiences might be affecting you and your marriage, is to consider your family stories – the ones your mother or father told about themselves or about you. The ones you tell to others about events in your early family life, and so on. First decide whether they were true or not. If not, what actually happened? If the story is one from your parents' life rather than yours, ask how it affected you; how much you carry it and use it in your marriage.

Daniel and Ann's marriage seemed to be getting to pressure cooker stage. They arrived looking tight-lipped, angry and hurt. They both were at the end of their tethers. They'd been arguing for years – about anything really – and the argument always ended with Daniel slamming out of the house. Once this had been just for a few hours, but now he would go for a couple of days. They came because of the rows, but it was this escape that seemed most interesting. It appeared that Daniel's father had frequently hit his mother during his childhood, and had actually been imprisoned for it at one stage. His mother's stories had all been about what brutes men were and in his young life there was little between one cross word and violence. So it wasn't so surprising that when there was conflict he would take himself away from it in case he acted with violence like his brutish dad.

But that was only half their story. Ann's father, a captain in the merchant fleet, had also been absent for most of her childhood. When he came back for his few days' leave the family would have great fun for a few days, and then tension would start to grow and he'd be off again to sea. Her mother's stories were to do with men being good for two things – money and sex – but not much else. The absence of a man for Ann was an absence of excitement, but also an absence of tension, and she had learnt how, with just a few hurtful words, she could make Daniel go. Just teaching them other ways to communicate and deal with conflict let them leave these myths behind with their parents, and begin to live their lives together as adults for the first time.

Some of the strongest family stories are about the differences between men and women – what men do and feel and what women do and feel. Because they're just stories, they can live right alongside contradictory ones, and also contradictory behaviours, so everyone feels slightly mad. For example, one family story I heard was that the father was a very great writer, and this talent kept the family going. The mother and the two daughters did everything to make the house suitable for such greatness, and of course he had a generous study in a flat that barely fitted the rest of them. The irony was that the father actually produced nothing, and the mother was an excellent writer, but kept it all hidden. She also kept somewhat hidden (but not so well concealed that it wasn't eventually discovered by her husband) a long affair with one of his best friends. Living a myth is quite likely to make those who do badly out of it get their own back in other ways! Now the daughters behave towards their husbands as if they are geniuses, but both of them also act in ways that affect the marriage adversely – so one is alcoholic and the other (despite an outward appearance of great respectability) smokes marijuana somewhat secretly. Talking about both your families' stories and how they might support each other, for better or for worse, is a very useful exercise.

We need to understand in more detail the ways early life can affect how we behave in adult relationships, not just so we can choose more successfully, but so we appreciate better why things go wrong later. Understanding gives us a chance of putting it right. In particular, in understanding how men grow to relate to women and women to men, we need to know the ways those little boys develop into men, and the effects this has on how the sexes relate in marriage.

Joining the Club

I TALKED recently with a teenage boy whose brief relationship with a girl in his class had just ended. He seemed upset, though it was coming out as anger. It was not, however, because the brief romance was over; rather, it was because he'd been told by a mate that she was saying she'd given him up. 'I gave *her* up,' he insisted. 'She's a real bitch, saying she dropped me. Now they're all saying I didn't know what to do.'

Rejection is terrible. Psychologists, psychoanalysts, developmentalists – everyone agrees that the most fundamental fear in young babies is of being abandoned. Unlike foals teetering within minutes of birth on their spiky legs, or tadpoles on their own from the moment of conception, infants have to be cared for over many years if they are to survive. The need to keep their parents with them is immense. With the help of a naturally attentive mother, little babies quickly learn to be bundles of joy and smile efficiently to keep their caregivers where they want them most – at their beck and call. Food when they want it, cuddles when they want them, warmth and sleep and the comfort of being clean. Without these the baby will simply die, and so it's hardly surprising that it will swiftly learn how to relate to its primary caregiver, which is usually mum. But the fear that underlies the attachment stays: for babies and young children, abandonment means death. That same fear tugs at us all sporadically or, in some people, continuously throughout our lives.

For most little girls, this close attachment to mothers as the main caregiver stays in its original form, however ambivalent the feelings that surround it might be. Virginia Woolf, in *Moments of Being*, says: 'Until I was in my forties, the presence of my mother obsessed me. I could hear her voice, see her, imagine what she would do or say as I went about my day's doings. She was one of the invisible presences who after all play so important a part in every life.'

For boys, however, the process is different. Although in some sense they also stay attached to their mothers, the closeness contains within it much more ambivalence, more complexity, and frequently as much rejection as there is attachment. At a certain point in their first few years – probably around the age of two or three – little boys have to choose sides, in order to declare themselves to be men. How this transition occurs – their experiences of their mothers and their fathers at this time – is going to be one of the most crucial points in their development. Up until that point they, like their sisters, have been closest to their mothers, the principal vessel for their love and admiration and the main supplier of everything they need. And then it all changes. Then they start to realize that mum and dad, boys and girls, are different and that they have to choose to model themselves either on their mothers or their fathers. And of course, for most of them it's no choice at all. Even from that young age most will realize that the power in the household belongs to dad; even then, chances are, they can appreciate that men are more admired, more welcomed, more privileged, than women are. There is a men's club and, if you're not in it, you're nothing. If you're not in it you're a cissy, a girl, a woman.

This choice that they have to make at such an early age is a tough one – stay linked to your loving, admiring mother and belong for ever to her lower caste of humanity; or reject your mum in favour of your dad and gain the goodies that apparently come to men. And this will happen eventually even where there's no father on the scene. Then the child is more likely to invent a father to emulate – perhaps one that has all the super-hero male qualities rather than the more complex picture that a real dad would present. For all boys, to become men is a case of cutting out the softness, the tears, the warmth, but belonging to the club. From this age on, and often even earlier, stereotypical male behaviours, such as we considered in the last chapter, are rewarded and female ones are punished – whether physically, verbally ('Don't act like a girl/sissy/old woman') or emotionally (by turning away or rejecting the child). Karen told me:

> What drives me more crackers than anything else Ed does is the way he tries to make the boys be like him and turn from me. It's not that he goes round doing macho things all the time, and he's not an aggressively male male at all, but he does things like nudge the boys and says, 'Watch out, your mum's in a flurry with her duster,' or he raises his eyes to the ceiling over something I've asked them to do and says, 'Go on, you know what women are like.' He doesn't even seem to know he's doing it. I can watch the boys hovering between being loyal to me and thinking that it seems more fun on the other side. I hate it, and I think it's so bad for them.

Girls never have to choose like this. They never have to leave their mums. Nevertheless, I suspect that some try to. They see where the power lies, who seems to have the most fun, and they see if they can join dad too. Usually this 'little boy's' behaviour is frowned upon and so quickly eliminated, but women who are first-borns often report that being a tomboy was allowed until a brother was born. Sasha, who's an only child, told me:

> My dad encouraged me to be a tomboy. I never wore a skirt and insisted on my hair being cut short, and he always backed me up. I went fishing with him, helped him build the workshop, went to football matches, and all that. It was fine till I started my periods and then suddenly everything changed and I felt relegated to my mother's world of sewing and knitting and cooking. I think I've felt cheated ever since.

But she went back to mum. In some sense she had never separated, not in the final way that boys have to do. In the book *The Way Men Think*, psychoanalysts Liam Hudson and Bernadine Jacot describe this separation by boys as the male wound. They point out that it has two stages: one where the boy 'leaves' his mother, and the second where he identifies with his father. The trauma of this move is unmistakable. As many adults know, even if you do the leaving, you often feel abandoned just the same.

> In stepping clear of the warm, symbiotic presence of his mother, the small boy may also leave unresolved a sense of loss and resentment; and perhaps, too, the fear of punishment or revenge. A consequence is that there will often exist in the male mind subterranean currents of violently negative sentiment, some [of which] . . . will focus directly on the female sex and on the female body. *Hudson & Jacot*

Behaviour that our society views as unmanly, they suggest, may be due to the failure on the part of little boys to cease identifying with the mother – perhaps because she is so strong that separation is too difficult. Heavily macho behaviour, on the other hand, shows a big leap away from the mother and strong identification with the father. Others may leave their mothers, but not identify with their fathers – perhaps because he was cruel – and so stay in a fairly androgynous state, expressed either through their work or through bisexuality: they know they're not women, but they're not too impressed with the world that's traditionally male. Hudson and Jacot also use the theory to explain why men choose particular careers. They have found that those who go into ultra-butch jobs, such as engineering, mathematics or surgery, show a much more fundamental rejection of women than do those who go into more artistic jobs such as architecture or music. They quote from the work of the psychologist Anne Roe who back in the fifties studied various types of scientists. She found that those in 'hard science' seemed to be able largely to do without personal relationships and, like successful businessmen, were very independent from their parents. Those who chose less rigorously scientific occupations like psychology, however, seemed to have much less independence, a number of resentments towards parents, and a preoccupation with personal relationships – much more what the theory suggests you would find in women. The authors' evidence for this comes from in-depth studies of individual men, their early lives and their adult relationships and careers.

This developmental step in boys' lives involves turning their back on mother in order to be truly masculine, leaving the world of women to pursue the obviously male – sport, finance, management, control. But this presents a very tricky dilemma for men: the more male they are the more they have had to turn away from (even against) mothers/women, despite also needing them sexually, both because of a biological need and because having a woman is seen as an essential part of masculinity. Taking a 'big step for mankind' then becomes the childhood foundation for the adult male's practices of locker room songs and pin-ups, sexually-disparaging jokes, pornography, and so on. Any need for women (especially non-sexual need) is despised in themselves and others, and has to be denied because it represents a return to mum across the gender Rubicon they left behind years before, but the other bank of which still remains seductive in its comfort. The call of the Lorelei, the sirens, always enticing men back. They abandoned her, but in doing so they were abandoned, and what they lost still beckons.

This difficult choice that little boys have to make in order to be Real Men, adds to the explanation of why men's greatest fear is not of abandonment per se, as it is with women, but of rejection for not being a male. Unlike women, they have already gone through one form of abandonment when they left the world of women to join that of men. They have survived it, but at a price: now all they have left is the men's club and membership of this is secure so long as they are seen to be, and to remain, clearly male. As I've said earlier, this isn't always easy: one of the definitions of being a male is having a woman, even if you merely love her and leave her. This means that rejection by women remains a fear for men, and the two drives – to be with a woman and to stay away from her – create a lifelong ambivalence for many men. Here's a wife's description of a separation after twenty-two years of marriage:

> Last September he left me and I have to say that we were both very unhappy and not communicating at all. He came home in February and stayed for one week

and said he felt 'hemmed in'. He later came back to stay and this lasted for three weeks, but it just wasn't working so he went again. He says he loves me, then he says he no longer wants to be close to me – but it's clear that that's causing him pain as well. I just wish he'd make up his mind, so I knew where I was.

Well, of course, she could make up her own mind rather than wait for him, but most women prefer not to do that. Unlike men, women stay with the fear we all are born with – simply of being abandoned.

Women's Deepest Fear

THIS EARLY but persistent anxiety about being rejected, of being alone, that most women know to some degree or other, has been interpreted in various ways throughout history, whether through literature, psychology or sociology. For example, W. Somerset Maugham in *Of Human Bondage* says, 'Because women can do nothing except love, they've given it a ridiculous importance.' In other words, that's all women are any good for, just loving. So that even when the only male-female relationships they've ever had have all been dreadful, still they go on to have another, and then another. In the bestselling book *Women Who Love Too Much*, Robin Norwood limits this proposition by suggesting that some women (the ones in her title) get into a repetition of poor relationships with problematic men (alcoholics, abusers, the physically or emotionally impaired, right through to sports fanatics) because they are trying to make up to their parents for the parents' unhappiness. They'd tried to make it right as children, and of course they'd failed, and now they seek men with problems so they can try again and hopefully do better as adults. And they fail. I have absolutely no doubt that this dynamic happens – I see it in psychotherapy over and over again – but I don't think it's restricted to women with poor or unhappy parents. More-over, if her theories are right and sufficient to explain what's happening, then just as many men with unhappy parents

51

should behave in this way. Some do, but most don't. What made the book a true bestseller was that almost *all* women recognized themselves in its pages. All of them were trying to help their partners and make things good for them, and not usually with good results. Not only do they find they are holding themselves and their partners back in the process, but also many men dislike that level of nurturing when they are adults and react to it pretty poorly. A much more fundamental reason for all this loving and helping behaviour in women is that they have not made and survived that early break, as boys have, and so they continue to try to please in order to avoid rejection. Anything but that!

Hudson and Jacot show not just problems but also clear benefits from the boy's break with his mum and identification with dad, seeing it as responsible for his greater sense of freedom and power to do things. It's this feeling of control and possibility for action which perhaps lets men leave a partnership with apparently so little thought, while a woman will often stay for years in an appalling marriage, initially trying to make it work, and later waiting hopefully for him to go.

On the other hand, it is the negative side of the choice to separate which makes it so hard for many men to make a commitment. The wail of the modern woman is how even New Men, ones they really thought they had something going with, suddenly turn tail and mumble things about not being ready. But it's not that they're not ready; it's that old memories are being stirred as the relationship grows more intense. They've been there before. They've gone through the pain of separation once already and may not want to risk returning to it, especially as it has old strings attached to do with dependency and smothering of which they have few fond memories. He'd like to say 'I love you', but he just can't quite get the words out.

My Better Half

THERE IS something else that might be at work in all this which involves the psychoanalytic idea of projection. This is a process where I hand over any feelings that make me feel uncomfortable about myself onto another person or group of people, and they may or may not take these in, and act in ways congruent with how I am defining them. In a broad sense this dumping of things we have been taught to see as unattractive or unpleasant or dangerous allows us to view some races as lazy, others as avaricious and mercenary, while we might then see ourselves as hardworking and kind – so it's a great basis for nationalism and wars.

But it can also be a very attractive basis for marriage. It captures the ideas of Plato who thought that the man and the woman were once one person but became divided and needed to find each other again. In this way marriage has the capacity to make you feel complete, but it can also make you go to quite destructive extremes in order to balance each other. So Robert told me: 'I'm hopeless with money; Marjorie does all that.' This view of himself allows him to be spendthrift and perhaps generous but to be dependent too, while Marjorie keeps a more than adequate control of the pursestrings, which gives her some power, but stops her being able to behave generously or spontaneously. Now we certainly don't have a biological or genetic basis for being able to handle money or not, but handing control over to one person, and financial impulsiveness over to the other, stops them having to deal with the feelings that meanness or extravagance may have for them. It also lets each of them keep the cast out feelings close by, safe in their partners, just in case they ever need them.

A dislike of certain emotions or behaviours comes from seeds planted, like everything else, in your childhood. Marjorie, for example, had a very spendthrift mother, which had led to frequent family rows, some financial shame, and finally to the breakdown of her parents' marriage. She could have learned to act in the same way, but she deeply feared the spontaneous part of herself in case it led to similar chaos. So in Robert she could play with that side of her nature but also control it. Robert had a remarkably similar background, with money again a feature of his parents' relationship. His father had kept his mother on such a short financial rein that her dependency and depression created a constant atmosphere of unhappiness and guilt within the home. Although he feared poverty – his father had taught him that – he could rely on Marjorie to make sure that his excesses would be happily kept in check. This sounds a very useful arrangement for everyone but of course it also means that one side of their natures – Robert's adult sense of responsibility and Marjorie's generosity – had to go unused.

This dovetailing of characteristics is one of the things that underlies our determination to see differences. So, if the world dislikes strong women (as it seems to do on the whole), then women are likely to project their strong part onto the man, and the man hand his weak part over to the woman, and – abracadabra – the stereotypical differences become magnified as if by magic.

I think, too, it might be involved in the two basic fears – of abandonment in the case of women, and of abandonment for not being a Man in the case of men – and how they work throughout our lives. If both sexes are born with a deep fear of rejection, and boys then actually experience this when they step away from mum, then chances are they are not going to be so frightened of rejection in the future: they've done it once and survived, not always well, but they have survived. What's more, for most of them mum was always there to return to: that makes separations so much easier.

Everyone, however – women as well as men – is perfectly capable of rejecting someone else. When the man and woman come together in marriage, she can transfer onto him her rejecting part – her own capability to be an abandoning person – because he's done it before and because she finds it such a very uncomfortable possibility in herself. If he accepts this (which he's quite likely to do because it fits with the view of the love-them-and-leave-them male stereotype), then maybe it could add to his own rejecting behaviour, making him perhaps even more likely to show this within courtship or in marriage. This means that he, rather than she, is the one more likely to turn away from the relationship towards other things – other women, sport, work – than she is.

Eric and Fiona had had a very tempestuous marriage for nearly ten years. She admitted herself that she clung to Eric like a limpet and his reaction, on countless occasions, had been to walk out – for hours, days or even for weeks. One evening at a party she found herself being clearly courted by a man she'd never met before. Next day she left Eric and joined her new lover. Eric was destroyed – all those times he'd said he wanted a divorce and now she'd just walked out with apparent ease. He sat outside her house for weeks, rang her constantly, waited for her after work. Then he met someone else. When she saw him with this other woman she became distraught herself and eventually they decided to seek help to get back together. This involved both of them exploring their own early experiences of attachment and abandonment so that they could see, as grown-ups, that you didn't have to be the rejector or the limpet. There was life in between.

If the thought of one of you carrying the rejecting behaviour for the other sounds fanciful, then think about whether you agreed with what I was saying about Marjorie and Robert and money. That perhaps was much more commonplace and acceptable. I suspect that, when we get to the idea of rejection, we are a bit more edgy about believing, and this is because the fear of being abandoned is so basic to us all.

But whether you accept this or not as part of the to-and-fro of relationships between men and women, it is the choice on the part of little boys that is the key to all the rest. It is this fundamentally important fork in the road that takes place at such an early age and that leads to all the important differences between men and women from then on, which has such vital influences on the relationships between them.

But we still need to explain why the choice to leave mum and to join dad comes when it does. Of course, it might be biological – the boy child might be programmed to respond differently to all that young petting and hugging from his mum – but if this is so, there is no evidence for it yet. There are, however, quite compelling psychological reasons to explain why the move occurs when it does and what happens when the boy finds himself over on the other side, and it's to those we'll turn next.

Chapter 4

Escapes and Ensnarements

Domination begins with the attempt to deny dependency.

Benjamin, *The Bonds of Love*

FROM VERY young a child learns to be ambivalent about the person who most usually takes care of him or her. Most often in our societies, this is mum. Even before children know that the face that hangs over them, the breast that comforts and takes away the pain of hunger, the hands that stroke them and make them clean actually all belong to a separate person, they already know that the absence of these wonderful things makes life feel pretty uncomfortable and miserable. As they realize that there are separate individuals to themselves, it's still likely that they see the angel who brings the goodies as very different from the witch who seems to take them away and makes the baby feel so miserable.

When She's Good
She's Very Very Good,
But When She's Bad . . .

THE REALIZATION which gradually dawns on the baby that this is one and the same person, who has a life away from them as well as being able to provide them with everything they want most, is a major developmental step for infants to make. Adults who haven't made it very well are those who see life – and especially people – as very black or white: a person is either all good or all bad. They are the sort of people who, if they are your friends or your partners and you put one foot wrong (as you will inevitably do), then you'll be cast out forever. They have to see themselves as always in the right, because if they weren't they would be always in the wrong. Very difficult for them, and even more so for those around them.

So babies have to come to terms with the fact that mum is both good and bad. Good when she's there for him, and bad when she's not. What's worse, he has only limited ways of controlling her – he can scream to bring her and smile to keep her there, but if she chooses she can ignore even this. However much he turns purple in the face and beats his little fists in murderous rage at her absence (or even at her determination to change his nappy when he really wants her breast) she has the power to do just what she likes. I suspect that men and women never fully recover from this hateful dependency and lack of control over the person on whose apparent whims their very existence rests. But as they grow older and realize that their fathers appear not to be dependent like this and, if anything, seem to be in charge, then boys can decide to step across and be like dad. Girls can't do this; to some extent they are always linked to their mothers, and, even if they're not too friendly with them, they stay more closely attached to them throughout their lives. They continue to use their smiles to attract, and their words to appease; though it's true that some, like men, still use tantrums too if they seem to work.

Celia told me about her son and daughter:

They're so different. When I told them that I had had
enough of cooking all the meals as well as working, and
that we had to share evenly, Jean simply took over a
couple of days a week. William promptly got himself a
flat and left! Round here they say you've got a daughter
for life, but you've only got a son till he marries. Well,
I think you've only got him while you're prepared to
be his servant. If you stop, he's off. No animosity – just
couldn't really see what was in it for him any longer, I
suppose.

The dislike of dependency is there to some extent in both boys
and girls, but boys have the chance to escape from it more than
girls do. They see a world of 'independent' men, of heroes that
leave the women far behind, of the powerful who can pick and
choose and buy what they want. Independence is part of the
definition of being a Real Man. So with power as the lure, and
dependency as the shove, the impetus to step across grows
stronger. If women continue to grow more economically and
emotionally independent, this whole process could become
more blurred, both for boys and for girls, as stereotypical
characteristics are seen for what they are, and men and women
discover their masculinity and feminity in other ways than they
do today.

But for now, although the construction is getting a little
battered, for most little boys it still looks better over there.
When they appreciate they may be able to join dad, most of
them take the chance. Maybe now they'll leave all that need
behind them so that then they can escape from those feelings
of being controlled by the person they depend upon. Now
perhaps they can start governing instead of being governed.
But of course things just don't work out that way overnight.
For a start, they need their mums for years yet. They still want
the food, the comfort when they're down, the clean PE gear
there just on time. They want it but they don't want it. They
love her for giving it, but they hate her for her power to give
because the other side of this is the power to withhold.

Jim was sent to me after an attempt to kill himself. He was
unemployed. His wife, Jill, worked very hard, but the sight of
his not working made her constantly complain about him.

He'd recently experienced impotence for the first time. In writing about his early family myths Jim said his father had all the power – mum and the kids just did what they were told. Asked if this was really true, the evidence for it came from the way his father would bluster around the place, declare himself the breadwinner and so on. The evidence against it was that, despite this, their mum always seemed to get her own way and would sometimes inveigle the boys into joining with her. Now he was unemployed and in a family where he was clearly not the breadwinner, and he felt that all his power, his potency, had gone and he had no right to stand up against Jill's anger.

In many households like Jim and Jill's, men hold the obvious power and yet women frequently hold the covert power. The means to obtain this has been passed on from mother to daughter through generations, but it is also the stuff of women's magazines and tabloid papers which teach you how to please him, cook for him, seduce him and so on – so long as he stays a Man. For both women and men this poses a difficult dilemma: women can get what they want from men by keeping them dependent, but if they're dependent they're not Real Men and so not so attractive. Men can only be Men by staying separate from womanly things, but they need women in order to demonstrate that they're Men. Whether it's true or not, men often see this form of women's sexual power as being to do with the fact that she can refuse him. Many men complain that they feel they have to paint the ceiling, dig the garden, choose new kitchen units, just so they can have sex. They feel their dependency on women is being rubbed in. From the sirens to Penelope, the wicked witch to little Gretel, women, whether good or bad, are seen as devious. And not surprisingly if this is the only route to power, but it sets things up to go wrong.

Many men never get over the problem of dependency on their partners, whether it's to meet their needs for comfort and security or to relieve their sexual yearnings, and it will come up again and again through this book. After all that struggle for power and independence, not only does she still have the key to his heart, but she has the power to open the door for others, not just for him: she can bestow her love elsewhere. She can do to him just as his mother did all those years ago when she was busy comforting his father instead of her baby son; when she wasn't there looking after and admiring him. Father, wonderful as he might have been, was the first man to get in the way of what he wanted most.

Love and Fear

> I want a girl, just like the girl
> That married dear old Dad . . .

Remember Oedipus? His father, Laius, the King of Thebes, was told by an oracle that it would be dangerous for him if he allowed any son by his wife Jocasta to live. So when she produced a bouncing baby boy he promptly stapled the child's feet together and left him on the mountain to die. Cruel in the extreme, but interesting that he didn't actually kill Oedipus. He gave him a chance, even if it was a slim one, perhaps because as a father he felt both love and hate towards his future rival. Anyway, the boy was rescued and reared by shepherds and then told by the Delphic oracle (troublemakers, these oracles) that he would in time kill his father and marry his mother. Although he tried very hard to avoid this, not knowing his parents made things difficult and so in time he found he'd done just as the prophecy had promised. What's more he was now King of Thebes and so sat upon his father's throne. A pretty awful truth to come to terms with, and, not surprisingly, he took himself off into the wilderness with various unhappy results.

Of course, myths aren't just invented from thin air: they exist in order to explain some fundamental truth about the human condition. Freud used this myth to explain the sexual feelings of a little boy (especially around the age of three) for his mother and the inevitable competition and desire to destroy that this brings out towards his father, whose feelings towards this new young rival are themselves often far from positive.

This is the age when the child wants to marry mummy. It's also, as we saw earlier, the time when he chooses to join the men's club. Why now? What happens around two years old that makes the boy decide it's time to split? Well, it's at this age, so developmental psychologists tell us, that he gets better at distinguishing things in general, and so it's now that he starts noticing the differences between the sexes. In particular, he realizes that (shock, horror) his mother has no penis. This is pretty frightening stuff for a young lad since his only explanation for it, so they say, is that she's been castrated. It might sound far-fetched, but we are talking about a very small child who now has language and is fast trying to make sense of everything around him. He still regards himself as the centre of the universe and so whatever disparities there are in that universe are compared to himself as the norm.

Although Freud talked a lot about women envying men their penises, I have to say I've never come across this strange phenomenon. They may well envy them their power, and power goes hand in hand, so to speak, with the penis. But I suspect that Freud was covering his own fear by turning women into potential castrators because of their envy. He told us: 'The unsatisfied wish for a penis should be converted into a wish for a child and for a man who possesses a penis'. Very convenient.

There is no doubt that the fear of castration is very common in men – just mentioning the word is sometimes enough to make them cross their legs – and this has been the case right back into antiquity which shows it must be pretty basic. In *Malleus Maleficarum*, the indispensible handbook if you were running the Inquisition, we are told that women who are witches '. . . deprive man of his virile member . . . Witches . . . in this way sometimes collect male organs in great numbers.' (Sprenger & Kramer, *Malleus Maleficarum*, 1489).

Women, I am sure, are very aware of these male feelings and do all they can to make him feel a Man; for example, by faking orgasms, telling him he's strong, good at work, and so on. Also, when things go very wrong for them – when women feel rejected or in a position to reject because they have someone else – they sometimes attack his sexual endeavours or attributes in a way that might very much feel like true emasculation. But she doesn't want your penis: she just wants to hit where it hurts most.

Whatever women feel about it, some psychoanalysts suggest that it is this crucial 'deficiency' in women that lays the foundation for the contempt the boy feels towards his mother, both then and, in terms of women in general, for all his life. Pretty strong stuff, but is it true?

I realize that, if I ask a man does he and has he always felt contempt towards women, he's bound to deny it. As Mandy Rice-Davies pointed out: he would, wouldn't he. Nevertheless, the word 'contempt' just doesn't ring true to me or to some of the women I've asked. I'm sure I would pick it up quite swiftly, and on the whole I don't. But maybe I've just been lucky. It seems to me that the idea of contempt fits in nicely with the thought of penis envy – as if men have something women want and this makes women inferior to men, or contemptible. But, as I said, I think that's wishful thinking too. If we think about what that small boy feels towards his mother whom he loves when he notices her lack of a penis, it seems to me it's much more likely to be fear rather than contempt. Who's taken it off? It has to be dad – he still has his, and anyway he seems to be in charge. Better join his gang and be one of the men as quick as he can.

It's at this point then, that the fear of being abandoned felt by all infants becomes superseded in boys by the fear of not being a man: if I'm not just like my dad, I'll end up like my mum. At first that means having no penis, but later the lack of a penis is more to do with the lack of any status, or power. Since he's seen that it's this tiny member that makes all the difference, it's this that he views as the centre of all his future power and dominance. But the reality he learns to avoid is that it's such a tiny vulnerable difference – just him and his little penis, separating him from the world of women.

From now on he absorbs all those messages of difference that the world throws at him: women are less intelligent, more neurotic, weak, silly, and so on. By the time he starts school the split is very clear indeed, thanks to tuition from the adults in his life and his alertness for evidence of difference. The differences are imposed within every major religion and within most cultures. In some places they're extreme, like the tribe where men live separately from women and undergo terrible ordeals to turn them into ferocious warriors (some would say not unlike our public school system). In others, the differences in power are demonstrated in ordinary domesticity: a friend of mine married a Greek engineer and had a daughter and a son. From the age of six the son had learnt to snap his fingers and say 'Water!' to her when they sat down to the dinner she'd cooked. A boy in more liberal parts of the world will learn from his father to wield his power more subtly. When he's older, he may add ways which are more financially, socially or sexually oppressive.

Of course, one of the ways to oppress and control is to show contempt and I certainly don't deny that many men do this towards their partners – sometimes by the bucketful – and to women in general. However, it comes closer to most men's experience to explain it as an offshoot of the fear and sometimes anger that they feel: fear that they may be found lacking in manliness (and who will know that better than a woman?), and anger at being dependent still on women sexually and in other ways, as they were once on their mothers physically. Many women complain about the man who leaves as soon as sex is finished, or the husband who rolls off and turns away. It feels like contempt to them. Men describe feeling low and empty and having to get away. Their behaviour is more to do with the fear, disappointment and dejection he feels at giving in, losing control and demonstrating his need. Nothing personal. Contempt, when it is there, comes in ways that are both blatant and subtle. Here's a letter from a sixty-year-old woman which described the ordinary common-or-garden variety:

My husband is going to retire next year and I'm dreading it. We were married in our late twenties and all through this time he's continued to tell me I'm stupid, that I can't think, can't converse, I'm boring, and so on. At any social gathering he puts me down publicly to such an extent that I now refuse to go anywhere with him (which makes me unfriendly, he says). In fact, I can see that other people know what he's doing and are embarrassed about it, but it doesn't make me feel any better. Over the last few months, probably because he's also dreading retirement, he's been worse than ever. I've coped because I have several hours each day when I can be myself, enjoy my friends and our activities. The thought of this ending is more than I can bear.

I have no doubt that this man has used his wife as a prop for his self-esteem right through his marriage. Because she has permitted him to do this (anything for a quiet life), nothing has changed and he has never learnt to build his sense of worth from more positive tools than those of crushing his wife. Now he is about to retire: when he finishes work he loses not only his definition of himself in a particular professional role, but he also loses the badges of masculinity like a company car and a nameplate on his office door. Small wonder that he is going to have to demonstrate the differences between himself and his wife even more clearly than he did before: I'm smarter than you, wittier than you, better liked, and so on. He shows contempt, but it comes from fear and a self-esteem based only on the ability to crush his wife. If she turned on him, where would he be then? Well, he'd be standing straighter than he had before, perhaps, even if it felt strange without a crutch.

The trouble with power residing so locally in one part of one's anatomy is how precarious this can make life feel. The ways this precariousness is played out in couples can be seen in the letter above, but is also a recurring theme in part two. I suspect it's at the roots of much of the violence against women – the rapes, the beatings, the psychological cruelty. If we could take away the idea that a sense of self as masculine dances only round the mythic phallus, then maybe men would cease to be so vulnerable to the fear of sexual failure, and that would make male-female relationships much less tricky.

Wicked Thoughts

WHEN THE boy takes the step to join his dad (and we have to remember that the size of this step varies hugely), from then on mother belongs to a different group. She is the

Other, and it's at this point too that boys have sexual feelings towards her: she's the one he wants to marry; he's her little man.

> I remember watching my mother dress through the crack in her bedroom door. I don't know how old I was – five or six I should think. She wore a corset and suspenders, I remember that. I'd slept in her bed right through the war, and I can always recall how good that felt. But when my father came home all that ended. And how!

I know it's terribly unfashionable to say that the Oedipus myth has any relevance today, and I realize that many of you will be adamant that no such lustful thought ever crossed your younger minds. That's fine; but I promise that many men still have no doubts that what they experienced towards their mothers was at some stage sexual, even if it only feels like wanting the comfort of her softness or a fascination with old-fashioned underwear! These stirred-up emotions that the boy feels towards his mother are in most societies of the world regarded as taboo, largely unspoken, frequently denied, as they are in the other direction, where she shows she has sexual feelings for him. There is nothing at all abnormal in these feelings – what is wrong is if the adult acts upon them. However, what is forbidden or seen as wicked, of course produces guilt, which in turn creates anger. Lust, love, guilt and anger – a concoction which can carry on into the adult world of men and contribute to the way he treats women in general.

Girls go through similar feelings towards their fathers, but they don't have to choose to change sides in order to do this: daddy is always the attractive Other. To be daddy's girl, they can still stay (and compete with) mum. In extreme forms this competitiveness is really simply envy and can be seen in those women who seem to be more interested in having affairs with married men than in having a man of their own. One woman I knew, the second of three daughters (which I'm sure enhanced the Oedipal issues even more), had a dreadful habit of going for the husbands of her friends, giving them a key in case they found their wives too intolerable. She told me she considered she helped her friends' marriages by doing this, which perhaps let her see herself as helping 'mum' rather than destroying her. In one family she even gave the two sons marijuana, again because, she argued, it was better coming from her than from some seedy stranger! She wanted control of everything that other women had. Her feelings towards her elder sister were still full of hate and envy, and this was dished up lavishly and destructively year after year under the guise of consideration to her friends.

More healthy competitiveness, usually seen as a male trait and so unattractive in females, is less able to be shown by women except perhaps vicariously through their husbands. I watched a documentary about men and their company cars where one man admitted total humiliation at being given a Maestro after he'd had a Cavalier. He and his wife had cried together at the shame of this and she had refused ever to enter the car again, letting him know that it wasn't big enough for her and he had to go out and do better. A modern version of Macbeth, perhaps.

Most men and women can handle all those early yearnings quite happily, and forget it ever happened. This is made much easier by parents who show quite clearly to their children that, although they're gorgeous, they are not available to them in any way sexually. In most families the mother and father make this unambiguous by being a very clear couple. But sometimes parents don't make these boundaries so well; for example, a mother whose marriage is poor might come to depend on her son almost as a partner, needing his support and closeness in ways that hover on the edge of being simply maternal. As an adult his old yearnings for his mum are then more likely to linger, usually unacknowledged because it's just too painful, but making close relationships with women problematic (see chapters eight and eleven).

The other side of the Oedipal triangle is the parent of the same sex with whom the child is temporarily a rival. Difficulties can happen for sons, for example, if the father leaves the home (through divorce or death) during their young years or later as teenagers when the rise of sexuality sometimes makes the Oedipal attraction guiltily resurface. If dad goes, then it sometimes happens that the son feels responsible in some way for his departure: he's won, but at the cost of someone he loved.

Chris was forty-two and still unmarried. He was clear that he was heterosexual, but he rarely had more than brief affairs with women whom he left the moment things looked serious. He'd done quite well in his career, but not fulfilled the early promise of an exhibition to Oxford. He sought help for what he saw as mild but constant feelings of depression, and to explore what he recognized as problems with women. In talking about his early family, he described the death of his father when he was seventeen: nothing seemed to have much point after that, he told me. It's not uncommon that someone stops 'competing' when the parent of the same sex dies at such an age. Exploring the guilt he felt about this – although he couldn't think of a reason for it – seemed to prompt a deeper level of grieving which he was later to say let him say goodbye to his dad in a way that allowed him to move on. He began to see his mother more regularly, having avoided her for many years, and began a relationship with an old girlfriend.

None of this might have been to do with Oedipal longings, it's true. I didn't raise them, but it's the way I understood what might be going on: he had to 'forgive' himself in order to let go of the past and start enjoying his own life, and that seemed to work. In similar situations, I've known successful businessmen to sail constantly close to the wind (and one finally to meet a force 9 gale and go to prison) as a way of risking or even destroying their success. In Johnathon's case, he had built up a very prosperous accountancy business, but had frequently taken a step too far and so his financial assets were always either amazingly good or else on the edge of ruin. Finally, when things were going really well, he got involved in a corruption scandal and ended up going to prison and losing his wife and children. In therapy later he talked a lot about his father, either with love or with contempt that he'd never 'made it' because he'd been a postman all his life – at least, until he'd begun to lose his faculties in his early sixties. Johnathon had spent years competing in a race his father clearly didn't even enter, and each time he seemed to be winning he'd make sure he tripped himself up.

Even without the sexual attraction to mum, a very large proportion of men have experienced competition between themselves and their fathers. But it's hard to know what they're competing for if we take away the maternal point of the eternal triangle.

Measurement Matters

IN FACT, most fathers don't die, or dement, or leave the family home. In this case the boy's attraction to his mother, once she becomes the Other and different from him, puts the son into competition with his father just at a time when he has chosen to join him to become a man. So although he's in the men's club, from the very beginning the one-up-manship is present: from such a tender age right on throughout his life he competes, first with his father and then with other men. At first it's clearly all to do with the main difference he's noticed between men and women, and so this is the time when the size of his penis (in fact, having a penis at all) is of major interest to him and to his peers. I remember watching two small boys (one three, one nearly two) stride naked through a lounge of dinner guests, the elder proudly showing off an erection while the younger stretched his foreskin as far as it would go, both shouting 'Big dick! Big dick!' Very precocious.

Performances such as these (perhaps not at dinner parties) are a normal part of growing up, as is the admiration they receive for their strutting and preening. In fact, some men never stop it. I once attended a conference about organizations where each day began with everyone sitting around in a huge spiral, and the director in the centre. The seat on his right was left empty for some time this morning, until a company director came in late, swathed in a sheet and flashing a big cigar. He sat down beside the director beaming at everyone, his legs apart, his cigar pointing this way and that as he gave us his opinions. It reminded me so much of the two small boys that I had to hide my face to stop myself from laughing out loud.

As demonstrated by the man who'd only got a Maestro, men's doubts about their penis size are common knowledge.

Big cars, big cigars, big guns: Freud's ideas about symbolism are part of everyday humour. When they're young, they only have their fathers to compare themselves with physically and, of course, they lose that competition at once. Later, during his teens, the size of a young man's penis can cause new doubts and fears when he realizes what he's expected to do with it and how important this performance is in terms of masculinity. To stay in the club it's not enough that you have a penis – you have to be able to use it frequently and effectively on women, and the only woman that you know at this time is usually your mother. Not surprising then that the old Oedipal yearnings may sometimes rise again around now, though analysts suggest they're never totally absent from a man's dealing with the opposite sex. In his book *Why Men Hate Women*, Adam Jukes says that his wife-beating clients all had their first masturbatory fantasies about their mothers. He presumes other men did the same.

In early sexuality (and sometimes later, too) it's easier to count the length of one's penis, the number of women conquered, notches on your gun, etc., than it is to be truly erogenous. If men were trying to please women, then a 'quick screw/another notch' is the last way to go about it. Women constantly and consistently say that they want the truly erotic, the widely erogenous, rather than the narrowly phallic. As Sam Keen says in his book *Fire in the Belly*:

> I have it on good authority that when women get together and talk about their lovers they don't speak much about hardness, speed, or numbers of orgasms. Instead they praise men who touch softly, who receive pleasure as easily as they give it, who are as comfortable in melting into the softness of communion as in thrusting vigorously in the frenzy of climax. My informal poll of women of all political persuasions reveals that they all agree that they would like men to slow down, take their time, enjoy the trip and not worry so much about the outcome.

So, for some men, if sex is not about giving mutual pleasure, then it is likely to be about conquest and competition and scoring high. If it's just a slip-up in trying not to depend on women, then the sooner it's over, the better.

In terms of his dealings with men, the blatant competition about anything so primitive as the length of his penis gets layered with age and the sophistication of western twentieth-century life: gone are the codpieces of Elizabethan times; impossible in a grey suit are the long curling decorated horns that the New Guinea natives use to cover their genitals. Instead the penis becomes the biggest cigar, the sportiest car, the largest desk, the best reserved parking space, the deadliest weapon, the biggest mausoleum.

I know when I first started clinical psychology and began to read Freud, I thought his idea about the Oedipus story being reflected in all male behaviour was the most fanciful thing I'd ever heard. It wasn't until I began to see the various patterns emerging again and again; for example, in patients like Chris who had lost a father at a critical age, in men who become impotent on marriage because they see their wives change from lovers into mothers (see Chapter eight), but also in the competition between sons and fathers that happens in both directions. As Oedipus's dad made clear, if it's a fight to the death, he's just as capable of playing foul.

The Urge to Compete

I'VE SUGGESTED that one of the forces to war comes from a need to demonstrate gender differences at times when these become most blurred: the men shall fight and the women shall weep, and then we'll be clear again about who's who and what's what. Another force could be seen as coming from the struggles with the father – the urge for ritualized competing between groups of men, usually in sport and business, but sometimes in battle. And in *Refusing to be a Man*, John Scholtenberg has taken this one step further, suggesting that men need wars as a result of their unconscious desire to kill off their sons: old men create a war to end the threat of youth. With so many potential unconscious shoves towards battle, it's hardly surprising that there are always at least half a dozen major wars raging at any one time.

Of course all these various propositions are difficult to prove or to disprove. Apart from the clients in therapy who say what they feel, we can only observe, for example, the ways many fathers use to attack their sons (both psychologically and physically), or witness the mess of guilt and anger and competition that is seen when a mother keeps her son as her 'little man' when his dad walks out. In this case, the desire to please his mum is paralleled by his rage towards her for being the cause of his guilt about his father as well as for making it so hard for him to cross over into the world of men.

Dennis was a teacher who had lived with a woman for ten years and had had two young children with her, a girl and now a boy. He was an only child whose father and mother had separated when he was seventeen. His life at thirty-five was still tied up with resolving differences between them since they had never finally divorced each other. His anger towards his mother was almost violent and yet his attachment was clearly just as strong. Within a few sessions of psychotherapy for his depression, I was receiving similar treatment to her – sometimes shown disdain, sometimes inappropriate dependency. What's more, it appeared from what he told me that his partner received the same. Had he had a male therapist, I suspect there would have been a fast demonstration of competition, envy and guilt. This transference of feelings from the past onto those of the present is the way psychotherapists and their clients learn to recognize the repetition of patterns, the links in the chains created when we're young that stop us living fully now as adults.

Part of the work we did concerned his excessive fears for the safety of his new son – how he was sure lorries might run over him as they walked along the street, that burglars might kill him, that he might fall down stairs with him, and so on. I suggested that it might be his own murderous thoughts towards his son that he was putting onto other people, and he found some relief in admitting these – what it was like to be usurped by his child in his partner's affections very much mirrored the feelings he'd had when his father came home after a temporary separation, for example. The other issue that we worked on was why he'd never married the mother of his children. He could come up with all the usual right-on stuff about trusting her too much to tie her to him with a ring, but he came to agree that these were just excuses. Actually, he'd never divorced his mother: they'd always been close, but when his father left home he felt he very much took over in terms of care and company, and this was still seen as his role.

Absent Fathers

ONE WAY that fathers can act destructively or like rivals to their sons is simply not to be there when the boy makes the step towards trying to be male. Although thirty years ago divorce was much more rare than it is today, the men were still very absent from their children's lives. They were at work, in the pub, at the football match, or in bed with mum. One way you can get a hold of where your parents were for you, is to get yourself quiet and relaxed and try this visualization exercise. You should take about half-an-hour over it.

> Shut your eyes. Imagine yourself at six or so – any early age you like – and slowly walk up to the door of the house where you lived. Open the door and go in. See your father – see what he's doing, where he is, what he looks like. Do the same with your mother. Who else is there? What are they doing, and where are they in the house? How does your father show his happiness? His appreciation of you? His anger? Do the same for your mother. How do you show your joy and anger to each of them?
>
> When you feel clear about what you've seen or not seen, say goodbye to each of them, and leave the house and walk back down the road. Open your eyes.

Ask yourself:

> How did I feel walking up to the house?
> Could I see both parents?
> Who was clearest?
> Was there anything significant about where they were in the house? Or what they were doing?

How did we show our joy and appreciation? (Did we show it at all?)

How was anger expressed (if at all)?

Who else was there; who should have been there but stayed absent?

Was it hard for me to say goodbye to either parent?

How did I feel walking away?

Some people can't see their fathers at all during this exercise. For others, he's a murky figure in front of a window or behind a newspaper. I've rarely had a very clear active and alive person described to me. In fact, it is perhaps the fathers of that era and earlier who featured in the thirty-six-year longitudinal study I discussed at the beginning of the last chapter: the one which said that close affectionate relationships with dad at aged five were very important in terms of the adult male's ability to be part of a stable family himself. The age of five wasn't magic – it just happened to be when the study took its first measurement. Chances are, the warm same-sex relationship is vital throughout the boy's early life, right till he leaves his teens. A warm loving man will have had a warm loving dad to model himself upon.

Although mothers have received most of psychologists' attention this century, fathers are increasingly seen as having an equal responsibility in their children's difficult behaviour or psychological problems – especially their sons. Longitudinal studies have found, for example:

- Fathers of sons with conduct disorders were more likely to be alcoholic or to have antisocial personalities, or both.

- Cold, distant relationships are predictive of adult suicide and cancer.

- Adults with older fathers are more likely to be depressed and stressed.

- Fathers take less responsibility for their child's problems than mothers do. Fathers are much more

likely to blame mothers for anything that goes
wrong for the child.

Although, if you have one of these fathers, you might be
grateful that he's absent, there is also increasing evidence that
fatherless boys may have more psychological problems, certainly than those in families where there is no serious conflict.
Many fathers today are more aware of the need to be around
for their children, but I still don't see great changes in how
much this awareness affects their actual behaviour. There is
research which shows that they absent themselves more from
home once they have children than they did before. And now
that between a third and a half of our children will lose a
parent, usually the dad, through divorce, chances are that
things are even worse than they were when those longitudinal
studies began thirty or forty years ago.

To see the way this behaviour travels the generations, we
need to look no further than the British royal family. When
Charles and his brothers first separated from mother and the
world of women to become male, where was dad? Probably
cruising somewhere. Certainly, he wasn't around with open
arms to welcome his sons. There are frequent reports of his
cruelty to them, and his choice of Gordonstoun School was
perhaps a part of the lesson that the world of men is categori-
cally harsh. Boarding schools are an extraordinary feature of
British life. They may be fine for boys who have already taken
a giant leap across towards masculinity, but for the rest, many
end up feeling that they are failures if they are attached to
another human. One man told me: 'They train you not to be
attached to anyone. I still distrust someone when they say they
like me or love me. I can't believe them. I can't believe they'll
stay.' The fact that Prince Charles could at least maintain a
long and intimate relationship with his mistress, if not his wife,
shows that he has not been too irretrievably damaged by his
early experience in terms of his ability to love.

But damage passes on, generation by generation. A friend
of mine is a picture editor on a morning paper. He's commented to me on how much he would like a photo of the royal
princes, Charles and Andrew, opening their arms to welcome
their own children. Instead, he finds over and over again

pictures of their sons or daughters flinging their arms around their fathers who stand stiff, hands kept carefully behind their backs. The catastrophe of the Windsors' relationships was completely predictable, given the research we've discussed. The desire of the boy child when he moves away from his mother is to be touched, loved and contained by his father, but all too often the father is too damaged and out of touch with his own emotional needs to be able to respond.

With all the competition that is involved in his relations with other men, friendships too can be difficult. I know we hear about great male friendships, but I suspect that is because they are quite rare. Freud was very close friends with Jung, and yet this is how his letter ended it: 'I propose that we abandon our personal relations entirely. I shall lose nothing by it, for my only emotional tie with you has long been a thin thread.'

So for many small boys, the absence of dad makes them behave in a more and more extreme male way, to try to become more of a cliché man, to enhance still further the distinction and separation from the world of women. They're setting out on such a lonely path, and some of them never find their way back, never manage to get close to women again, and certainly not to men. Remember David Bowie's first hit, 'Space Oddity'? The spaceman is drifting further and further from earth: 'Here am I sitting in my tin can, far far from home. Planet earth is blue and there's nothing I can do.' I wonder if he wrote it as a song for men? The fact that he's made it, that 'the papers want to know what shirt he wears', is irrelevant as he drifts away without human contact.

Chapter 5

Don't Be a Mister In-Between

Blessed art thou O Lord our God, King of the Universe, who has not made me a woman.

Daily prayer for Jewish males

WHAT WE have seen from the previous chapters is that most little boys step away from their mums and over to their fathers. How far they step and what effects it has in practice may depend on any number of things. For example:

- If mum is able to let him go and dad is there to help him be a man with encouragement, then he will make a good transition; for example, he'll be confident that his masculinity does not depend on rejecting or despising women.

- If mother is much stronger than father, or she turns her son into her little man, the boy might not step so far into maleness, or he may stay put and show more characteristics that we see as female.

- If his father is very domineering, the boy might choose to take a giant step to join him, especially if mother appears weak and dominated herself. He may grow to be one of those rather ineffectual men whose self-esteem depends in turn on bullying his wife.

- Where dad's a bully, but mum has strength he might choose to stay put in between the masculine and feminine – as genderless as possible – if it looks too unpleasant over there with the men.

- If dad is absent, then he may still imitate other men or invent a fantasy dad to emulate. The result may be a parody of masculinity, a he-man to the nth degree, but alongside this, fatherless boys sometimes show an adult rootlessness, or lack of purpose, searching perhaps for an image to hang on to.

- If dad competes with his son to meet his own emotional needs, then the son may follow suit, or, if the competition is really damaging (fathers always win), then he might lose much of his self-confidence about being a man, and either be crushed or go to the other extreme with ultra-male behaviour towards anyone he can control.

Much of what we learn about being masculine or feminine is complete by the age of four, though it's heavily reinforced throughout our lives. Parents respond differently to boy and girl infants right from the time they are born. Boy babies learn quickly that they can get mothers to interact with them through movement, while girl babies do it by making sounds or through eye contact. Parents are much more active with the boys, more boisterous and noisy, and they are more likely to interact verbally with girls. Even the smallest difference between boys and girls will be rewarded, particularly in the boys, by mothers and fathers keen to produce Real Men. Whereas a greater variety of behaviour is usually tolerated in the girls (from tomboys to Shirley Temples), boys are created through the time-honoured process of reward and punishment, primarily to be different from their mothers. Their acceptably male behaviours are more rigorously reinforced, while female ones will be stopped promptly: 'Accentuate the masculine, Eliminate the feminine', the song might have said. 'Be a big boy; don't cry; don't be soft; chin up son.'

This produces a much narrower range of behaviours for boys than for girls, and this continues through much of their lives. Part of the feelings present during men's mid-life crises are to do with resentment at the straitjacketed existences they feel they have been living up till then, and this is often tinged with envy towards women for seeming to have more choice. In reality – and depending on how you define it – most women have less choice than men, but they are more likely to try out various options, perhaps because of necessity, rather than following a set course. A conflict between career and family may be difficult but it implies a choice, and it's one which few couples give to the male partner. The man's narrow pathway is built of stepping stones to some form of power, but at a certain point he often finds that they are crumbling away or that they end in nothing. The way some men talk during this mid-life period sounds as if they feel betrayed, conned by the whole construction of their masculinity by outside forces. Quite often the only one left to blame for this lifetime of apparent fraud is, of course, the wife. But the reality is that the indoctrination and initiation came early and came from every side.

Teaching Toddlers

AROUND THE age of three, boys and girls begin to teach themselves how to be different; for boys the flight from woman begins and is the foundation for the definition of being a Man. The greater the differences between their parents – the more conventionally feminine is mum and the more obviously masculine is dad – the more rigidly this lesson will be absorbed. A boy learns he can be aggressive up to a point, while a girl learns to turn her natural anger and aggression inwards, laying the early foundations for the possibility of adult depression. Both parents work unerringly at teaching little boys and girls what they must do and mustn't do in order to exaggerate the differences so that they, and especially others, will be very sure about their gender. Most of their instructions consist not so much of being told what boys do, but what they don't do – and what they don't do is act like girls.

Boys don't cry.
Boys don't like dolls.
Boys don't cling to their mums (or their dads).
Boys don't hang around with girls.
Boys don't play skipping.
Boys don't scratch people.

And so on. On the other hand:

Girls don't fight.
Girls don't lark about.
Girls don't show off.
Girls don't compete.

While girls are taught to be good, boys are indulged by having a blind eye turned to various so-called male behaviours. If someone hurts them, they are certainly allowed to hit back just as hard or even harder; in most families they are actually expected to do this. Girls are comforted but not encouraged to retaliate. Rather than fight or compete they are encouraged to relate and to be friends. While girls are often reluctantly permitted to be tomboys, boys are never allowed to be sissies.

Superman and his Sister

A PERSON'S sense of self – that they are distinct, different and (hopefully) worthwhile – develops most strongly in this same toddler age of around two to three. This is the time that the child displays the power it feels as it starts to talk and become skilled in dozens of new things each week. When they strut up and down being superman or superman's big sister, the parents respond to show their child that he or she is wonderful, magnificent, powerful, and so on. To ensure a good strong sense of self-esteem they mirror the child's confidence and omnipotence, and make absolutely sure there's not a gram of kryptonite to cause any doubts along the way. For both sexes, being allowed to show off and act daft, being allowed to enjoy being male or female, is what lets them later, when they're men or women, speak up confidently in meetings, take on daring ventures, make fools of themselves while they learn the skills they need, be happy to be a man or a woman. It should be a wonderful age for a parent to watch, but what happens all too often?

Well, in Britain I suspect that the words 'Don't be silly!' 'Don't show off,' 'Grow up, you're a big boy/girl now' occur rather more frequently than does the admiring mirror, and start echoes of childhood for most of us. Rather than the recognition of their worth, we often greet behaviour like this with cold stares and condemning words. Partly this is to do with our culture, where making a fool of yourself is considered a humiliating experience to be avoided at all costs; and, in some families, it's also due to the feelings of competition that are aroused in fathers by the young boy who's suddenly declaring himself a man. The lad says, 'Hey, Dad, I'm one of you. I'm in your gang,' and the dad might say, 'Oh, no, you're not.' Similar feelings may be aroused in mothers towards their daughters, but there is not the sharp transition in girls that happens in boys and so the declaration of their gender is not so obvious.

Heinz Kohut, an American psychoanalyst, regarded this period of development as key to the ways men and women behave when they're adults. Ideally, this strutting and self-admiration will be reflected back for a few years, until the child can believe in himself or herself – until the mirror belongs inside them, to use when they want it. But then, again ideally, the parents should start to fail occasionally to be so adoring, so that the child learns better to use and depend on his or her own mirror, rather than to depend on someone else to hold it for them. That's just a way of saying that good self-esteem is given to you first by the admiring gaze of your parents, and later by the failures in this which help you to learn to admire yourself rather than always relying on others.

So what if it doesn't happen? There are a number of stages in this process where things can go wrong. For a start, the mirroring may never take place at all, perhaps because a parent is depressed or, more often, because they actually condemn the superman behaviour. With girls being rewarded more for their good behaviour than for action or performances, this is far more likely to happen to them. Mothers will often be keener to smile at the antics of sons, than they will at their daughters. Many women grow up with very little sense of self as a result; the boundaries that make up 'me' are flimsy, flakey or absent. They only know they're real when they blend in with someone else, someone strong. And how does a man show he's strong – just in the ways that we let him. These might not be very pleasant for his wife, but she's blended with him; she doesn't know she can be a separate rejecting Other who can set her own limits and say enough's enough.

Men can also have no real sense of self. A father (or even an elder brother) who finds his 'rival' son too much of a threat will let him know that anything less than strength makes the boy girlish or gay. At the same time, he is being shown, usually more by 'goodnatured teasing' than obvious violence, that he is weak and clearly not a Real Man. He cannot blend with the opposite sex, as women do, because that would be like drinking poison. His strategy is much more difficult – to blend, mix, fraternize with Men, while carefully ensuring that none of his behaviour could possibly be seen as homosexual. He has to act something that often he doesn't feel at all, and so he grows up with little idea of who he really is.

His strategy is to build a parody of a self – all Man, bought off the shelf from a selection of behaviours favoured by society and by his parents, in particular his dad. But it's not easy. Like David in chapter two, who felt an imposter in his high flying job, they can sit and cry in terror at the thought that they will be found out – that they're not what they're pretending to be. In relationships with women, as she tries to blend with him, he moves further and further away to escape from a self that smacks of female.

These are the men with what Kohut called 'brittle grandiosity'. They look hard, shiny, puffed up with a shell of tough masculine symbols to surround them, and very frequently an entourage of women to polish and prop them constantly. Very frequently, they run big companies (or hope to soon), or street gangs, or operating theatres, or whatever. Like any brittle shell, every now and then one of them is broken, cracked, shattered, or they go to gaol, or kill themselves with remarkable deftness. These are the Peter Pans, created as much by female admiration as by male cruelty or absence. For them, the mother's mirroring of their strutting performances may have never stopped, and as an adult is taken on by wives and mistresses. The boy has learnt that it's only grandiose acts that get admiration, and that the praise has to come from others rather than himself. Without the external admiration he would fade away like Tinkerbell or, for that matter, like Robert Maxwell. He looked so big and solid, but the threat of imminent humiliation was undoubtedly enough to make life seem impossible.

What this means in terms of relationships between men and women, is that, for these men, their apparently boundless confidence is actually dependent on receiving sufficient reflected glory from their wives and girlfriends. These men, like Maxwell, are likely to be the womanisers; but unlike the Don Juans who really don't like women at all, these are men who actually seem to love women because they are the source of that extra confirmation of their greatness. But with the men around them, they usually spend their time competing with a ferocity that often lets them win.

Schooldays

BECAUSE OF the importance of male (that is, not female) behaviour, what boys do quite a lot of is to jockey for position with other boys in terms of male activities. This competitive behaviour shows itself in who's tallest, strongest, fights better, hates girls more, can pee the highest/furthest, and so on. The competitive flashing of penises as badges of belonging is as much an entrance ticket to the world of men as funny handshakes are to the Masons, or compulsory dirty songs to the rugby players, both of which are extensions in some ways of these first gatherings. Unlike girls, boys go round in large groups or gangs or, later, clubs and societies. Girls, with their undiminished fear of rejection, are into relating more than competing and so socialize in groups of two or three; boys, needing to be as high up the hierarchy, as far away as they possibly can from the divide that makes you a girl, need large numbers for safety. Although someone still has to be bottom, at least large groups ensure that the probability of its being you is very much reduced! (Small wonder then that the institutions and organizations that men create are conspicuous by their hierarchies of status and power.)

Once the boy has stepped across and signed up for the men's club for which the only membership requirement is that he is clearly a man, then there is likely to be constant jockeying for position in that club, especially for those who have any doubts about themselves. As we saw earlier, when they become adults, men's competition with each other is less about the size of the penises and more about penis substitutes like the make of car, type of woman, size of desk, position round the board table, numbers of the other gang they've beaten up, and so on. The more wobbly is the foundation on which they claim their rights to be a man, the more of these substitutes they are going to feel they need.

School, in the form of both teachers and pupils, is an even more rigid divider of boys and girls into segregated units than the parents could ever manage. In fact, for those parents who have done their level best to treat sons and daughters alike and to decry anything that smacks of the macho in their boys, school can undo their best efforts within days. The most efficient way we have to make Real Men is the traditional British public school where they are herded together away from the influence of women. But even in the old primary school down the road from you, you can still see Boys and Girls engraved in stone above the gates or doors. You might think this was simply history, but studies show just how subtly the segregation continues. Barrie Thorne's observational research of classrooms and playgrounds, *Gender Play*, describes how teachers attach gender to all their group instructions: 'You boys be quiet'; 'Girls, sit down'; 'Ladies, this isn't a tea party'. Playgrounds often appear segregated even though they're not, with boys taking up the most space for their team games; girls play with girls, and boys play with boys. For boys in particular, the socialization centres on making sure there is no doubt they're masculine. Bullying those who show any remotely female traits is one way to keep lads in line. For example:

> My son has been bullied since he was eight, first because his hair was said to be too long, and so like a girl's, and later because he was slight and developed later than other boys. He is now thirteen, and physically terrified of children and young people: I feel him flinch if we get near them in the street. He wears his hair in a crewcut, but he still cries with despair each Monday morning. He's been bullied by both boys and girls – the current term of abuse is pea-prick – and I'm noticing that he's now starting to bully his young sister.

It's not just long hair or long eyelashes that bring the boy to the attention of the bully; it's also relative weakness. Many people despise weakness in others because they fear it in themselves. It reminds them too much of the humiliation of being dependent and small, at the mercy perhaps of a big brother or a father. This certainly continues into adulthood, and you can see it especially in wives' letters about their husbands. For example, here's a letter from a woman whose husband has started to have panic attacks at work and now wants to give up his job:

> The extra worry is that I'm losing respect for him too. I married a man full of confidence, in control, clear in his direction. Now I am married to a shaking wreck, and quite frankly I'm losing my desire for him as well.

Women may keep men firmly within the corral of masculinity just as much as men, it seems. They have been taught to be excited by differences as much as the man has, and any slips in the barricade lead many to turn off with amazing speed.

Almost Adult

As adolescents, the sexes reach new heights in their rejection of the other. Young women become bitches and slags – any of the myriad of abusive words that the language holds for females once they reach puberty in order to separate out the genders once and for all. But boys don't escape either, especially not those who develop late or slowly, who are small still, hairless, voice still a pipsqueak, genitals unchanged. For them the nightmare happens every day as well: the promise of masculinity is just not becoming a reality. They listen to the chants of poof, fairy, pea-prick, and other forms of abuse, and think that probably they could be true, after all. Boys learn to live in the narrow gully between femininity and homosexuality. It's like those Japanese fish that have to be sliced so that you can eat the exquisite part of the flesh, avoiding by a whisker the part that is deadly poisonous. And every now and then someone dies.

This experience is frequently aided, I have to say, by the gym teacher. He's the father-substitute that will iron out any of the crinkles left that aren't overtly male. Didn't your dad encourage you to smash your head onto someone else's in rugby?, he'll ask. Oh well, I'll do it for you. Of all the figures on the road to being a man, this one is held in greatest dread. He's the one who can pick up the scent of fear and shame from the length of the rugby pitch and expose it with the most humiliating of words or exercises. I have had male clients in tears of rage when they remembered the public treatment they had in the gym class. What is so amazing when you think about it is that the boys and girls continue to go to school, to attend gym, to do their best to make friends. The fear of complete rejection is even greater than the physical and psychological fear of being bullied.

In terms of our adult behaviour, the different ways that the fear of abandonment develops for men and women have profound effects on how they come to relate. Men have to demonstrate their masculinity to the world as frequently as possible, and we know that this involves the types of clichéd behaviours we saw in chapter two: they mustn't show emotion, become depressed, show they don't know something, fail, or be too kind or caring. They must favour rationality, not rule out aggression, and do their best to win. To be really secure in the club they need to appreciate pornography and to deprecate women, even those they love. For some, their whole sense of self and self-esteem rests upon the notion that men are different and obviously superior to women: nudge this, and the pack comes falling down.

Being a Real Brick

WOMEN ARE good at propping up men. They learn it with their mother's milk. They have seen the little signs of adoration and admiration that mummy gives to daddy and that make him puff up a little bigger, and many are quite willing to do the same for their man too.

Apart from any other societal pressures, the envy that some mothers feel of their daughters will make sure they force them to conform to being stereotypically feminine or else to feel guilty that they're not. In other words, woman-woman envy acts to keep women 'in the ranks', while male-male envy acts to drive men into the firing line of life rather than be rejected for not being man enough. Denise described her mother:

> Any time we argue, she says to me: No wonder Doug finds you difficult. Bloody cheek. I'd never have said anything like that about her and dad. She says similar things about her girlfriends: 'Oh, he's so easy going, and she really is hard on him. She doesn't realize how lucky she is.'

Of course, while women remain financially dependent on men, it is in their interests to maintain male self-esteem and to stop the man leaving her and her children without support. Small wonder then that both men and more traditionally-minded women join together via organizational cliques on the one hand and the engineering of guilt on the other to try to stop

women earning too much money and so becoming independent of men. The glass-ceiling that exists in organizations as a
transparent barrier to women's reaching high-powered jobs
has a number of elements in its subtle construction. Many of
them are created by men in the boardrooms (the business
version of the locker-room), but there is no doubt that another
element comes from women: not just those who know their
place and frown against others who aspire to different things,
but also to those other women who find it so difficult when it
comes to it, to even apply for the top jobs on offer. Even in
these women, apparently ambitious as they are, the fear of
ruining the game of differences affects them, usually unconsciously. Two that I know well have recently been working
towards very senior positions in their organizations. One of
them left the preparation of her application to the last day that
it could be handed in; the other read the last date wrongly and
missed it altogether. At the final hour, all that preparing and
determination was yanked back by their own unconscious need
to keep things as they are, to protect the status quo by staying
well away from the club that supports it.

The rules and strictures that are used to guide and divide us
into genders also influence two very important learned differences between men and women, differences that profoundly
affect the relationships between them. One is to do with the
way they think about the causes of events in their lives, and
the other affects the ways that the two sexes talk to each other.

I'm All Right;
You're All Wrong

O NE GENDER difference that may come from early learning
and that helps maintain the status quo is called attribu-
tional style. The study of attributions, or the causes that people
give for what happens to them, has become a very important
field in psychology. The idea behind it is that the way you
think about things affects the way you feel about them and
therefore the way you act. In chapter two we saw how certain

ways of thinking were often found more prevalent in women than in men and were linked to depression, which in turn leads to further feelings of helplessness and inaction. To show more clearly how attributions work – how particular thoughts cause particular emotions and then different behaviours – think about yourself walking alone along the edge of a field, close to a wood. From nowhere you feel a sharp blow to the back of your head. Imagine what you immediately think – what cause you give for what has happened.

If your immediate thought was that a boy had thrown a stick or stone at you, you would probably feel angry and turn to fight or tell him off. If you thought it was the wind blowing a branch off a tree, you would feel very little more than irritation and rub your head and go on walking. If you think at once that it's a robber you'll feel fear and run as fast as you can. So each explanation causes a different feeling and a different action. Children learn particular causes from their own experience and from parents teaching them about the causes to give for things. So a child grows up to trust people or not, to believe that unhappy events are down to them or to others, to find something frightening or challenging, to see difficulties as controllable or uncontrollable and so on.

There is research evidence, for example, to show that one of the reasons for women dropping out of mathematics and science, is that, when they make mistakes they tend to blame themselves and to see things as uncontrollable and unchanging; for example, at their first poor mark they think I must be too stupid for science. In fact, seeing things as uncontrollable, unchanging and their fault is a style that is more likely to be seen in girls and women as a whole, certainly in terms of achievements like exams or job interviews. Ask a successful woman how she did so well, she often tells you it was largely luck. Having done it through skill, diplomacy or tactics that might make Macchiavelli blush are simply not revealed, perhaps because at some level doing well is something she's ashamed of or fears: it hurts male pride and where will we all be then? This means of course that it's hard for those who ask for clues to learn the tricks of the trade.

It's all a matter of learning. If a person, child or adult, is told constantly (even subtly) that she or he is not good at something, not particularly lovable or attractive, the causes they give will soon start to reflect that whatever goes wrong is probably something to do with them – something to do with their characteristics (looks, lower intelligence, personality) which are essentially unchangeable.

Now, I'm not saying that this is how all parents treat their daughters, or how husbands treat their wives; of course it isn't. But it's clear from almost every society that we look at, that women are seen as, at the very least, inferior to men in almost every way. As we saw in the previous chapters, in many societies they are simply not wanted at all, dreadfully abused if they are allowed to live, and, even in our own society and in spite of all the evidence to the contrary, they are regarded as less intelligent and more irrational than men and so given a smaller slice of every cake that's going. Whatever parents or partners are like, this constant subliminal force coming from society as a whole is bound to colour the way many women think about themselves in relation to men at every level of their interactions.

In the letters I receive, where the marriages are still intact but unhappy, there is no doubt that these women are much more frequently blaming themselves for what happens in their marriage and feeling that there is nothing they can do about it. And this has been suggested in research too (for example Rusbult's work in the States) which also shows how much women try to make things better. They are much more likely to put up with bad behaviour from husbands, and to feel helpless in altering things in any way except by trying to change themselves. Putting things right in this way – or trying to – gives them a sense of control, but it also continues to teach the man that the fault lies with the woman, and that he need do nothing to improve the situation.

However, research also shows that when a marriage is on its last legs, wives are quite capable of lashing out blame on the husband rather more than husbands do on wives. Certainly it's true that when I see a couple who are at the end of their tethers about their marriage, the blame tends to fly pretty evenly in both directions, though usually far more freely from the woman. I think that what causes this is that, in those early days, despite all her apparent self-blame and attempts to cure, she is also building up enormous resentment at the apparent inability (which she is helping to foster) of her man to change. Once things go too far, once the last straw lands, then all this resentment and rage pours out and the man inevitably wonders what's hit him and tries to escape.

Boys and men, unlike women, are taught to hit out at things, control them, drive their aggression outwards toward someone or something else, and this results in the causes they give for things that go wrong being more external and controllable. As boys they are more likely to throw their blame outwards. So one woman I know was told by her son who'd just failed all his exams, that this was because she'd pushed him to study which made him refuse to do a thing! As a man, any argument with his wife is likely to be seen as her fault rather than his. There are some men who blame everything in life on their partners, causing them great misery, but also ensuring that their own lives will stay as bad as they see them, since, by holding the woman responsible for the problem, they lose all their own power to change them unless they leave the marriage.

Carol is in her early thirties. She left her career as a teacher when she got pregnant by Robin and married him. Now she was suffering quite severely from depression. She told me:

> My husband is a solicitor and he hates his job and always has. He wishes he'd done medicine instead. He says that I've ruined his life because he didn't do medicine only because of the difficulty of having a wife and young children. He gets very angry and throws things at me. He hasn't hit me but he pushes me up against things. I have tried to help – I've written to all the medical schools and got prospectuses and found out which of them don't mind mature students. I've even contacted UCCA for him and filled out all the basic stuff, but then he missed the deadline for sending them in.

It's obvious, isn't it, when you're outside it? Carol's husband is a man who feels acutely dissatisfied with his life but hasn't the courage to change it. And he won't find it until he takes responsibility for himself rather than blaming his wife and family. Alternatively, she could refuse to take any more of the blame on herself (which is what she eventually did). This way of distributing fault is extremely convenient, of course, since the woman is very likely to see what's happening in exactly the same way: he blames her and she blames herself.

Of course, if the relationship gets difficult enough and he has the opportunity, the man is much more likely to leave (though not divorce) the woman than vice versa. If the fault lies with her, then getting someone new should change things for him. Moreover, he has learnt to act rather than to relate, while she has learnt that, as a woman, she should try to be good and pleasant in order to please. In addition she's learnt that, chances are, she is intrinsically in the wrong, perhaps for being born, and so is much less likely to see anything as changing unless she manages to change herself – to get slimmer, bigger breasts, longer legs, be better company, not take over the conversation, be more interested in sex (but no more than he is), and so on. And all this, for many couples locked in the status quo of male-female relations, is modern marriage.

These then are the differences that make the difference. It's not the biology of sex and gender that causes us problems; it's not even what we do with our biology. It's the way we're taught to think about ourselves as men and women that leads us to the difficulties that happen in marriage and the problems we have in resolving them. In particular, it's the way young boys learn to think of themselves as men that brings the greatest unhappiness to them and, as a result, to the women in their lives.

Talking Different Languages

THE COMPETITIVE behaviour that comes from that first step across when they had to compete with dad, runs right through men's lives. It gives the world good things as well as bad, but it adds another dimension to the problems of marriage – one that goes to the core of getting along and of mending things when they go askew. It affects the language that we speak to each other.

Poor communication is the thing that often comes out tops

in predicting marital breakdown. It's the most obvious aspect of things going wrong between them, but it's also what they need most in order to put things right. The foreignness that men frequently say they feel about women, and women sometimes feel about men, is illustrated for them by the differences they show in their language. The wail of many women is that their partners won't talk to them; the men, on the other hand, feel they do talk where necessary, but that there isn't anything else to say. Their talking is to make a point; women's is to make relationships. Most men stopped learning to relate – to know about another person at a number of different levels – when they left the intimacy of their mothers as young children, and chose to join their dads. Women (and those men who were more ambivalent about their choice) continue the struggle to understand and get close to others for most of their lives.

A writer who has done much to explore the different languages that evolve from this young experience is Deborah Tannen. In *You Just Don't Understand*, a book which explains why we find it difficult to talk to the opposite sex, she describes some of the ways these differences happen. For example, an old school friend of Josh's phones him at work because he's in town. Josh at once invites him to stay the weekend with himself and Linda, his wife. Linda's upset about this – she's working away all week and looked forward to a weekend together. Worse, she would never invite anyone without checking with Josh first. When she says this, Josh answers, 'I can't say to my friend I have to ask my wife for permission!' This, Tannen points out, would show the friend Josh wasn't independent, not a real man.

> To Linda, checking with her husband has nothing to do with permission. She assumes that spouses discuss their plans with each other because their lives are intertwined, so the actions of one have consequences for the other. Not only does Linda not mind telling someone, 'I have to check with Josh'; quite the contrary – she likes it.

Other incidents she talks about are the way husbands go out and spend large amounts of money on an item, while their wives would never do that without consultation. I had a row with my husband recently, and I realize that it fits within Tannen's ideas. I was going to New York the next day and I had to work late that night. I asked my husband would he iron my shirt. He blew up – did I think he had nothing better to do, and so on. When we talked about it later (in an expensive phonecall), he apologized: 'I don't mind plastering the walls, but I didn't like to have to do a woman's job, I guess.' Equally, I realized that I didn't at all need that particular shirt ironed – I had plenty to go with – but I was feeling a bit miserable about going, and I wanted a sign that he cared. Plastering walls wouldn't actually have been quite the same.

Deborah Tannen sees most of the purpose of male talk as a man establishing his place in the male hierarchy. For women, on the other hand, the point of talking is to relate. Although she doesn't discuss the causes of this, it can be seen in terms of the almost inevitable competitiveness that we've discussed above. Men's competitive behaviour is usually not with women but with men, so their talk of any sort – about sport or gadgets, women or theories – is likely to happen much more with other males than with women. And this is what the research shows us. On the whole it shows that men talk much more than women in either male groups or mixed sex groups. Women, on the other hand, talk very freely when they're in an all-women group. When a man and woman talk together as a couple, then the man has nothing to prove and so the point of conversation, of talking things through, is absent; while for the woman it is paramount.

As Tannen points out, this can be a major stumbling block in making things better when they go wrong; in fact, it can make things pretty tense and troubled in the first place. One woman wrote to me:

> Last month I learnt that my husband of fifteen years had been having an affair. He'd told his best friend who had told his wife when they were having a row and then she'd told me. I knew things hadn't been very good – we really had been drifting apart for much longer than he was with her. When I confronted him about the affair he admitted it but told me it was over

and he knew that it was me he loved. Somehow or other I believe him, but I still feel terribly hurt by it – especially being told by someone else – and I want to understand it and for us to learn to make our marriage better. But he doesn't want to talk about it at all. He just keeps saying it's over and why can't I let bygones be bygones, why do I keep raking up the muck. At first it seemed like a chance, even though it was devastating, to put our marriage onto a better plane, but now it's making it worse and worse because of his refusal to talk and, I suppose, also my need to really understand.

Tannen points out that women tend to go for the metamessage – the one that underlies all the others – so this woman is taking her husband's difficulty in discussing his affair as meaning he doesn't care enough about her pain about what being told feels like, let alone what it's like to be betrayed. For her, the whole business has made her question first her marriage but then whether he loves her enough to 'make it better'. She wants to turn it into something even better – something they can work on together – and he, concrete and keen to avoid anything emotional, would be much happier just to snip it away from their lives for ever.

Of course, she may well have chosen him in the first place just because he *was* the strong silent type. Most of our movie heroes fit the bill, with Clint Eastwood playing it par excellence. Why on earth should hard silence seem so attractive, when women's real pleasure comes in the actual relating, the discussion of feelings and the warmth of understanding? I have no doubt at all that this is a real example of looking for our fathers. Most women have had absent fathers, whether this was because they were away fighting or away working. Boys have them too, but they are set to copy them, not to find ways to relate to them as sexual opposites. What women do with such distant figures is imbue them with whatever we want them to have – power, mystery, strength, justice – usually all the good things that, as women, we might feel ambivalent about in ourselves. Small wonder that this big figure who comes home intermittently and sits silently behind a newspaper while his meal is prepared for him becomes the fantasy figure of female yearnings. When she gets her strong silent type, she then sets out to relate to him as she could never relate to her father. This time she will get close to him, though last time she failed.

She fails this time for two reasons. First, because of his determination as a man to act differently to a woman. She relates and shows her neediness: while they're talking and making things better, she thinks, he won't leave her. He does the opposite, becoming more detached as her need grows. The second reason is that his primary purpose for talking is to demonstrate some form of masculine power, to establish his place on the hierarchy. In the letter above, the husband has done this by having an affair and then by telling his friend; it's established and it's over. Why talk about it?

This difference in the purpose of language can be seen in the way men often use 'I' when a woman would use 'we'. In *That's Not What I Meant!*, Tannen says:

> When Mark announces, 'I think I'll go for a walk,' Harriet feels specifically uninvited, though Mark later claims she would have been welcome to join him. She felt locked out by his use of 'I' and his omission of an invitation: 'Would you like to come?' Metamessages can [for women] be seen in what is not said as well as what is said.

Women's need to relate, their urge to make things good, and their propensity to look behind what is said for the underlying and often negative message, comes directly from their fundamental fear of abandonment, still resident in most of us right from our earliest days. For men, on the other hand, this fear only becomes apparent in relation to not being thought a man and so it is in these conversations – with other men – that he will talk and talk in a way that competes, that hopefully lets him win over others, as he'd failed to win once upon a time over his father.

So, as they did when they were girls, women talk together in one-to-ones or very small groups because it is the establishment of the bond that matters; while men talk in larger groups:

because they need a rung on the hierarchy, the more rungs there are the less likely it is that they will be at the bottom! Who caught the biggest fish, who drank the most and held it, who has more notches on his pistol?

Chapter 6

Men's Feelings
for Women

There are only about twenty murders a year in London and many not at all serious – some are just husbands killing their wives.

Commander G. H. Hatherill, Scotland Yard, 1954, quoted in
A Misogynist's Source Book, Fidelis Morgan

TODAY ONE in four of all violent crimes are domestic, including 100 women killed annually in the United Kingdom by their partners. Violence to women takes place nightly on our television screens, in box office hits, and behind the four walls of houses in your street. It's so common that people stop seeing it as violence. A study by Jeff Hearn from Bradford University showed that men often downgrade the importance of violence by redefining it: it doesn't exist unless there's clear physical damage and the police are called in. 'I wasn't violent. I picked her up and threw her against the wall' one man told him. The mental violence that women find so painful is usually overlooked completely. For example:

> My husband had an affair with someone I thought was a close friend – that was bad enough. But one night he came home after having had intercourse with her, got straight into our bed and had intercourse with me. He

had not showered so you can imagine my horror – the smell of another woman on his body. I went into the bathroom and scrubbed and scrubbed so hard I had red weals. I felt so dirty. The scrubbing went on for weeks until I went to see my doctor, but I couldn't tell her the real cause. She sent me to a clinical psychologist.

Please note: she becomes the mental health statistic; he doesn't.

Misogyny in Practice?

I T'S QUITE fashionable nowadays not just to think that men have difficulty with women, but that they actually hate them, and experiences like this woman's reinforce this view. It's a central theme from articles in magazines through to learned books by psychoanalysts. In 1993 Adam Jukes, a psychotherapist working with men who abuse women physically, wrote a book on the subject, extending the hatred from these male abusers to all men, including himself.

If you think about the situation of women in the world, you might very well agree with this view, concluding that this dreadful state of affairs is to some extent a result of the extremely negative views of women taken by men. Could it be otherwise when you consider the facts concerning the levels of violence against women, from infanticide in India to granny-bashing in Britain? Or when you look at our organizational statistics and see all those men at the top and the women at the bottom, despite knowing there are no intellectual differences between them. Or you study the cultural practices that, until very recently even in the west, have treated menstruation – women's normal bodily function designed for the joint pro-creation of children – as something akin to leprosy. Or if you just consider the adjectives used stereotypically to describe women compared to those used to describe men. From chapter two we know that the ones referring to women are generally seen as less desirable, while those describing men are seen by both sexes in a much more positive light.

It is certainly not surprising then that little boys are keen on becoming men: in the light of so much misogynist evidence, apparent to even a three-year-old (let alone the fear they may have when they notice that girls have lost their penises), deciding to turn your back on such an apparently short-changed group seems to make good sense. But do they also make this choice because of more negative feelings? I choose not to be a Buddhist priest because quite frankly I don't feel up to such a difficult life, both physically and financially; however, I have nothing but respect for those who do. So choosing to leave the ranks of women is not enough in itself to make boys and men feel vitriolic towards them, or to want to exclude, or even abuse them.

I don't believe that all men are misogynist – not at all – but I do think that they suffer universal fears that can prompt them into acting hatefully towards women if they are sufficiently frightened. What's more, some of these fears are being aroused much more strongly by the shifts that are taking place in our society. The potential then for an avalanche of hate is clear. We need to examine in more detail what it is about men and women and the relationship between them that underlies this potential for hate.

The Fear of Being Dependent

SOME DEPENDENCY feels fine: it doesn't worry a psycho-logically strong man or woman at all to let themselves be looked after at times, or to rely upon each other for comfort or help. But even so, most people begin to grow uneasy if the giving is just in one direction. Psychologists talk about the finely balanced feelings concerning reciprocity – a sort of natural balancing act between feeling that you are giving as much as you are getting and vice versa. Just think about family Christmases and you see at once that they are an epitome of the feelings we have about each other right through life. For some people actual dependency – knowing you need someone who's not your servant to supply you with some essential element of life – is quite intolerable. Especially to men. Masculinity depends on control, not on need.

As I described earlier, babies and little children depend upon their caretakers – usually their mothers – for their very lives. Without them to provide the warmth, comfort and food they would have no way of surviving, and this state goes on for many years. Mother then becomes the most important focus for little boys and girls, the main recipient for all feelings, both good and bad. This, however, is relatively new. Before this century, unless you were born into the middle classes or above, when you would have nurses and governesses, most people relied on a large number of caretakers who were part of the extended family. To some extent at least, this must have dissipated many of the intense and frequently negative feelings that men and women show towards their mothers today, feelings that are at least partly due to a determined rejection of those earlier experiences of need. However good the mother was, there will always be times when she hasn't been good enough, when needs haven't been met, and when disappointment and the humiliation of having to ask has been painfully felt.

Where a mother has been more negligent, vindictive, or absent (even through death, let alone divorce), then a deliberate rejection of dependency is likely to be much more an issue throughout the son's or daughter's life. Boys may become the sort of men who say: 'I have been so let down by a woman, I am never again going to get close enough to one to have it happen again'; or even the type who decide: 'I am going to punish every woman I come across because of what my mother did to me.' Not that these decisions are consciously made, but still men do recognize during therapy that that is precisely what they've been doing.

However, unlike men, it is rare for women fully to turn their backs on these feelings of dependency. They certainly may like it no more than men do, but they rarely choose to try to leave it all behind them. The issues faced between mothers and daughters through their lives are usually centred around dependency: daughter depends on mother when she's young, struggles to escape throughout much of her adult life, and then has mother depend upon her when she's middle-aged.

'I am too dependent on my mother. I know that and I hate it, but I can't seem to stop it': something I've heard on

101

numerous occasions over the years. Such women complain about their need to phone their mothers whenever anything goes wrong, whenever there's a problem with a boyfriend or if they're having difficulties at work. They have never managed separation during adolescence particularly well, probably because their mothers never let them but also because girls, unlike boys, never have that earlier experience of separation. Because the daughter stays attached throughout her life, she is much more obviously influenced by her mother than most sons are. If the mother wants her to stay that way, she has plenty of time to teach her that, not only is it wrong or foolish to separate, but also that the girl is unlikely to make it on her own, to manage without her mum. In this way the fear of abandonment that all babies are born with continues in girls and in women to a lesser or greater extent depending upon how willing the mother is to let her daughter go. If it does continue strongly, then it won't just be separation from her mother that causes the woman problems, but also the absence (or just its threat) of her boyfriend, her husband, her children.

Of course, this can happen to boys too, but it's more rare. These are the boys who made little effort to join dad when they were infants, and so who now stay linked for ever to their mums: the mothers' boys discussed in chapter eight.

Many male and female clients who describe other difficulties with their mothers are still actually concerned with issues of closeness and dependency. These are the ones who will be damned if they'll do this for their mother, make one more compromise, put up with this or that behaviour. But they too stay linked, even if the chain is anger.

And being dependent certainly does make you angry. This anger is perfectly apparent in the infant when he first decides he will feed himself, and you try to do it for him just for speed. Puce-faced tantrums are inevitable, as well as food all over the kitchen. You see it just as clearly in adolescents as they struggle to free themselves from their parents, whether it involves becoming an anarchist or wearing twinset and pearls. And you see it in British workers who are kept dependent – short of information, without knowledge about the whole task, without recognition of their adult skills. I see it in women who are being made dependent on their husbands: kept that way financially, or because they can't drive, or because they are made to feel they aren't strong enough to act or think for themselves. Given permission within therapy, the rage they can sometimes give words to is quite terrifying. Dependency and anger go hand in hand.

Often these women don't even seem to know they are angry: that timid tight little voice is only contradicted by the glint in her eye or by the clenched fist as she tells me how good her husband is really. When I get letters from women asking for advice, many will tell me awful facts about their partners' behaviour, and then will say that they'd really like to help. It took me quite a while to realize (by taking my own pulse) that I was being asked to carry the woman's anger for her so she could stay well-behaved and helpful. I was supposed to write back about how beastly he was being and how she ought to kick him out as hard as she could. Now I concentrate on her feelings and let her work out for herself what she should do about them!

This anger over dependency happens in men too. Not usually towards their mothers, because for the most part they've left them years before, but towards women in general and wives in particular because closeness to them reawakens those early feelings and makes them realize that the escape to dad was by no means complete: they still need woman as much as ever. All those yearnings and needs that were left at mum's door are transferred to the wife: 'With these needs I thee wed, but I'm furious to find I still need them.'

Wanting to get close to women means recognizing that you need them. For some men, like the MP Ken Livingstone, who has made no bones about preferring the company of women, this is no problem. They can be dependent when they need something, but independent when they wish. They can enjoy the company of women and feel grateful for what they are given. Letting oneself feel appreciation and gratitude like this are actually very mature emotions, and not enormously common I'm afraid. For what I suspect is the majority of men, there is a fear that closeness or commitment will demonstrate their need for something female, and this is far from comfortable. There are a number of things, he realizes, that he could easily get dependent upon once again.

• **The comfort of women.** This has always been seen as a dangerous lure for boys and men, and one to extricate yourself from as soon as possible if you want to be a man. Hence we have schools like Gordonstoun, Outward Bound movements, the cut and thrust of the boardroom, the institutionalization of the hard and rugged. Anything far from the softness and tenderness that epitomizes True Woman. Of course, man has always had pretty ambivalent feelings about this dark, soft, warm comfort, portraying women just as frequently with images of decay and corruption. For example, there is a statue on the Cathedral of Worms in Germany that shows a comforting, bosomy woman, dressed demurely, with a little soldier clinging to her ankles. Around the back of her, however, we see her whole body is being eaten by toads and snakes. Clearly, it tells us, you can't trust any woman. Their softness can corrupt you if you're not extremely careful, but nevertheless the warmth and comfort of which they are capable never ceases to beckon. A man could get attached to that.

• **The inspiration of women.** Muses are female. Women not only create geniuses by giving birth to them, they also provide the inspiration for them to attain that pinnacle of excellence. Like Dante and his elusive Beatrice. Part of the disappointment that forms the mid-life crisis and turns many a man against his wife has to do with the failure of the woman in the long run to have produced in him the genius that he was sure was there. Of course, he'd never do this if he hadn't been taught to lay his blame outside himself, and preferably at the feet of a woman.

• **The need for sex.** Men realize that, unless they become homosexual or celibate or stick to masturbation, they will need women for sex for the rest of their lives. Once again they find themselves dependent on a woman, and it feels pretty awful: women, it appears, hold the Ace of Hearts after all. One man told me: 'It's all right for you women; you can get sex whenever you want. You just have to crook your little finger. Men have to do all the work in trying to get you to agree: they have to court you, buy you flowers, be nice to you all night. Or pay for it. Of course it makes us angry.' And it makes them seek alternatives. Some find that paying for sex is an alternative to feeling they have to ask for it, though much of the violence towards prostitutes may well come from the fact that the dependency for women remains despite the fee. Others continue to enjoy or even prefer masturbation. As one man told me: 'I usually wank on my own after sex with Susie. I like it better in fact, because I'm in control.'

The loss of control that takes place for both men and women during orgasm can cause problems for both sexes, and some women in particular make sure they don't enjoy sex too much just so they don't come, since the loss of control is so frightening for them. It's perhaps even more alarming for men, since part of their definition of masculinity concerns being in control of things. It's rather unfortunate then, that they have been given a sexual organ which seems to have a life of its own. Not only does it occasionally fail to do what it should during sex itself, but also it does just the opposite when the man is trying to be serious. I am sure that one of the reasons why women are not welcome in the world of work – except where segregated into typing pools or on conveyor belts – is that men find the sexual arousal that their presence creates problematic since it's beyond their control. Controlled if anything, by women. Not too much surprise then at the article I read recently where male executives in the States are apparently being told to masturbate before they have a meeting with someone from another company, if that person is going to be female. Distraction due to an irrepressible organ might just lose him the deal.

Some writers, like the psychoanalyst Lederer, in his book *The Fear of Women* see post-coital depression, or the dip in mood that comes after sex, as being to do with feeling drained dry by the woman, but I suspect that it's more to do with the fact that he has once again let control slip from his grasp and given in to 'letting her have her way with him'.

The adult dependency upon women for sex is seen by Lederer as again awakening the feelings that the young child has for his mother. Here's how he describes the male orgasm (something we women find hard to imagine):

> . . . that other sheltering insertion, . . . bringing with
> it a sense of peace and completeness comparable to

immersion in a warm, long-forgotten ocean; a state of being before thought and before pain, an oceanic feeling less nostalgic than that which overcomes us in nature, but equally related to the mother: the visit home, the only way we 'can go home again' before that final homecoming of death.

It is of course true that in sex men always to some extent return to what Freud called 'the homestead whence we were evicted'. So it's not surprising that their feelings about this may be somewhat ambivalent. The move of some men towards celibacy is often described as the only way they know to get beyond these. Richard said: 'We stopped having sex four years ago because I wanted to. I loved Marguerita and somehow it seemed more and more that love and sex were incompatible. I was always fancying other women, and I resented her for so many of my problems. Since I absolutely decided to stop sex all this has gone.' William, an Australian lawyer, found he'd completely lost his libido now he was on a particular drug. Rather than be overwhelmed with concern, he told me:

It's actually the most wonderful relief not to have that constant twitch between my legs. I work so much better, I can concentrate, and I really enjoy women's company more. It's as if some barrier has been raised between us. I know it's easier for me because I don't have to be like this for ever, and so maybe I'm appreciating it more, but honestly it's such a treat to be able to use all my mind instead of just a bit of it.

The ambivalence men have about wanting and needing sex affects their relationships with women quite enormously. Partly this is due to the need in itself, and partly it's because women are then made witness to the man's potential or real inadequacies. I'm certainly not suggesting that celibacy is the solution to this, but it might be a necessary step for some men in order to untangle their emotions and start to live differently whether sexually active or not. I don't recommend that the husband comes home cheerfully one day (which happened with friends of mine) and announces that he's now a Buddhist and so celibate. I do suggest that you make any decisions together as part of a way of working through any problems you might have.

A Fear of Weakness

THERE IS no doubt that some men in all strata of society take their anger out on women both physically and in other less brutish ways. Men do feel angry about their need for women and women's capacity to say no to them. They have been taught that masculinity is about controlling, but here they are being controlled. But it isn't just about control. This behaviour has to do with the same things as all other forms of bullying: it is also a fear and hatred of weakness. In bullying, the aggressor sees the weak point in the victim – perhaps we all have one or perhaps victims have some ether which makes them stand out as having a really vulnerable spot, a true Achilles heel. Certainly, child victims usually find the same behaviour whichever school they go to, and often it happens in a string of foster homes as well. Women can also find themselves in the same position, with a stream of abusive partners.

Of course, all bullies, almost by definition, go for someone smaller or weaker than themselves, and so a traditional marriage can be a perfect place for them, especially if they make sure their wives stay poor and close to home. Here's an example:

> I have had a very difficult marriage as my husband is very critical of me and has always been a bit of a bully and hands out plenty of verbal abuse on occasions. I am basically quiet and find his shouting and language difficult to cope with. For example, we went together to a concert in a town I did not know and after the concert he vanished. I waited and waited for him until there was no one left. I had no money for a taxi and a couple were about to drive me home because they were

sorry for me, when he drove up hurling abuse at me,
saying I was unintelligent and he wasn't my guide dog
(I have cataracts and so don't see well at night).

Not surprisingly, you find that these bullies have been bullied,
humiliated or abused themselves when they were young. You
could say then that they are copying this behaviour, or that
they are seeking some sort of retribution. But if it's retribution,
why don't they go and beat up their fathers or whoever it was
who hurt them in the first place? The reason is because being
beaten or teased viciously when you are young is always a
humiliation – it emphasizes your smallness and your weakness,
and it is this weakness that you grow to hate, more sometimes
than you hate its perpetrator who may have been also loved or
admired. When later you are bigger and stronger you then
attack weaknesses wherever you see them. You are really
attacking your own small area of shame, but you do it to
others because the sight of their smallness or weakness awakens
your own early unhappiness. This is the dynamic of the bully.

Just as in the school playground, there are two ways of
handling constant bullying: you either have to get out of the
situation, and sometimes that is quite appropriate; or you have
to stand up to the bully. The woman who wrote the letter
above went on to say that, even after twenty-five years of it,
she had managed to change things by fighting back verbally.
The abuse had almost stopped, and they were getting on much
better!

Some husbands are bullies and so, for that matter, are some
wives. But most are not. Most have had good enough parenting that lets them become reasonably loving, allows them to
get reasonably close. Nevertheless, we have all been small and
weak at some point and our dependency upon our parents
highlighted this. When boys step across to join their fathers,
they renounce (as well as they can at that age) their dependence
on their mothers and the weakness that it demonstrates to the
world. As a result of this, most men are pretty unforgiving
about weakness in themselves and rarely compassionate about
it in others. They may not attack it physically, but still they
turn away from it. I once looked after a bitch from an animal
rescue home. She'd been beaten by men and cringed whenever

one came near. When I popped round to my neighbour's with her on a lead I watched this pleasant reasonable man's face contort at the sight of her cringing form and saw his leg moving back to kick her. I moved away hastily. Later we were talking about childhood and he told me about being beaten by his father when he returned from the war to find this new little usurper in his place. The humiliating brutality of this large strong man had made my neighbour hate fear and weakness in others or in himself more than any other trait.

And women stereotypically are seen as weak: physically less strong, emotionally fluttering, more likely to burst into tears, and so on. Men hate this weakness because it reminds them of their own small vulnerable centre which they despise. But women dislike weak men too. Taught that they must control their own aggression and wrath, many women rely upon men to be aggressive for them. Mandy, who's eighteen, told me:

> I went to a disco with Sean and the bouncer on the door wouldn't let us in because he said they were full up. Sean was arguing with him, but very reasonably like they were having a chat. I could feel myself getting hotter and hotter. I didn't want this – I wanted Sean to hit the bouncer. I know it sounds awful, but I really wanted it. When he didn't I felt let down somehow. I didn't let Sean touch me that night.

This dislike of apparent weakness might be to do with the woman's use of men for vicarious aggression – and certainly the white feathers they gave out to non-fighters in World War I were precisely a result of that – but also they will occasionally have a similar root to men's in representing a fear of their own weakness. For example, another woman, middle-class and married to a professional man who had to go into hospital for a small exploratory operation, told me that the sight of him lying there pathetic and immobilized horrified and disgusted her. 'I couldn't bear him to look so weak and ineffectual. I actually felt physically sick at the sight. While he was in hospital, I slept with someone else.' No wonder men go on fearing weakness, fearing failure: not only are they likely to be banished from the world of men if they show such behaviour, but women too are egging them on to be strong, also with the threat of rejection. And women means mothers, girlfriends and wives.

The Fear of Failure

So IF men dislike weak women, does this mean that they are more likely to go for strong ones? Well, if you're a strong woman you'll know that the answer is very rarely going to be 'yes'. It appears to me that men are very often attracted to strong women, but then find them much too difficult to handle. Watching female friends and clients go through this difficulty over and over again, it is also apparent that the men often leave them in particularly vicious ways. One woman, successful in business but not so lucky in love, had been going out with a man she really liked for just three months when they went skiing together. After a few days of being constantly in each other's company, he very blatantly began to flirt with a young pretty girl in her late teens and finally made it clear to everyone in the party that they had had sex. When the woman protested, he launched into a dreadful public attack on her, dragging up any vulnerable points he could think of and inventing others such as how hopeless she was in bed.

This initial attraction and later distaste for apparently strong women is an example of the conflict that men feel between their fear of weakness on the one hand, and their fear of sexual failure on the other. Many men find the subjugation of a less obviously strong woman is in itself arousing sexually, so that they can perform with confidence only in these situations. Almost all hard pornography is concerned with subjugation of one kind or another, and I would suspect that most men who use it would at some stage have felt abused themselves. These men are somewhat less secure with a woman who knows what she wants, who expects reasonably frequent satisfaction, and who is confident enough not to be demolished by his absence. This is not a woman who will cling to him, make him work too hard, expect the perfect provider. But it just might be a woman who sets other standards – sexual or emotional – which he might fail to meet.

The conflict reflects the two extreme images of woman that have existed for the last two thousand years or so: that woman is pure and chaste and that sex is actually unpleasant for her, so men have to wheedle it out, rape, or go elsewhere; and that woman is essentially wanton and can't get enough sex to satisfy her. These quotes are a good illustration of what is often called the Madonna-Whore paradox:

> If she is normally developed mentally, and well-bred, her sexual desire is small. If this were not so the whole world would become a brothel and marriage and family impossible.
>
> Krafft-Ebing, *Psychopathia Sexualis* 1920

> A well-bred woman does not seek carnal gratification, and she is usually apathetic to sexual pleasures. Her love is physical or spiritual, rather than carnal, and her passiveness in regard to coition often amounts to disgust for it . . .
>
> Dr O. A. Wall *Sex and Sex Worship* 1932

On the other hand:

> Women are evil temptresses
>
> *al Bukhari*, Islamic text

> Give not the power of thy soul to a woman: lest she enter upon thy strength, and thou be confounded.
>
> *Ecclesiastes, Holy Bible*

> Of women's unnatural insatiable lust, what country, what village doth not complain.
>
> Robert Burton *Anatomy of Melancholy* [1577–1640]

> An unusually sexually promiscuous young lady.
>
> Judge William Reinecke, on a girl, aged five, who had been sexually assaulted by her mother's boyfriend, Wisconsin USA, 1982

This fear of the lustful, insatiable woman has an unpleasant ring of truth for many men today: over the past twenty years we have read numerous articles in magazines like *Cosmopolitan* which appear to encourage women to become more demanding and more predatory in their sexual activity. The achievement of orgasm is seen as an absolutely equal right, and many women would want not just one, but several. It's such a subtle balance, all this, between the woman feeling she is sexually inadequate, boring but pure, because she can't have orgasms easily—an inevitable result of her tendency to blame things on herself and of men to blame things on others – and then switching to appearing rampant when she discovers by accident that her body is actually capable of multiple orgasms almost to order. In this situation she can appear to turn from Madonna to Whore almost overnight.

The myth that women are really nymphomaniacs was created by men perhaps by projecting their own lust onto the woman or girl. As we saw earlier, projection is a useful psychological defence that stops us owning the less than pleasant bits of ourselves and seeing them instead in others. Spouses do it to each other, parents do it to their children, one department, one race, one country does it to another, men do it to women, and vice versa. We all know about it instinctively. When a British judge says of an eight-year-old little girl who's been raped that 'she was no angel', we know really that, as well as declaring himself to be in the same club as the rapist, he is also projecting his own lust onto the girl. We know that's true, thank God, without needing a psychologist to tell us.

This is a real heads-you-win-tails-I-lose situation for women, and it can't be much fun for men either. The reality is that women are both good and bad, sexy and dependable, caring and demanding. Having the Madonna or the Whore allows these men not to fail sexually: either she hates sex and so can't be satisfied, or she can't get enough – and so can't be satisfied. But having these split views of women in society, in the media, and in their parents' minds when they raised them, tends to make many women mould themselves one way or the other. Whichever type of woman men go for, they are going to be troubled: whether it's by the constant reminder of everything they fear most in themselves, or by the threat posed by the strong woman that they will be shown to be not as clearly masculine as they would like. In both situations, the root fear is that they will not be found to be the strong, constantly randy stereotype of manhood that is basically the only one acceptable.

This fear is not of women rejecting them (though that plays a part) so much as it is of other men finding out that they are in some way not quite male. Whenever a man tells me about his wife having affairs, his main concern – greater even than the possible loss of the woman he loves – is that other men might laugh at him. Simon came for help with his panic attacks. In case you're lucky enough not to know what these are, a panic attack is a terrifying hotchpotch of physical symptoms like pounding heart, cold sweats, nausea and so on which generally means that a person has to leave wherever he is, wondering if he will die on the way.

Simon had his first one during a party when he saw his wife wink at another man across the room. She denied it, but that's irrelevant. The wink was followed by the sound of a man laughing and, instantly, by his panic attack. He left at once, sitting in the car hugging himself in terror until she came to see what had happened to him. Like depression, panic is a useful sign that we have touched upon some fundamental fear. I frequently find that women get them when they experience a hint of real anger or strength in themselves in relation to their partners; men, on the other hand, may have them when they feel the possibility of being seen as weak or as a sexual failure. Men frequently treat panic in the same way they treat depression – with alcohol. Honestly, it doesn't work.

So the mythical insatiability of some women means not just that the man will eventually fail her – in particular, that his penis will not get hard or stay hard – but also that she will then seek other men to satisfy her. And word will get around. Most nations over the centuries have created laws to protect men from this indignity, and many Muslim countries decree the stoning of adulterous women. Even in the west it seems we can easily be lured into similar safeguards: in her book *The War Against Women*, Marilyn French points out that in Connecticut an old law was revived as recently as 1990 which allowed the prosecution of adulterous wives, and three women were arrested under it before it was repealed. Such laws have nothing to do with protecting the family – all the evidence shows that an absent father is just as likely to affect a child as an absent mother – but everything to do with protecting the man. Every man knows that his place in the club, his power, depends upon such things being secure.

Fear or Hate?

IT'S CLEAR that men have many reasons to fear women – whether it's because they dislike the thought of dependency or weakness, or whether they view women as having the ability to show them up as failures in some way. Lederer tells us: 'And yet – in the unashamed privacy of our consulting rooms we do from time to time see strong men fret, and hear them talk of women with dread and horror and awe, as if women, far from being timid creatures to be patronized, were powerful as the sea and inescapable as fate.'

Whatever the cause, the organization of the sexes into mothers and fathers, sons and daughters, wives and husbands with the power consistently but tenuously handed to the male, is bound to make men worry about what options are left to them if they lose that power. The trouble is that, at least until recently, women's only true power was the ability to take away men's power, whether by fostering his dependency or denying him sex or making him feel a failure because he couldn't satisfy her sexually or economically. That makes woman always a threat, always something to fear.

In fact, there is another power that women use over men – or rather over boys – and that's the power to use them sexually. I realize that talking about the sexual abuse of boys by their mothers or big sisters is not very politically correct from a feminist point of view: let's face it, it's only been very recently that the enormity of men's abuse of women and girls has come to light, and we don't want to put a shade on that by raising new issues. But this abuse exists and I suspect that it is far, far more common than any of us could imagine. Asking round a group of four men recently, I found instances where it had happened to three of them, though only one knew that it was clearly sexual and clearly perpetrated by the woman rather than by himself as a child. In this case his elder sister had seduced him when he was twelve and she was sixteen, and had continued to do so for three years until she went to university. If it had happened the other way around, it would have been called rape rather than seduction. How is he now? Well, he's not so bad: he's risen quite high in his job, and is still rising; he has five children to whom he seems pleasant, if usually absent; and he's had three wives and countless mistresses. The mistresses are usually someone well known to the wife – a close friend, a neighbour, a sister. I don't know what the dynamic is – he's not my client – but it seems to me that he both loves women and hates them, longs for them and despises them, wants them close and rejects them.

The second man's father had left home shortly after his birth. The mother was always described as a saint the way she cared for her daughters and her new little son. And no doubt she worked hard and life was difficult. But her son began to share her bed on and off from the age of two until he was about seven, when he stopped (he doesn't remember why). When he was thirteen and puberty was shaking him around day and night, he began again to get into his mother's bed, this time when she was apparently asleep. He would run his hands over her body, and rub himself against her till he came. Who seduced whom? The woman passive, even with her eyes shut (though he and we know that she could only be awake), and he being forced into the active role, so that he felt the defiler of the saint. His adult relationships with women, including his wives, have been the results of a turbulent mixture of guilt and anger: his extreme guilt towards his mother is played out by anger towards women, followed by guilt, and so on.

The third man knew that his mother used to come to him at night and pull down his covers and just look at him: enough to give any young man, supposed to be asleep, an erection. Her own marriage was very unhappy and now he can only imagine that she became aroused watching him.

In *Broken Boys/Mending Men: Recovery from Childhood Sexual Abuse*, Stephan Grubman-Black describes similar relationships – situations where the woman, either without a partner or with

115

one who gave little love, has used her son as some sort of substitute husband, blurring the boundary in a way that confuses the boy and the man he becomes.

We don't know how many men have had experiences like this when they were young but the figures for child sexual abuse overall are horrifying. In the United Kingdom community surveys show that around 12 per cent of females and 8 per cent of males have received unwanted sexual touching before they reached adulthood, and a national survey in the States found 27 per cent of women and 16 per cent of men reporting sexual victimization in childhood.

Certainly the vast majority of abuse comes from men and not from women, but these accounts show that women cannot shun all responsibility. It's still very hard for boys to admit to such acts or even to count it as abuse. One young man told me that when, aged four, he asked his mother why she had no penis, she showed him her genitals. Perhaps she thought it was a liberal thing to do, but it strikes me as a vicious act that was potentially arousing and so bound to create the guilt he feels today. When a woman does the abusing, then the retaliation in adult life is perhaps more direct, more understandably aimed at women in general; but male-male abuse contains just as much complex humiliation, and so both are likely to make men hit back at anything they see as small and weak, the abused part of themselves that they'd rather forget. Any form of victimization, physical or sexual, is likely to make men behave badly towards women, whether through the depression that it causes and that in men often comes out in violence or destructiveness, or because it makes them feel an even more desperate urge to be masculine in all its stereotypical ways, and they need a woman to fulfil this.

So do men hate women? What most men feel towards women is varied and complex, but we cannot deny that, for many of them, it contains a large element of some sort of strong negative emotion. Although few women actually experience this as hatred, there is no doubt that such strong feelings do exist for many men, often made even more complicated by love and guilt. What I have tried to explore in this chapter is the ways that these extreme negative feelings are underpinned by a fear that doesn't belong to the present, but is rooted in early relationships with mothers and fathers. Learning to recognize what belongs in the past is an essential step in freeing yourself from its chains and beginning to live more peacefully in the present. We only seem able to tackle hate by incarceration and punishment – by approved schools, divorce courts, or by abandoning the bully. Research demonstrates consistently the uselessness of such methods in bringing about change; hate, if anything, seems to grow as a result. But research also shows that we can tackle fear much more effectively, primarily by helping people to understand the fear, to appreciate that it belongs to something that has gone, and to face and get close to the symbol of this fear today. To conquer fear like that, face-to-face, you have to be a hero. And why not?

Part II

In Practice . . .

Chapter 7

Waving or Drowning?

Wife (to husband): Do you love me?
Husband (from behind newspaper): I'm here aren't I?

Joke drawn by Calman

BEYOND ANYTHING else – beyond all the sadness of affairs, the anxiety of sexual difficulties, perhaps even beyond boredom and cruelty – comes the silence that stops couples understanding what is happening to them, what hurts and why, and how they might change it. One thing that we know about why some marriages work and why others don't is that, where there is poor communication between the partners, the relationship is both more likely to fail and to be less satisfying even where they stay together. If we're going to create anything good for the future out of the upheavals that are happening today in society and in our families, then speaking about them, confronting the myths, refusing to live a lie, is the first task we face.

Whereas the following chapters deal with the more specific problems of marriage that come out of our early experience and our socialization, and offer ways to think about these, this chapter deals with the communication problems that underlie so many of the others, and suggests ways to improve things:

121

what stops communication and what helps it to flow again. Although it's directed towards helping difficult times in relationships, it won't hurt to tackle some of the exercises together even if everything's swinging. If one of you refuses to join in, then it should still be useful for the other one to work on this alone.

Being There

THE GREATEST silence of all comes from the absence of one partner from the home, and the latest research shows that measuring the time that couples are actually in each other's company is the best predictor of success. Even when you take into account that some of them work long hours or go away on business, it's the ones who still make time to be together that stay together best. You can't communicate too well unless you're there – phones and letters are useful, but they are prone to dangerous misunderstandings that happen less when you're face-to-face. Of course, what being together means is that you have the opportunity to communicate. This might not always be chatter – couples who have been married for quite a while usually value simply being in each other's presence. Even when you are angry with your partner, you often need their presence in order to put some shape to what you feel. This very primitive form of communication, just by the presence of someone you love, goes right back to those earliest days of all – to the safety that the baby felt when it knew its mother was there in the room, close by.

As your relationship lengthens you build up a whole form of communication by tiny signs – a pet name, a song that takes you back, a raised eyebrow that signifies some old joke, and so on. This is a language shared only by the couple, and hard to understand by an outsider. It's one of the things that makes losing a partner so painful, having no one left to talk to in your secret language. I have no doubt that this is an important part of communicating in any successful marriage.

But in some marriages, the silences are painful rather than

loving, and the ways of communicating are indirect, loaded with malice or dissatisfaction, or stuck in a dreadful groove which makes life seem like a time-warp from which you long only to escape.

The Budgie as the Message

S OME COUPLES use a go-between to dilute the difficulty they seem to feel about communicating face-to-face. Any of you who have a dog or a cat will probably recognize the importance of being able to direct your message to the pet instead of your partner. When our dog died we found it quite difficult for a while not to be able to say things to each other indirectly: 'Oh, dear, Jet, he's not in a very good mood today, is he?' That sort of thing! We had to learn to say it to each other instead. As for the old family habit of kicking the cat, or making sure the goldfish fails to thrive – what else is this but a way of delivering your message to someone other than its true receiver?

More serious than using the pet is using the children: 'Tell your father his dinner's on the table,' is often not half as innocuous a demand as it sounds. 'Don't bother mummy, darling. She's in one of her sulks.' Worse still, is when we deliver not just the message but also the emotions we feel towards a partner to the children instead. Sasha told me:

> Elliott would end every confrontation by going out to the pub, slamming the door and taking the car. I'd be left full of anger, trapped in with the boys. I know I took it out on Andy [her eldest son] – he looks like Elliott and acts like him a lot of the time – and within minutes we'd have got into a row. It made me feel worse, it solved nothing, and it must have hurt Andy.

Certainly part of what Sasha was doing was venting her anger – communicating her feelings – to her son instead of to her husband. But also, as we'll see in chapter eight, Andy might have been helping in this by being naughty so that his mother and father could diffuse some of their feelings about each other through him.

When people go for help, whether individually or as a couple, it is communication that they are seeking: both the opportunity to be able to talk to another person about what is happening for them, and to be listened to, and for that person to be able to do his or her utmost to understand and to pass that understanding back. With couples, the therapist or counsellor initially becomes the go-between, acts as a funnel between them, catching any possible communications, verbal or non-verbal, and passing them on to the other partner so that they are clarified or no longer missed and left to reverberate and bounce endlessly and dangerously around the room like a squashball out in space. After a while, the couple is taught exercises to make them more aware of what is being said, and what is not being said, and what effect this has, so they can learn to do without the go-between and communicate together more directly.

Back to Square One

WHEN COUPLES get into difficulties in their marriages, they are usually very well rehearsed in what they feel at the moment – what they dislike most about the other party, what's making everything go wrong. When they talk about these things, with or without a go-between, they relapse instantly into accusations and formuli. However it starts, it quickly disintegrates into a well-learnt script: I say this and you say that so I say this then you storm off, and so on. So it's no use using what's happening now to start to learn how to communicate. It's all too negative. Much better to go back to the very beginning.

Sit together, preferably facing each other on two chairs with nothing in between you. Toss a coin for who'll go first. That partner tells the other what it was that caused the first attraction: 'When I first met you I was attracted by your . . .' When this partner stops speaking the other can repeat those attributes back: 'When you first met me, you especially liked me because . . .' You do this because communicating is not just about giving the message, but also about accurately receiving it. Write down the list of attractions under your name, and repeat the process the other way round. What you have now is two lists of attractions. The following example is based on a couple that we'll call Jean and John. They'd been married for eighteen years; they described themselves as 'stuck', but they came for help when John had confessed a brief affair, heavy drinking and when, for the first time, he'd raised his fist to Jean. Here's their lists:

JEAN WAS ATTRACTED TO JOHN BECAUSE OF HIS:	JOHN WAS ATTRACTED TO JEAN BECAUSE OF HER:
Humour	Secret smile
Affection	Cheerfulness
Strength	
Romantic gestures	Carefulness
Spontaneity	Containment
Sad life	Sexiness

When you have a list for each person, you will need to explain just what you mean. How did Jean 'know' John had strength? And vice versa? What were the signs? What was an example? What did Jean's secret smile mean to John? What did he think she knew? Did Jean feel she could 'fix' John's sad life? It sounds like a soap, but without these questions how do we know just what we mean? What John meant by 'strength', for example, might be very different to what Jean recognized in him. For John it meant that Jean didn't constantly have to have him around, that she let him go out with the boys, that she had her own career. For her, it meant that she could lean on him, depend on him, let go of some of her independence. No wonder you could smell the disappointment that hung between them!

When you feel you're clear about meanings, each of you should go on to say why each of these characteristics was important. This is more difficult, because sometimes they might reflect aspects of earlier relationships. For example, Jean said: 'I didn't know my father, but I'm told he was strong and romantic, and I thought you were like him.' John said: 'My mother was depressed and I seemed always to be trying to make her happy; it was nice to have someone who seemed cheerful instead.' Jean's containment or self-sufficiency might also be a relief after the neediness of his depressed mother.

But not everything belongs to the past: it might be that Jean felt her carefulness – about money, or jobs, or clothes – was nicely balanced by John's more adventurous or even impulsive actions. She could get some excitement from him, while he could hold himself tethered safely by her. They could see quite quickly that his spontaneity, constantly fuelled by alcohol, had become an emotional and financial problem to both of them, while her carefulness had caused her to restrict her life almost to the point of paralysis. The next step is to work out which of these attractions is still present, which were never really there, and which seem to have faded away. Some of them might have gone, but could easily be begun again; for example, Jean could explain to John what she means by 'romantic behaviour' and then he could agree to introduce it once more. John could explain to Jean what he found sexy and work out ways together that it might be recaptured. He might also agree to tell her when he wants to make love rather than behaving badly to let her know that something's wrong (just as he did as a little boy when he wanted his mother's love and attention). Equally, she might learn to read his non-verbal messages more accurately, rather than use non-communication as a reason to withdraw her attention still further.

Mind-reading

I F YOU don't spell out just what you mean by words like 'romantic' or 'affectionate' or 'strong', then you can be pretty sure that your partner will have a different definition to you. Rather than communicating them clearly and directly we hope those we love will recognize our needs: if they really loved us they'd know just what we wanted. They'd easily be able to read our minds.

This longing for mind-reading comes partly from an unreal expectation of what love can produce, and also from a fear in each of us to say what we really want. Why do we fear it so much? Certainly for some of us, like Jean, it comes from the disappointments of childhood, when what she wanted – her father to come back to them, her mother to show she was loved as much as her brother – was simply never granted. In this marriage now, with all its hopes and dreams, how could she bear the disappointment of asking for something funda- mental and not being given it? So, instead of building on the initial love between them, she builds up her own little fortress against disappointment: her work and her ability to earn good money enables her to pour scorn on her husband when really what he wants is the sort of admiration his mother never gave him. Her denial of her need for his strength helps to destroy its possibility; moreover, her mother so admired her brother's strength, that Jean was left with envious feelings that stopped her really taking it from John. At the same time, his need for her strength implied the possibility of weakness and he helped to deny this with the manly flamboyance of alcohol, affairs, and now violence.

Explaining what we mean by words like 'affection' can also untie some of the strings that attach us to our past. What we wanted when we were youngsters is not going to be possible fully to replace now we are adults. You need to spell out what you see as affectionate adult behaviours: 'I want you to kiss me when I come home; I want you to look at me when I speak to you; I want a reply when I say I love you.' Without spelling these things out, John saying he felt affectionate would not be good enough. And that's what you're trying to communicate: just what's 'good enough'. You're grown-ups now; about most things you're perfectly realistic. So this is the time to leave behind the longings that come from imperfect parenting – and most of us have had this – and the dreams that they are turned into by our society, and to decide precisely what is good enough.

If both of you are communicating as fully and as carefully as you can, then this first exercise will take quite a long time. It will certainly be more than enough to start you off. Some- times couples need no more than this: it can reawaken in them the warm feelings they had for each other that they thought were gone, and this small rekindling can be enough to help them on their way to developing these characteristics in an adult way. Whether it has immediate results or not, however, isn't so important as trying together to communicate honestly and to understand something about your partnership. At the end of the session tell your partner how you feel. I suspect that many of you will say 'sad', because it is sad to leave things behind and, inevitably, you will find that some of those early attractions were never there in the first place: what you left behind actually belonged to the longings of your childhood. Don't try to talk each other out of these feelings, but just give each other a hug if this feels OK.

The exercise led Jean and John towards some actions which took them out of their rut. John joined AA with the conviction that he had to know how he felt without alcohol. He resolved to find other ways to ask for things, other than by behaving badly. Jean decided to try telling him what she needed from him, and to dare to put a halt on the expansion of her work so that they could spend time together. She resolved to begin to separate her envious feelings towards her brother from those she felt for John. Big tasks, but changing just one thing in a marriage changes everything, and so once one of you dares to do this, nothing will be the same again. Frightening? Well, weigh it up – the safety of the status quo, or the possibilities of change.

Strong Silent Types

BUT WHAT if the feeling you're left with is frustration? You've done the exercise, and still you feel he hasn't been open with you. He's backed off from things you really wanted to get into, for example. I'm referring to a man here because we know (from chapter five) that men do communicate in a different way to women, and this can drive both of them to distraction. You'll remember that while women talk to establish closeness, and expect men to do the same, men talk when they have something to say. This doesn't mean they don't talk a lot – they do – but it will frequently involve something to establish their position as a man; to ensure they stay superior or, at least, that they are not humiliated. Since they are not usually in competition with women, there is less need to communicate with them. This doesn't mean they don't love them, however. You're not going to change such a fundamental gender difference overnight: certainly not beyond simply recognizing it and treating it with humour. It's this recognition that lets you watch your usually silent husband talking endlessly to his mates, and to realize that this doesn't mean he loves them more than he does you. It lets you decide that, rather than keep demanding your version of intimacy from him, you'll get that sort of relating from your women friends. But there are also ways that you can encourage this process more determinedly. Here's a few tips for both parties:

- Understand the differences in communication (see p. 93)

- Teach yourself to recognize other ways that he or she is communicating – those that are different to how you do it.

- Men have to be taught that learning to express feelings and distress is not a sign of weakness, but of strength. Women have to be sure they believe this if they are to teach it.

- Men might learn to see the metamessage – that she is not saying what she wants quite as clearly as he would. For example, 'What a lovely day for a walk,' means 'I want to go for a walk'. It will help them too with understanding their daughters, and female colleagues at work.

- Women might learn to tell themselves that love is shown in any number of ways, and to train themselves to notice what these are.

129

- Women need to express their needs very clearly. Ask yourself why you don't; what you fear? Ask too what you have to lose if they're not being met anyway?

- Men and women could use some of the exercises in this chapter in order to communicate, initially in a structured way.

Sometimes men who seem to have learnt how to talk in similar ways to their wives can cause even more consternation if they then behave unexpectedly. This was the situation of Tim and Fay. In the three years they were married he had seemed to chat away quite happily about plans for the house, for children and so on, but deep down he was dreading the increasing responsibility. When he left she felt betrayed. Despite apparently being able to talk in the female way – where discussions of houses, nicknacks and children implied an intimate future together – her husband was unable to tell his wife his real feelings, of being unhappy and over-burdened, just like any other uncommunicative man. He could not see that there are many steps in between talking intimately like his wife did and saying nothing at all except goodbye.

Reading Between the Lines

THERE ARE ways to communicate other than words, and these need recognizing. You'll remember from chapter three that research has shown that boys show their unhappiness in different ways to girls. Girls who grow up to be depressed are more withdrawn and self-punitive; boys, on the other hand, are much more likely to be obstreperous and wilful. If you have a boy who's constantly behaving badly, the only way through it is usually to put your arms around him and love him for a while, until he can find the words to talk about his unhappiness. Maybe a man who behaves badly is doing the same thing? I know he should find better ways of communicating, but maybe he just hasn't learnt how. Maybe he, like so many men, was taught that expressing feelings other than anger was simply unmanly. Perhaps, if you love him enough, it just might be worth addressing his pain, trying to find out what's happening to him through love rather than through anger and retaliation. It's just an experiment. It might not work. But it's worth a try. Perhaps.

You can use the following exercise to learn to appreciate other possible ways of communicating:

The Woman: Whenever your partner irritates or upsets you by something he says or does, recognize this and try to work out what he's really trying to say. Don't tell him when you're doing it, but make a note of what conclusions you've come to.

The Man: Try to be aware of when your partner is doing this exercise. Note down what it might be that you said or did that upset or irritated her, and how you noticed that it was happening.

Depending on the frequency of her irritations, you might want to compare your notes daily or weekly or somewhere in between. Then swap round and reverse the exercise and compare notes again. Tell each other what you have learned from this in terms of how each of you communicates and how you could do it more clearly.

Wanting to Hear, but Not Wanting to Know

THE OTHER reason that your male partner might not be communicating with you is because you don't want him to. Even women who complain that their husbands never say what they feel or never talk about what's happening to them, often come to realize that they simply don't want to hear the words. If, as a woman, you've had a father who expressed his anger or disdain very clearly to you, you might very well not want your man to do the same. In some way, the woman cuts off the expression of feelings in the man, just in case the words contain messages she cannot bear to hear.

After a few initial tries, John was at last trying to tell his wife what he'd felt over the last few difficult years together. Each time he spoke I saw Jean's head turn away ever so slightly. John would tail off again, and look hopeless. 'What are you frightened that John will say?' I asked her. It took some time. Her head hurt, she said, trying to get beyond the anger to the fear. 'I think that he is going to tell me he will leave me,' she finally wept. Over the next few weeks we managed to explore her feelings of abandonment, something that was a feature of her childhood.

Other people for whom anger and aggression were a frequent part of early family life, fear that, if they speak they will get terribly angry, or, if they let their partner speak he or she will blow up in ways a parent once did. Again, this stops communication. Equally, men are sometimes afraid to communicate with women because they feel they're too fragile to take it. So John also hid his fears and concerns from Jean just as he'd learnt to do from his depressed mother when he was a boy. He coped with the inevitable unhappiness that came from this bottling up process by drinking heavily.

To summarise what might be stopping communication:

- You may be expecting too much: we all like different levels of communication and varying amounts of contact.

- Your partner may be communicating in other ways to you and you're not noticing.

- You may be blocking communication even though you want it.

- Your partner may not dare to communicate because of the fear of upsetting things.

Expressing Yourself

BLAME CAN ROAM around a marriage or even round the whole family in ways that are destructive and useless in terms of change. If I blame you for everything, I become your victim. If I take all your blame onto myself, then I might be powerful, but again nothing will change. Research shows that it can actually cause marital unhappiness in the future. Other research (by Gottman and Krokoff) also followed couples over a period of time. They found that wives who did what the husband wanted and were always pleasant early on reported, as did their husbands, that their marriage was wonderful. However, when they were followed up it was found that they were then much less satisfied and the husbands had withdrawn from them. The couples they followed where the wife had said she was able to show anger during any rows actually improved their marital satisfaction over the period of the study. Good news for saying it the way it is!

The importance of good communication is vital. It's not what you say but the way that you say it. This affects even the order of the words you use to describe what you're feeling. For example, if you say: 'You did this, and you did that, and you made me feel so miserable,' you might be expressing your feelings, but you're losing all your power in doing it. You're staying the victim. If, on the other hand, you say: 'I feel very angry when you do that', you are keeping the power, the right to be angry, and saying what provokes it, without demanding in any way that your partner change. The order of the words – always starting with 'I' – is important, but so is the recognition that your partner doesn't have to change. Jean was asked to express her feelings to John about his drinking. She said: 'I hate you when you're drunk because you get so withdrawn from me. But you don't have to change.' You can imagine how those last few words can stick in the throat! But the reality is that John did have the right to choose whether to change or not, just as Jean had the right to say how she felt about it, and maybe what she might do in reaction to it.

Accepting that there is no way we can make a partner

change is part of the communication. It's particularly necessary with women because of their tendency to try constantly to make things all right within a relationship. The structure of the words is also important to stop the woman being a victim of the relationship, and to stop her trying to gain power by seeing herself as having the key to his behaviour, as knowing the only route to his happiness.

Perhaps the most useful communication exercise of all for couples (and families as a whole) is for each of you to make one angry or resenting statement each day, and one appreciating statement. For example: 'I resent you for not backing me up when I disciplined our son', and 'I appreciate you for putting your arms around me when you knew I was upset.' They may be as mundane as, 'I appreciate you for remembering to buy salt!' This exercise is important because it first opens up the correct form of expressive communication; second, because it begins to teach the other partner just what it is that is appreciated or resented. Without that we're hoping, guessing, but certainly not mindreading.

For those of you who find the expression of angry, negative feelings particularly difficult (and this is often the man!), you'll find that once you have got them out in this way, the appreciative and loving feelings flow much more easily. As Daldrup and Gust point out in their book *Freedom from Anger*, bottling up resentful feelings is like keeping your foot on the soft pedal – everything else gets repressed too and so joy and enthusiasm and gratitude and love can't be felt the way they should be. Expressing your anger lets all the rest flow too.

Keeping in Touch

B EFORE ALL those words, before we had learnt to talk at all, our mothers and fathers communicated with us by touch. We could easily understand love that passed through fingertips and breasts. Even when we began to label things with words, we learnt the importance of 'keeping in touch', of being 'touched' by someone kind, the value of a 'hands on' experience. Now we are more scientific, we know through research what we should have known instinctively, that stroking and massage brings about wellbeing and reduces pain in any number of conditions; stroking pets, for example, reduces blood pressure. But you don't have to use a pet as a go-between to stop you touching your partner (could that be why the British have so many pets?). You can undoubtedly reduce his or her blood pressure by massage, and chances are you will find you create a new openness as well. Touching each other will work where words fail you, so when you or your partner seem irretrievably stuck, touch his hand or stroke her face. Communicate that way.

Talking Dirty

How do you use some of these strategies to talk more openly about sex? Well, partly they will help you to some extent to understand why discussing aspects of your sexual partnership is difficult: what it was in your childhood that has made it that way. That's a good beginning, but it may not be sufficiently satisfying in the long run. More than that you need to be able to convey to your partner what you want in terms of sex, and for them to be able to let you know whether that's available, or whether they'd prefer something else instead. Discussing it is just as much an area for give and take, compromise, and mutual enjoyment as is any other form of problem solving. Agreeing on what you want is no different, for example, to planning a special gourmet dinner: who gets to decide on first course, main course, and maybe a dessert that you both find irresistible. Quite often, of course, beans on toast is just fine for both of you!

Part of this process is to do with setting boundaries – not in your head, but out in the open. If a particular form of sex upsets or hurts you, then you have to make it very clear that that's out. Making this explicit with unambiguous words stops the hope and disappointment of the expectant partner. Not making it clear means that the pressure continues, and chances are anger on both sides isn't far away. Feeling guilty about refusing may make you feel anger, and so on. The difficulty for women is that, having never experienced that sharp distinct boundary between themselves and their mothers, they are never too good at knowing where the boundaries should lie: what's acceptable for them and what isn't. Their boundaries are always being penetrated.

Because men have taken that first step away from mother, and created that first important boundary, they are unlikely to find this much of a problem. They are clear about what they're willing to do. More worrying is the point that part of what we consider stereotypically male behaviour features being in command and sometimes even the humiliation of women. So some apparent desires are really just ways of insisting on your maleness: 'I must be a man, I do this', or 'I must do this because I'm a man'. The other problem that we've talked about before is the woman's tendency to blame herself (at least early on) when things go wrong, sexually or otherwise. This can allow the man the dubious privilege of being able to blame her for all his sexual ills: 'If only you let me do X, Y, and Z, everything would be all right.'

Well, it won't. No marriage problem is cured by a particular type of bonk; no sexual difficulties are eased by pretending that they are all to do with the other person. John admitted his anger towards Jean with great difficulty. Remember, he'd had a depressed mother, so expressing negative feelings directly to a woman was definitely not part of his repertoire. What he felt angry about was her determination (as he saw it, and it might have been true) not to notice his overtures for sex. He showed this anger eventually by having an affair which (surprise, surprise) he was able to communicate to Jean by way of a confession, although it was in truth a punishment. Her reaction to this was neither to forgive the confession nor to take her punishment like a woman, but instead to withdraw even further into her job. The threat of violence was the next step in this escalation of despair; the unpicking of these miscommunications and the introduction of ones that were clear and honest provided building blocks for a more hopeful future.

Saying It Like It Is

HERE ARE SOME strategies that might help communication about sex:

- Notice how you suggest sex. Are you asking explicitly? Hinting broadly (or even narrowly)? Behaving badly? Think about why you might find it so difficult just to ask. Is it because it shows your dependency, your need? Practise asking explicitly: you'll find you're still a man for all that (and how nice to be a man who no longer has to have tantrums to get what he wants!). If as a woman you ask for something specific, again notice that this hasn't turned you into a harlot overnight. If her asking makes you, the husband, feel uncomfortable, try to work out why.

- Make explicit what you appreciate or dislike about sex, using the exercises above. Tell each other what you feel when this is expressed: excitement, anxiety, relief, fear? Make sure you discuss these feelings, and try to understand them rather than argue them away.

- Decide on your own what your personal limits are in terms of sex. These may change, but they're what you want today. If you can't tell these directly to your partner, then write a letter.

- Women need to be able to give the man permission to fail. She needs to convey to him that (1) sex is only part of marriage; (2) physical comfort and contact is an important part of sex; (3) penetration is only one way to be sexually satisfied. But she needs to believe it first!

137

- As a woman, stop faking orgasms. Yes, it makes him feel a man, but he needs to feel that in himself, not because you've been dishonest with him. Faking gives you a secret that you'll spring on him in bad times. And maybe wish you hadn't.

- As a man, experiment with other ways of getting close: through words, through touch, through play. And for some of you, make sure you are not communicating anger through sex: words will work much better.

- When everything feels unhappy, stuck in the groove of some awful damaged 78 record, then resort to touch alone. Hold his hand, stroke her head, knead his shoulders, massage her spine. When words fail, we can re-parent each other best through touch.

Chapter 8

Love and Marriage

Love must always grow greater or grow less.

Code of Love from the court of the Countess
of Champagne, 1174, quoted in
J. Langdon-Davies, *A Short History of Women*

STATESMEN, PSYCHOLOGISTS and writers of all sorts have
been predicting throughout this century that marriage
would not be with us for much longer. Its inevitable
demise was attributed to the likelihood that the institution
would become increasingly unnecessary. Marriage was very
useful when, with children to be reared and women prevented
from owning property or the means of being economically
independent, the family unit ensured that women stayed close
to home and were kept dependent upon men.

Until Victorian times, love and romance were an absolutely
unnecessary ingredient of marriage, whatever class you were
born into. People married because their families and their
society wanted it – in colonial America, for example, where a
small population was a problem, single men were regarded as
lazy and could actually be fined for not marrying. For working
class couples in Europe and for colonial couples in the States,
men and women worked and lived side by side, and the family
was a useful economic unit. Although the traditional division
of labour – women working at home and men away – is usually
thought to date back to the hunter-gatherers, it was in mid-

Victorian times, with the establishment of factories and out of home working, that the first real segregation of the sexes began, with women sometimes staying home to raise children and men going routinely elsewhere to work. Perhaps it was this separation that heralded the beginnings of romantic love: if you don't see much of a person, you may well start to fantasize about his or her wonderful qualities in ways that would have been abruptly curtailed by the reality of working side by side. Certainly it's just since then that love was seen as a necessary and sufficient reason to marry.

Nowadays no one in the west marries in order to survive physically, and one might therefore expect the urge to marry to have decreased. Once women get to work in jobs economically equal to men, once they can own their own property, once society allows them to have children without having a husband, then one might think that marriage would die. Really, what's the point? Well, it seems instead that the prophets were wrong. Although there has been a slight decrease over the last fifty years, around 90 per cent of men and women in the States, and almost as many in Britain and Australia, do still marry at least once. And the reason they give more than any other is that they are in love. The problems with this are obvious: if you marry for financial or protective reasons, then so long as these continue to exist there is no reason to be disappointed with one's lot: economic expectations are easy to define and so equally easy to audit. However, if you marry for love, then there are all sorts of potential problems on the way: love is full of undefined expectations, our meanings of love are going to be extremely individual and rarely expressed, and so transgressions, real or imagined, are bound to be myriad.

Romantic Love

THE RELATIONSHIP between love and marriage is as strong, or perhaps even stronger than ever. This might be because, despite all the superficial changes that have come about over the past few decades, men and women are still pretty segregated. Even in big organizations, the hierarchies with men on top and women on the bottom (the old mission-ary position of organizational structures) ensure that men stay distant and powerful, and so inevitably romantic. This is why power seems sexy: we create attributes for what we can't see and ignore what we can see. Of course, for many women, this reawakens earlier experiences of distant dads: the fathers of young children, generally absent for much of their waking hours, frequently assume romantic and powerful qualities. Some believe that the modern emphasis on romantic love stems from a general feeling of alienation in our modern society and the oasis of hope that marriage represents. Both theories, if true, represent a big burden of expectations for any two people to carry – to make up for something that should have happened when we were young, or that should be provided now in our society.

So far this book has been pretty short of references to love, and this isn't going to change much, I'm afraid. I've read whole books by psychologists on love, where they never quite define it, or define it in so many ways that one gets confused. The best we can do, it seems, is to look at the behaviours and feelings that are associated with love, and try to link them to individual experiences. Then we can at least have some idea of who might be a good person to fall in love with, and whom you should avoid like the plague. If only . . . In terms of the type of love one sees in long and happy marriages, I prefer the American analyst Harry Stack Sullivan's definition that it occurs where the security and well-being of your partner is as significant to you as your own security and well-being. This is not a totally selfless love, but it's equal – you care for him or her in the same way that you care for yourself.

However, it's romantic love that nowadays prompts most of us into marriage in the first place, and it's romantic love that holds the key to why things go wrong. The Oxford English Dictionary is really most unflattering about romance itself. It uses words and phrases like 'a picturesque falsehood', a mental tendency to be influenced by romantic tales, which themselves are 'remote from experience, quixotic, dreamy'. It seems by definition that this isn't a time when your feet are exactly firmly upon the ground, or when you're at your most practical and critical best.

How do men and women know that they're experiencing romantic love? They describe various signs:

Passion. Most people describe a passionate feeling for the other: full of painful longing, a hunger, a tugging at the heartstrings. If you've ever been to a Passion play, you'll know that it is a state always associated with pain. Its emotional strength is a sign that it is pulling on old wires that create urges and upheavals as strong as they did when rompers and rattles were the order of the day.

Unity. People say they long to merge, to be one with the loved one. They lose the boundaries that make them separate and independent people, and return to the psychological state of the infant who feels incomplete without its mother's constant closeness.

Insanity. They are mad about the boy, crazy for her, crackers over him. It's a state that makes you out of kilter with those around you, that stops you working or behaving like an adult, that makes you impulsive and wild in your actions if they will possibly gain you the unity that you long for.

Sexuality. Although people often like to keep love and sex somewhat separate, there is no doubt that they are intimately linked, and most people talk about deep sexual yearnings for the person they are in love with.

In addition, women (and occasionally men) talk about **dominance** – the man taking charge, swooping them up, being in control. Lynne Segal sees much of women's dissatisfaction with men today as having its roots in their ambivalence about dominance. In her book *Slow Motion* she discusses the feminist Ann Oakley's venture into fiction (*The Men's Room*, for example, which is full of romantic but ultimately hopeless men). She says:

In writing of men's perfidy, she [Ann Oakley] laments: 'Promising sublime intimacy, unequalled passion, amazing security and grace, they nevertheless exploit and injure in a myriad of subtle ways.' For sure, sublime intimacy, unequalled passion, amazing grace are not what men can deliver. Nor women either. And yet, they remain what most women (and, in fact, large numbers of men) weave their obsessive and foredoomed dreams around: the problem is no more than the projection of our own desire onto the loved one. . . . Might not feminist disappointment in loving men stem partly from the incompatibility of their own romantic longings with women's conscious pursuit of equality? The object of romantic desire is, by definition, he . . . who dominates and disappoints.

Who first taught these little girls (even these little feminists) that men were dominant and disappointing? Father, of course. Most children have never had enough of that alluring distant figure and, for girls in particular, this image of the opposite sex continues throughout their lives making any attempts by 'New Men' to change into something different doomed to failure in the romance stakes.

What we can see about the words used to describe romantic love – even its sexual aspect if you believe that this is a big ingredient of early childhood – is that they are all in some way taking you back to the feelings and emotions of your first few years, even to the time before you could talk. Many people have commented that men are more romantic than women, meaning that they experience these emotions more strongly. This is not surprising: for them the experience which is awakened when they love someone belongs to that period before they joined the men, the intense early years when all that really mattered was mother, a period that writers like Melanie Klein have even labelled psychotic in its primitive emotions. Mad with desire. But also it was a period when babies learnt that having mother close has a bad side as well: she is in control, she can go away and leave you; so much pleasure always has the risk of so much pain.

143

Although both sexes experience this, its reawakening for men can be much more painful and passionate because the feelings are linked to that period of abandonment when he left mum and stepped across to dad. I suspect that the bigger this step was – perhaps because dad wasn't really there and so the characteristics he took on were just stereotypically male, or extreme – the more intense the period of romantic love will be. In the book *Men Who Hate Women and the Women Who Love Them*, Susan Forward talks about misogynists as being particularly charming and romantic during the courtship period. Every night is 'some enchanted evening'. He makes his woman feel that 'her prince has come'. But I don't think that misogynists are a race apart. It's all a continuum where how far they move away from mother, and the type of father figure they identify with predicts the intensity of the adult experience of getting close again, but also the possibility of seeing women as some remote and contaminating enemy in ways that we saw in chapter six.

So there is a difference between the images of romantic love for men and for women. For women the image comes from the absent father, and the fantasy is powerful, strong but also disappointing because he's not here; for men, perhaps it comes from mothers who *are* there and meet almost all your needs, but are ultimately smothering and disappointing. Although all romantic love is essentially a totally selfish endeavour for both sexes, men and women are trying to acquire very different things from it. Nevertheless, because they're looking for love now which actually should have happened in the past, each party is primed eventually for disappointment. This doesn't have to be a bad thing: it might actually be very useful, both for the individuals concerned and for the marriage itself. If we feel disappointed and start to look at why this is, and where the expectations came from then we can leave our disappointment behind, where it belongs, back in our childhood, rather than blaming it on our present partner. It is the possibility that marriage gives for individuals to address and perhaps heal early relationship difficulties which psychoanalysts like Janet Mattinson see as the cause of the institution continuing today.

That Old Black Magic

WHAT IS it that casts the spell? What attracts a man to a woman and a woman to a man? The answers to that depend upon whom you ask. If you ask a biologist they will put it all down to whatever best ensures the reproduction of the species or, more narrowly, the carrying on of one's own genes. Everything about courtship is seen in this light, so they give as evidence the fact that women prefer men to be slightly older, that men like women to look capable of childbearing, and so on. Attractiveness is an ingredient (by definition I suppose) that is important for both sexes nowadays, but particularly for men. Women can produce far fewer children in their lifetimes than men can which makes them more choosy, more particular about their mates, so they might go more for wealth, stability, and so on. Men, the biologists tell us, are more inclined to dart around sowing their seed wherever they can because they are never sure that the child produced from one woman is their own: increasing the number of women increases their chances of carrying on their genes.

That sounds logical, but in practice it doesn't seem convincing. I don't see all men as rampantly fertilizing the female population by any means; and are women really more choosy than men about their mates? I think not. If they were, I'd be out of a job! What's more, men fall in love with men, and women with women; in fact, in ancient Greece men fell in love with men, but *not* with women, suggesting that society has quite an influence over biology.

Psychologists and sociologists see love and the choice of whom we love as largely a learned behaviour which has certain emotions attached to it, again by learning. Our main teaching experiences come from our very early relationships with mothers, fathers, siblings and others, and we go on to have this early learning reinforced or changed by what society, literature, life events and even schooling teach us. For example, if I've learned as a little boy to love my mummy, but then she is taken away one night in an ambulance and I never see her again, my experience of love will be that it doesn't last, that

145

you can't trust it, and that it's so associated with pain that perhaps it's best to avoid it completely in future. This would be more likely to occur if no one talked to me about what had happened. I would then tend to invent my own explanations such as 'She didn't love me, really' or 'Women can't be trusted', or 'I am unlovable'.

Nevertheless, this man might still want to try again – even again and again. Many of us seem to marry someone who gives us the opportunity of righting something which once went wrong. So a woman might go on seeking out problematic men in order to make them happy in ways that she felt she'd never managed with her father when she was young. Recent research supports the idea that women who have been treated violently as children go on to choose violent husbands. On the one hand, their idea of 'love' is something angry and abusive; but also they may be seeking out fresh chances to make that first childhood relationship succeed instead of fail.

Although some might choose a man or woman who will replicate mum or dad in all their glory or gory detail, another strategy that people sometimes choose is to marry a person the very opposite to the parent who caused the early pain, but it doesn't always work straight away. For example:

> I've been married for four years to a man who is really very nice and kind, but so boring. I know that sounds awful, but I can't help it. I know I'm falling out of love with him at a rate of knots and it's making me so unhappy. I'm being a complete bitch to him, and all he is is understanding – I could scream. Needless to say, there's another man on the horizon (my boss at work) who I know is not at all nice and I'm trying desperately not to give in. My father was a nasty brutal man who made all our lives a misery and I really felt I'd got away from all that, but it seems I haven't.

This woman has gone for the other extreme (very sensible!), but the problem is that her childhood experience of 'love' is painful and brutal, and so she cannot equate what she feels for her husband as love. Trying to reduce the negative effects of your childhood through adult relationships can work if we really understand them, and appreciate how much our present feelings really belong to the past. But this is often very difficult to do alone. The man described earlier, for example, who was so hurt by his mother's unexplained disappearance, might seek out a woman who seemed to have the loving attributes he remembered in his mum, or in his vision of what a mum should be, but then go on to punish her unmercifully for the wrong 'she'd' done him. Because the idea of his mother is likely to be romantic and unrealistic, it's also probable that he will put more and more demands on his wife, none of which will ever quite satisfy him because the dissatis-faction he is feeling belongs to the past rather than the here-and-now.

A number of women clients I have had over the years have seemed to long constantly to find a man with whom to share their lives, but have failed consistently. I know you can justify this with the thought that all the decent men have been snapped up years ago, and so on. Just the same, whenever an attachment does begin, it is quite quickly seen as unsuitable in some way – married, or the wrong class, not good enough in bed, just plain boring. It's often been difficult and distressing for them to see, longing as they do for the perfect partnership, that they are sabotaging their own happiness either by choosing men who cannot marry them, or finding those that they decide will in some way be unsuitable. These women have invariably had very strong, often cruel and violent fathers whom nevertheless they admired enormously. They looked now for men who would emulate daddy, but they knew unconsciously (and sometimes also consciously) that daddy had hurt them, and he really needed avoiding. They're attracted, but they run away, and so they're stuck alone in a no-man's land of their own making.

So our choice of whom or whether we marry can be very much affected by our early experience. Another way that this can happen, psychoanalysts tell us, is that you choose someone with a similar background to you, but who will carry for you the result of that background – for example, anger, or insecur-ity – which you find too uncomfortable to carry for yourself. In *Marriage Inside Out*, Clulow and Mattinson, analysts from the Tavistock Clinic in London, tell us:

Love of the other as a complement to the self is often quite conscious, with opposing social skills and personality traits openly admired. The calmness, even dullness, of one partner may be containing and useful to an excitable other, just as the more emotive response of the latter may engage and bring spontaneity into an otherwise stable and ordered life. However, in the search for wholeness one partner may choose and use the other to express a feared or unrecognized part of the self, and this, by definition, is unconscious.

They go on to describe how one partner can carry the anger of the other one who is particularly afraid of the strength of her or his rage. In other words, we hand over the emotion or characteristic to the one who can handle it more safely. This sounds convenient, but it can stultify both the individuals and the marriage unless each partner tries on the overcoat of the other – the characteristic they've handed over. This is similar to what I described in chapter three when one person wearing the security overcoat can make their life narrower and narrower, while the partner who wears the wild and flamboyant one can easily go right off the rails. One might be depressive, while the other one is manic, for example.

The Predictors of Success (and Separation)

ALTHOUGH MOST of the vast number of people who marry every year expect to live happily ever after, one in three marriages in the United Kingdom and half in the States will end in divorce, usually within the first five years. In Britain, for example, 10 per cent end during year one. In the States, psychologists Sally Cate and Rodney Lloyd have studied the reasons that marriages last or fail. Their summary of the research on this shows that whether or not a union is more likely to end in a long and happy marriage depends upon a number of factors.

- **Age.** Teenage couples and couples who marry over thirty are more likely to divorce.

- **Longer courtships.** It seems that, if you marry in haste you *are* more likely to repent at leisure. However, they also point to new research which shows that ultra-long engagements are equally bad news, especially the sort where the couple keep falling out. In both these cases, where the marriage still lasts, the couples are less happy.

- **Higher levels of education.** The better educated you are, the more likely it is that your marriage survives. This might be because education, where it's good, goes hand-in-hand with improving levels of communication.

- **Good communication.** Research has consistently shown that the ability to communicate well together before marriage is an important predictor of success. This doesn't just mean talking a lot, but also listening, building on the conversation, and picking up the other person's mood, enthusiasm, and so on. Poor communication is certainly the biggest bugbear that people raise when things go wrong.

- **Personality characteristics.** Longitudinal studies, following individuals or married couples up over several years or even decades, show a number of early factors to be important for men:

Lower neuroticism.
Higher impulse control.
Greater conventionality.

For women, we find:

Lower neuroticism.
Higher impulse control.
Greater conformity.

In other words, almost identical (and also what some of you will probably regard as simply boring!). Other research has shown that marriages last better when couples are similar rather than very different – birds of a feather, it seems, really do stick together – but these longitudinal studies again suggest that they ought to resemble each other in these rather conventional ways rather than both being on the wild side, for example. Other studies have suggested that less intelligence and less ambition in women seems to be a predictor of a stable marriage. Yes, well, it would, wouldn't it! We haven't quite reached the stage where women are allowed to be bright, ambitious and loving all at the same time. I don't find much of this research particularly impressive: saying that two conventional stable individuals stay married longer seems to me not to be saying very much.

- **The quality of childhood.** If your parents had a happy marriage, if the child had warm relations with them and with his or her brothers and sisters, the marriage is likely to be longer lasting and happier.

As we saw in chapter three, the importance for men of a warm, affectionate relationship with their father when they are little is increasingly recognized as a significant factor in their ability to form lasting adult relationships. Certainly, Harlow's experiments with monkeys raised with wire 'mothers', with or without a terry-towelling covering, compared to those raised with their real mothers, showed that both their social and sexual adult behaviour was severely damaged if the young monkeys had missed out on the comfort and care that came from mum. Whatever way we look at it, for both men and women early love seems a pretty important precursor for later successful adult relationships.

- **Spending quality time together.** The very latest research on the subject points out that by far the best predictor of a long and satisfying marriage is simply the number of hours you spend together. This study looked at a whole range of couples, from those who worked long hours to those who hardly worked at all, and it was the ones who actually made time to be together that reported the happiest and longest marriages. Of course, it just might be that spending time together is a reflection of how well you get on, rather than vice versa, but it's more likely that it's the bottom line: if you don't give each other time, you'll never learn to communicate, to work through difficulties, to enjoy mutual experiences, and to help each other to develop, learn from and overcome early troubles.

The Honeymoon Period

WHEN MEN and women fall in love and during the early days of marriage, they temporarily step back into the world of the mother. This is the time when a couple might use babytalk and spoon food into each other's mouths; when they kiss things better and stroke away any anguish; when they want to make babies of their own, more to play with than to parent. It's a time when the man feels he can do anything with this woman at his side – she's the limb he felt was missing, the prop that will help him to stand tall and even win the race.

Although for both of them, this is a stepping back to childhood, for women it is not a foreign world. Instead, it's an extension of the relating and getting close that makes her world complete, and she believes that he feels that way too. For men, however, it is a true regression: by stepping back into childhood he has also entered again the world of women, and in particular of mother. The taste of this warm, comforting, sometimes smothering world is both alluring and terrifying. It is this that awakens for him what he gave up, what he can get again, but at the price of dependency.

The End of the Honeymoon

IN THE honeymoon period dependency is fine – both of you can be children again, and children can be as dependent as they want. But then it ends: it wouldn't be a honeymoon if it didn't. The total feeling of unity evaporates and each person is left in the glaring spotlight of separateness. For some individuals the doubts that can accompany this occur even prior to the marriage, and they busy themselves with preparations and ceremony as a way not to think about what they feel. For others it can come within days as a sudden carelessness sets in and you see your partner in this new uncomfortable light.

For women the honeymoon may end when the romantic knight in shiny armour drops his visor and cuts himself off in a way that hurts. For men, it happens when the perfect mother that was around for the groom makes a mistake or gets a little careless. Just like his real mother, she forgets to praise his achievements every time, she doesn't always want him close, and she gets up and dresses for work just when he's feeling a bit lost and in need of a cuddle. Even where she did nothing apparently wrong, if the man has had a far from perfect early childhood – a mother, for example, who was hardly ever there for him because of work or even death – then he is likely to create more and more demands for demonstrations of her love. Joanne told me:

Jack had no father and his mother had to go out cleaning. She left him with anyone who would have him, or else she'd put him in his pram outside the house where she was working. Because she was so poor and couldn't help it, he won't admit this was wrong. He doesn't seem to realize that for a baby this just isn't good enough. I realized eventually that he was trying to get me to fulfil endless demands, but whatever I did it wasn't enough. Early on the demands were about giving up my job and looking after him but, when I'd done that and more, the demands started to be sexual – more and more bizarre things. They would be like obsessions – he'd go on and on about this one act – wanting me to shave my pubic hair or have a friend along as a threesome – and when finally I'd do it, within weeks he'd have thought of another one.

Eventually Joanne sought help and began to realize that the requests would be endless because she wasn't the one who could fulfil them. Until Jack could admit that he wasn't loved by his mother as a child should be (not blaming her, but stating a fact), he couldn't let go of his yearning.

But in most new couples it's not so extreme as this, and the results are not so obvious to see. In most relationships, the women don't try quite so hard as Joanne and their careless slips make the man withdraw: he's been here before and he's damned if he's going to put up with disappointments like that again. He chose to leave his mother, and now he'll mirror the act by distancing himself from his wife in much the same way. Back to work, back to sport, back to the boys where he'll be more than welcomed.

So the honeymoon ends because his new 'mother' fails in just the same ways that the first one did. But the other side of the coin is the conflict he feels about his dependency and his old needs (and new ones) that now are reawakened. For many men, the conflict is again resolved by turning his back on the woman, putting away his toys, and returning to manly things. Now he will take over, take up his crown, be distant, absent, just as his father was to his mother. You are either smothered by mother/the wife, or you are rigidly separate from her – there is no other way it seems to him. But it's so sad. Major Tom, sitting in his spaceship, drifting far, far from home says: 'Tell my wife I love her very much.' 'She knows.' So sad and so lonely.

The man's decision to separate again can be a dreadful blow for the woman too. It often seems so abrupt, and she is left wondering what on earth she's done. Agony aunts' postbags are full of letters like this one:

I have been married for three years and we were the ideal couple to all our friends and relatives, and I thought so too. It was only at Christmas that we were planning our long-term goals together – buying a larger house with a garden, having children, his career, and so on. And then last week he came home one evening and said he was going – that he didn't like married life any more, he wasn't ready for all this responsibility, he didn't feel old enough to be with just one woman. He even said he wants to start being with the boys more. I can't believe it. I am completely devastated. I wonder if he's mentally ill? How can anyone change just like that?

Well, he's done it once, and he can do it again. It just isn't so hard for men to walk away. What has happened is that these two have entangled themselves to a point where he feels smothered by things wifely and weighed down by things traditionally husbandlike. When one drops out of role, the other is left not knowing what to do at all.

Mummy's Boys

ALTHOUGH RESEARCH shows that close early relationships with the parents are predictive of a more stable relationship, there are gender differences in terms of what the relationships with parents are like once the couple are actually married. The research seems to indicate that it is much more important for wives than for husbands to continue to report a warmth with parents; in a man, a very close intense relationship with his mother that continues into adulthood appears to predict lower marital satisfaction.

Certainly being married to a 'mother's boy' can cause great distress to some wives, and can even wreck any chance of a good sexual relationship, since many of them find sex pretty difficult, especially sex within marriage, as I'll explain later. On the other hand, women who are not at all happy about sex themselves, at least when they are young, may marry a man who's abnormally close to his mother in order to safely relieve any pressure on her that she might find in a less attached man. Unfortunately, if her own sexuality develops, as it frequently does, a real triangle of resentment may be created for her, the husband and her mother-in-law.

Other women choose mummy's boys because they are so different from their own aggressive, forceful fathers, while the close relationship the man has with his mother may awaken a yearning that she has never experienced. For example, Deborah and Andrew came for help at a point when she was threatening to walk away from their twenty-year marriage for ever. In a separate interview she described Andrew and other key people in their lives:

> My husband is very quiet and unemotional, and not as demonstrative as I would like him to be. I was young when I met and married him, and I guess I thought he would change. He has a completely domineering mother who does her best to hang onto him. His father is kind, weak and boring – the anything-for-a-quiet-life sort, and I think Andrew copies him. The trouble is I feel I'm behaving like her: I get into terrible rages, and quite often have a bust-up with her. My own father was loving and demonstrative, but also angry and impatient which upset me a lot. Maybe I avoided it in choosing Andrew.

With help, the couple worked together on who carried the anger. Deborah, it seemed, had enough for both of them. This was partly to do with the fact that she had experienced a very noisy, angry form of love from her father and both wanted it and didn't want it in Andrew – which rather tied him in knots – but also they gradually came to realize that it was pretty convenient for him if Deborah took on his battle with mother. She could lash out in ways he'd never dared to do. He had no experience of doing that himself, and no role model in his father, but that didn't mean that he enjoyed her domineering and interfering ways.

Change for them came by deciding that they would act as a team, a partnership in handling mum, rather than leaving it all to Deborah. Over the course of a few months, he learnt through role playing some assertion techniques, and some ways to express negative feelings, and he put these into practice with his mother. He complied with requests to initiate things (outings, affection and even sex) himself, and the couple planned a move further away from his parents. Deborah practised handing over responsibility to him in certain situations, and living with the consequences. There was a lot of goodwill between them to make it work, and it did.

Of course, the problems of mothers' boys can be explained too by the idea that these are the boys who never stepped very far away from mum at all, and this to some extent might explain their sometimes lacklustre libidos. However, there is another aspect of mother-son relationships which can spoil sex not just in mothers' boys, but in men who to all intents and purposes are rigorously masculine, sexually enthusiastic, and may even express a less than friendly relationship with mum.

No Sex Please, We're Married

'HAS YOUR husband got a headache?' I asked in a recent magazine article, and promptly had a mailbag of women saying yes, yes, oh yes! Some of them described a gradual decline of sex over marriage, some said that it had never happened, either before or after the big day, but a sizable portion fitted the bill for sex outside marriage but none within. In other words, they had had a very full sex life with their partners right up until the moment they said, 'I do', and from then on there was nothing but excuses.

> Physically we couldn't get enough of each other and after five months he asked me to marry him (we'd been living together for the previous two months). I said yes and then things began to change. He got angry a couple of times and was violent (just hard shoves). Suddenly

sex didn't seem as important and I had to start asking. I postponed the wedding, but he said he would look a fool, and we got married. On the honeymoon I had to ask for sex, and I noticed that he started to compliment other women on their looks but never me.

Living together, it seems, is not enough to really test out marital compatibility. That plain gold ring still means something psychologically much more powerful than just sharing a key. What is happening here is that old Oedipus has reared his head again, just when it seemed that mother had been left behind for ever. If you remember from chapter 4, the little boy (and frequently the older boy too) experiences sexual yearnings towards his mother. Gradually the idea 'I want to marry my mum' becomes overladen with guilt: that it's simply not done, and any slight expression of desire is usually dealt with swiftly to help him learn. Even in those boys where mother was clearly ambivalent herself about her feelings for her son, the boys still had no doubts that what they experienced through her behaviour was wrong, and all of them felt guilty about it. But then, the boy grows into a man, probably leaves home, and most begin to have sexual relationships with the Other Sex – with real women. All this is fine; everything seems normal and healthy. All thoughts about mum are a million miles away when he's in the arms of this sexy woman who is unattached to him. It's so good, he falls in love and secures her to him by proposing marriage. It all seems so natural. But a transformation takes place when she says, 'I do'. It's as if the Bad Fairy comes down and touches her on the shoulder with her drooping wand. Suddenly he finds he no longer fancies his wife; all his urges have vanished; they've not even waited till the honeymoon is over. As Freud said rather sadly: 'Where they love they do not desire, and where they desire they cannot love.'

What the Bad Fairy does at the wedding ceremony is to change his sexy girlfriend into his wife; to transform her from wicked woman to untouchable saint; to reincarnate her from lover into mother. It all comes back to him:

- mothers are good/pure/asexual

- you don't have sex with your mother

- you have sex with Other Women

- Other Women are wicked

- wives are good

- your wife is like your mother

- so you don't have sex with your wife!

Tortuous but logical enough for a philosopher to confirm. Of course, lots of other reasons are put up for the failure, as we'll see in the next chapter, but essentially this is what's happening, and unless it's recognized it will sour a relationship irreconcilably. If you think that some other dynamic might be involved in this, rather than a confusion over mothers and wives, here's another letter:

> On our honeymoon my husband told me I was useless
> in bed and masturbated in front of me. He also called me
> by his mother's name while we were having intercourse.

Some women go through a similar dynamic in relation to their fathers and new husbands. Perhaps this is the source of that phenomenon which men frequently comment upon, that she cuts her hair off as soon as she's married, and often puts on weight. This might be some sort of shriving for the sin of fornicating with this symbol of father: an attempt to make herself as unattractive and as asexual as possible. Melissa told me:

> I had had a fabulous sex life with Alan. I could have an
> orgasm in seconds if I wanted one. It was all so easy.
> We even used to leave the office and dart home to my
> place at lunchtime for a quickie! When I married I went
> on the pill (ironic that!). But from our wedding day on
> I just stopped fancying sex. It would take sometimes an

hour of pumping away to make me come. Awful dreary stuff. We blamed the pill, but we also slipped into affairs within the first couple of years. I was still on the pill, but sex was good again. It took a divorce and then another marriage to make me appreciate the pattern, and so I went into therapy.

Melissa's relationship with her father had been as ambivalent as those I described earlier for men with their sexually needy mothers. It's the hidden area of sexual abuse: nothing actually happens, things are left unsaid, but the girl knows that something is wrong, and she takes the guilt onto herself. In Melissa's case, the father had been outrageously jealous of all her boyfriends, making each courtship an assault course. He had enjoyed taking her out for a drink, and would comment happily that he expected everyone thought she was his girl-friend. And as a photographer of note, it wasn't that surprising that he took decorous but nude photos of her, saying that she ought to have her loveliness captured because it wouldn't last for long. Surprisingly he didn't share this pleasure with her mother, but hid the photos away, so that Melissa knew she was sharing in some bad secret. This type of sexual abuse, like that of some mothers towards their sons, goes unrecognized and so it is much more difficult for the woman to realize the effect that it has on her future relationships with men.

Reproducing Ourselves

ALTHOUGH PRODUCING babies confirms most men's images of being a Real Man almost as much as it does women's idea of a Real Woman, these bundles of joy can still be a catalyst for problems. Although almost all the evidence shows that children (especially those under six) do help marriages to go on longer, a similarly conclusive series of studies shows that the quality of a marriage deteriorates when a couple starts a family. Compared to childless couples or those where the kids have left home, couples with children are simply not as happy. In fact, if you plot marital satisfaction over the first twenty-five years you find that it deteriorates steadily for the first ten, and then improves over the next fifteen.

It seems that the positive affection that is around at the beginning of a marriage declines rapidly towards the end of pregnancy, and this lasts over the nine months following the birth. Marital satisfaction, I'm afraid, goes down alongside this and continues to do so for women and especially for men, over the first couple of years, while psychological distress goes up. What an awful picture: it's enough to get any couple leaping for a new supply of condoms! But it's not just a gloomy prognosis: knowing the facts can stop you blaming each other and let you plan how to counteract any difficulties. Since most couples do have children, it's important to try and work out why it happens.

If we think about the ways that men and women behave when they are newly married – those described earlier – we can see that much of this period is to do with re-parenting by our new partner. The woman becomes everything the man–child could ever have wished for in a mother, while the husband shows all the strength and love and dependability that she longed to have in her father. And then a third person comes along, and sometimes a fourth and a fifth. The perfect playmate becomes the perfect mother and shifts her whole attention from the centre of her life, her husband–son, to a new child, and then wonders why he acts as if his nose is perpetually out of joint.

The effect of this newcomer on him is likely to be worse where he has experienced it before – for example, where he was the elder and so only son, and then 'lost' his mother's love when the second child was born. This will pull a string for him that reawakens old despairs, old jealousies, and perhaps make him behave as badly as he did when he felt like an abandoned toddler years and years ago. Particularly if the baby is a son, the man may feel like a displaced person (as Dennis described in chapter four) and spend more time at work (as research shows most new fathers do!) or transfer his affections to a lover who will continue to treat him in the way that he so recently rediscovered and then lost.

Again, similar things might happen to women who have daughters; certainly it's been shown that the mothers of young daughters are decidedly less satisfied with their marriages than are those with sons. On the whole, it seems divorce is less likely to happen in families with sons than in those with daughters. It seems that very little has changed since Henry VIII invented new ways to gain a male heir.

Just occasionally, though, things go the other way, and a child can work hard to keep a couple together. This is invariably unconscious on the part of the child and, although it may be effective, it is also very damaging. They achieve this inadequate union by getting ill or getting into trouble and so diverting the high emotions, especially the anger, from the couple and onto the child. Malcolm told me:

> June and I were in the throes of separation. I'd been having an affair, and the kids knew about it – June made sure of that. Sam [the eldest] was angry with both of us but just said we'd have to sort it out for ourselves, but Eddie put a lot of work at first into trying to get us to make up. Then he seemed to lose interest. The next thing we knew, the police were at the door saying he'd been caught taking ecstasy with a gang from school. Of course, there was a great furore and it took all our attention for some time, especially as I felt so guilty. I stopped the affair. But then when things started to get out of hand again, we 'discovered' he'd been doing it again. Luckily that's all it took for us to realize what he was up to, otherwise things might have been even worse. I don't think he knew what he was doing at all. He was just unhappy and angry.

Other children might try to 'fix things' by having severe asthma attacks, or accidents, by promiscuity, stealing, and so forth. If there is real conflict and unhappiness in your marriage, do watch for signs like this in your children. It's all too easy to be so engrossed in your own battles that you fail to see what others are up to until the writing is on the wall.

Great Expectations

MUCH OF what goes wrong, especially early on in marriage, is that the expectations that we carry with us from our culture and especially from our parents, are thwarted. We tried to get away from this type of woman/mother, and we find she's there; we wanted a romantic strong husband/father – one who was there rather than absent – and we find he doesn't take charge and can't communicate at all.

Because romantic love is essentially selfish, the expectations that cause the problems are rarely of ourselves, but of our partners. We could usefully parody Kennedy's inauguration speech as a way to help our marriages, whether they are ailing or not: 'Ask not what my partner can do for me, but ask what I can do for my partner.' How can you actually show love by caring for the security and wellbeing of your husband or wife as you do your own, as Harry Stack Sullivan suggested that you should in his definition? Here's an exercise based on those suggested by Lederer and Jackson in *The Mirages of Marriage*. You could both use it now and then as a litmus test of your marital behaviour.

- Briefly list three instances of your own loving behaviour toward your spouse during the last week.

- List three instances of your spouse's loving behaviour toward you.

- List three rotten things you have done – intentionally or unintentionally – to your spouse in the last week.

- List three rotten things your spouse has done to you during the last week.

- List something which you have asked or nagged your spouse to do or improve in the past week, but which he/she hasn't done.

- List something which he/she has asked or nagged you to do or improve in the past week, but which you haven't done.

- List three times recently that you have told your spouse you appreciate him/her.

- List three times recently that your spouse has told you she/he appreciates you.

Unrealistic expectations of others are more likely if we find it difficult to accept the less than wonderful aspects of ourselves. Owning up to these really helps. If we can see ourselves as capable of good acts as well as not-so-good ones, then we will find we're more tolerant when others fail. And if we choose a partner to replicate or rectify something from our early life, then we have to realize that using him or her in this way is bound to be tricky. So be prepared for hard work. It won't be easy, but it may be possible: whereas once we were impotent because we were just children, now marriage can be the place where old difficulties are tackled and overcome – but not without a struggle.

Chapter 9

The Priapic Prop

'Women have served all these centuries as looking-glasses possessing the magic and delicious power of reflecting the figure of man at twice its natural size.'

Virginia Woolf, *A Room of One's Own*

WHILE ALL of us, men and women, long to have recognition and appreciation – especially if we missed getting enough in childhood – many men tend to get it and to expect it much more from women than women do from men. As we saw in chapter five, their sense of self is sometimes quite brittle and fragile, created by and dependent on the praise and attention of women. Some women, at least for a while, will nurture, protect and prop that brittle, grandiose self, like Wendy did to Peter Pan, repairing his ego as often as she did his shadow. But a man's self-image has been forced to depend most criticially on that one physical difference that symbolizes all the others. This is what she knows needs propping most. Some do it consciously, like faking orgasms, each of which becomes a bullet in her armoury should anything later go wrong between them. Others, particularly those with a very fragile sense of self themselves, act unconsciously taking on the problems of their partners, blending with those who rule. This chapter is about the collusions of marriage, the *folies à deux* that lock couples into often painful and unrewarding dynamics, ones that offer little to either

164

partner, though perhaps less to the propping wife than they do to her husband.

Erecting the Phallus

FOR MANY males, the early step away from mother towards father is fraught with anxiety. It's all very well deciding to cast your lot in with dad, but in so many families, even nuclear ones, for much of the time father simply wasn't there. How is a young lad going to learn what it means to be a man? He may well identify with his father, but then only get very small glimpses of how he should be in order to be masculine. Because of this he will go for small clues and magnify them. If he looks for the obvious differences, what might he see?

- Dad is absent.

- Dad is emotionally distant.

- Dad has more money (often much more) than mum.

- Dad works and *his* work matters.

- Dad gets the car more than mum. And, of course,

- Dad has a penis.

All these things seem to give dad power that mum just doesn't have, but none of them is possible for a child, except the last. It's that little penis that forms the foundation of his power all through his growing up period. It leads to all the rest. It's the key, and without it – functioning as it should – he's nothing. So much power dependent on such an unpredictable member is enough to make anyone anxious. Therefore the other aspects of difference – the absence, the distance, the money, the car, the career – throughout his life are stacked around the central core to buttress, protect and enlarge it. What they create together is a symbol of power – the phallus itself. More than anything, he needs a woman to prop up and enhance this phallic construction, but the woman then is privy to any failure in his potency, a witness that needs nobbling if his sense of being is to survive. So some men, riddled with doubts from feeling that they have only an insecure grasp on their masculinity, set about devising ways to nobble the wife, just in case she laughs, just in case she kisses and tells. Just in case she finds him inadequate and wanders off to someone else.

Never Quite Right

I've been married for thirty-five years but on sexual terms with him for only twenty. By 'sexual terms' I mean allowed to touch him. When I married I was gregarious, intelligent, had a good career and loving friends. My husband and I were very different, especially in appearance: he was pretty and I was pretty ugly, as he told me often. I started without a high opinion of myself physically but soon after marriage I felt as if I was a monster species of some sort that no normal male could mate with.

Our sexual relationship has always been a disaster, when it happens at all, although he flirts constantly with our friends. He does it because he wants to alienate them from me and cut me off from all sources of help and solace. I realized after some years that he would not let me into his sexual feelings because it would give me a hold over him – it would make him vulnerable – and obviously he felt that I wanted to master him as much as he wanted to master me. It went on because I couldn't believe it would fail if he realized that I wasn't his enemy and didn't want power over him. I felt if I tried hard enough and was loving enough, things must come right. Everyone had disapproved of our marriage and I couldn't let them know that they were correct, could I? Now we've both retired and he's around all day. That, I realize, was my life.

Like the woman in chapter two who was dreading her husband's retirement, the partner of this woman has quite systematically attempted to destroy her self-esteem. Letter after letter comes to me describing the extraordinary array of methods used to achieve this. The stories they tell are always so clear, so unambiguous, set down now in pen and ink, that you wonder how the women could possibly have fallen for it. But they do, over and over again. This happens for a number of reasons. First and foremost, they have the traditional tendency of blaming themselves when things go wrong. And second, they believe that if they (which means her, not him) work at the relationship long and hard enough, it will eventually be good. This is where they have been taught to see their power lying: in making it better for the men.

> I have been married for six months to a man who said he loved me very much up till then. Because we are Christians, we didn't make love. Now I am still a virgin, and he never tries to make love to me. When I ask him why not, he says my breasts are too big. I am only slight but I have dieted strongly and now I am really quite thin and my breasts are very tiny, but he says they are not right. I don't know what to do. I am a GP and I see my patients with their families, but not me. What am I doing wrong?

How, she wonders, can she make her breasts any smaller – that's what she seems to be asking for help with, despite her medical qualifications. It is, of course, a pointless question. Men don't stay chaste (nor do they wander) because their wives' breasts, hips, chins or any other part of them are the wrong shape. They may kid themselves they do – that if his wife was more or less curvy then his libido would soar. But it isn't true. So what's her husband up to? He may well be completely impotent, and this is the ideal excuse; or perhaps homosexual, but hoping that he could marry anyway. He may, on the other hand, be simply very low in self-esteem, and very envious of her qualifications and status. If he attacks her by withholding sex and telling her she's undesirable, as the husband in the previous letter was doing, then he may even break her to the extent she ends her career.

An extreme form of this treatment is gaslighting, which I mentioned in chapter two. Here, the man gradually drops more and more innuendoes (and even plays actual tricks) to convince his partner that she is going mad: that she isn't too strong, doesn't remember too well, is suffering from a neurosis, is just depressed and so can't make decisions, has severe hormonal difficulties, is going mad. It's a determined way of destroying her sense of self, the autonomy that he (and sometimes she too) finds so threatening. Every time a man tells a woman she's stupid, mad, a neurotic wreck, or any of the other terms of abuse that feature in many of the letters in this book, they are attacking her self-esteem and pushing her towards depression. With some men it's methodical, with most of those who do it, it's just careless.

Of course, all these examples seem fairly extreme. Most men are not so insecure about their masculinity that they have to resort to such behaviour. But at various times in their lives (often when their careers are going less well), men will use their wives in subtly destructive ways. Here's a few:

- The backhanded compliment; for example, 'You look better than you've looked for ages,' or 'I really should have appreciated you more when you were young. You were so lovely then.'

- Flirting with other women in front of his wife. Then saying, 'Come on, it's only a bit of fun. Where's your sense of humour gone? Where's your charity?'

- Casting doubts on her abilities to do things: aspects of work, study, sport, driving, etc. This may happen when the woman looks as if she's genuinely enjoying the activity, or if she expresses any sort of doubt about her ability. This is then picked up on and magnified as though sympathy is being given: 'Look, you don't have to do it if you don't want to. I won't think any less of you if you stop.'

- Restricting her financially and certainly making sure she has less than him.

- Telling her after she's clearly enjoyed a party that she really shouldn't laugh so loudly/brag so much/ dress like that and so on; anything which sows a seed of doubt about how people saw her.

- Implying that she's a duffer, neurotic, at the beck and call of her hormones, or just hopeless.

Some of these are easily recognized. Others merit more attention, sometimes because the women seem to go along with the tactic and so it's hard to see what the problem is. The prop is almost invisible.

Driving Him Crackers

THE PROPORTION of women owning and driving cars is growing fast, and for young women there is likely to be no issue at all surrounding who takes the wheel. But it's not the case for everyone. The psychologist Dorothy Rowe has suggested that a good cure for female depression is to open your own bank account and to get a driving licence. I would only add that it's *using* the driving licence that matters most. I'd passed my test in Australia but never bothered to drive: it was easier to let the man take the wheel, and they were only too pleased to do so, and as a result I didn't drive for years. When I finally decided to get a British licence so that I could be properly mobile again, I couldn't believe the freedom it offered. It changed my life for the better far more than degrees ever did! I remember driving over Snake Pass with the sunroof open, the sun shining and the Rolling Stones playing loud, and thinking that this must be one of the best experiences of my life. All that freedom; all that independence.

But also, all those jokes. What we joke about a lot gives us a clue as to what disturbs us. So there's no doubt at all that male society found women's driving extremely disturbing. The jokes were designed for just one reason: to stop women from doing it. You still hear them today in any club, but they reached their heyday in the fifties and sixties as a desperate attempt to take away the skills that women had acquired during the second world war. Then it was quickly apparent that women could drive not just cars for generals, but also large trucks and buses. That rocked our notion of difference quite dramatically, and the jokes over the next thirty years were designed – OK, unconsciously – to take away the confidence of women at the wheel. In the end, this has failed to happen, but many, many women in their forties and older don't drive because of the effects of this joking and all that went with it. Lisa told me:

> My father taught me to drive. He was fine for ages, quite patient and easy-going about things. I learnt very quickly and put in for my test. As it approached, he began to get tenser and tenser, much more critical about everything. It brought back memories of how he'd been with my mother. I remembered sitting in the back with her driving and him criticizing more and more until she cried. She gave up after a few of these lessons, and never went back to it. The day before my test he was really horrible to me, ripping away at my confidence until in the end I got out of the car and walked home. I didn't sit my test for another five years and even then I found it very hard to drive if there was a man with me.

What does women's driving mean to men? Over the years I have heard three meanings. You might have others.

- It goes against differences. Cars are mechanical things that men by tradition understood and women didn't. Moreover, women were considered to be less spatially accurate, so more likely to drive badly. However, now that engines are more complicated so that neither sex understands what's under the bonnet, and now that insurance companies give better deals to women because they have fewer accidents, this urge to maintain difference has much less weight. But the strength of the need to believe in it can still be seen; for example, men will often hold onto the handle when they're in the passenger seat, and flinch as they approach crossroads. These tiny displays are done by the nicest of men, but continue to have a subtly undermining effect on women's confidence.

- A man told me recently that he actually finds it arousing to be in the passenger seat when a woman's driving. I talked to other men about this and some of them agreed. This was news to me, and so I asked why. Maybe, they suggested, it's because the woman is in control: a bit like being tied up and spanked perhaps? I've no idea. Anyway, we know from chapter six that being constantly aroused by women in situations where they are not supposed to be, is something that some men find at best an irritation and at worst a reason to turn against them. It demonstrates a lack of control which some find unsettling. Perhaps this is part of the urge to keep them out of the driver's seat.

- The reason I find most frequently rings true is that cars mean freedom, and that's something that many men fear to give to women. Why? Just in case they run away – as simple as that. One of the greatest problems for men, perhaps the initiator of our tradition that a woman's place is in the home, is that they can never know for sure that the baby is theirs. Women need tethering so you know where they are and what they've been up to. Let's face it, if a man knows what lascivious thoughts and even acts he is capable of, then he feels pretty sure that other men have them too. And his wife may be the object of them. Men who are worried about their own sexual abilities fear giving freedom to their partners in case they find someone else. It's the same reason that some might try to stop women working or being financially independent.

These fears work together to a greater or lesser extent and in different combinations for quite a large proportion of men. They form the impetus for the snide remark as well as the carefully honed joke. For many young women, they fail, but even among these, born since the sixties, I witness some giving up the driving wheel once they marry, and alongside this I see a growth in their dependency and a droop in their self-esteem. Why do they give it up when it's such fun? Undoubtedly there's the pressure I've described above, but also there is often the voiced or unvoiced feeling that she needs her man to feel strong and that her dependency helps this to happen.

In addition, a number of women over the years have told me that they are equally afraid of the freedom that driving offers because they too worry that they might find someone else. For the same reason, women have told me they're scared to work. Where on earth does such an extraordinary idea come from? Well, partly it's picked up from the man's fear of his own less than superman potency, and partly from her own irrational belief that comes from the dark ages and goes against all the evidence, that women are deep down loose and sexually voracious. As Aristotle reminded us: 'Females are naturally libidinous, incite the males to copulation, and cry out during the act of coition.' Give them an inch and they'll take a mile.

Shelly believed this. She had stopped driving because she was sure she'd harm someone; she had stopped working because she was sure if she continued she'd have an affair. She'd once kissed a man at an office party, and now she worried irrationally that her son was not her husband's. She had no boundaries, was convinced that any contact would lead to penetration of something that would defile her and her family. She'd had a dreadful abusive childhood, primarily from her father, and was allowed nothing that was hers alone, no secrets, no sense of self. But still she had the grit and strength to choose a deeply caring though anxious husband and to get psychotherapy. Learning that her needs were not damaging and overwhelming, and that she could say no to men, was part of the treatment.

Laughing all the Way
to the Bank

I WOULD also go along with Dorothy Rowe's other piece of advice – women should open their own bank accounts – though I realize that it's not always easy to put much in. One of the main fortifications to male power for centuries has been to hold the purse strings, and to curtail women's freedom by doing so. The following letter shows that this method is far from consigned to Victorian melodramas, but is alive and well and living in Shropshire:

> We've been married for eighteen years and have two teenagers. I feel that my husband treats us very unfairly. He seems to live in the past and he's getting worse as he gets older. If any of us want anything at all (from a pair of shoes to a holiday) we have to be really 'good' or it's refused. I work in our business three days a week and he pays me £45. I have to clothe all of us out of this. If we go out or on holiday, he always says he's 'taken us' – not that 'we went'. Nothing in the house ever gets replaced, he turns off the heating, and he hides the fan heater. Can you tell me whether I expect too much?

She doesn't need telling. She knows very well that he's in the wrong, but she wants me to be angry with him instead of her. It's easier that way.

Women over the last decade or two have taken more and more control of their own money. Or have they? They certainly earn far more than they used to and in some parts of Britain there are more women working than there are men (though partly because they'll work for less). But even those with a good personal income, their own business perhaps, still get themselves into financial trouble with their partners.

> I am writing in a crisis. My husband and I run a business together which, like most at the moment, is

struggling somewhat. Last night we got burgled and now I discover that he never bothered to renew the insurance, although he'd told me he had. I'm dumbfounded, but when I look back I realize it's always been like this. He's been casually negligent with my money again and again. It was my business which he joined five years after we married. I'd achieved a lot, but I've let him take it all away over the twenty years we've been together. Why did I stay? Why did I let it happen when I know what he's like?

Just as with the way that many women let their partners take the wheel when they drive, so too they let them take it in financial terms. Men who feel shaky in their self-image are again more likely to restrict their partners' money in order to restrict her freedom. They'll either do this by giving her too little, or, if she has an income of her own, by draining it away. And still she goes along with it! Her own need to see men as more powerful, as in charge, as strong (just as daddy seemed to be) makes her hand over her hard-won wealth and then wonder why it is that, rather than increasing his strength and abilities, her husband instead becomes even weaker. His reliance on her prop drains away any strength he might have mustered had he been left to learn to fight for himself. It's tit-for-tat: she protects his greatest fear by making him appear a Man, while he protects hers by staying put in the relationship, by not abandoning her. At least until someone who makes him feel even more like a Man comes along!

A Woman's Place is in the Home

WHEN I first started training as a clinical psychologist, I was given, like all trainees, female clients who had been suffering from agarophobia, often for many years. Agaraphobia is a fear of open spaces; agarophobia is a fear of the market place, but it doesn't really matter what you call it: basic to both is a terror of leaving the house. Usually it starts with having a panic attack in a supermarket, and avoiding going there again, and gradually the avoidance spreads to everything outside the home. Some simply stay put, with their husbands doing all the shopping and gardening and posting of letters. Some manage to be driven out in the car by their husbands if they're wearing sunglasses; others manage to make it to the dustbin to get rid of the rubbish. Over the years all but one client has been female, and all have been married. Without exception the husbands have been wonderfully kind and helpful to their wives, and haven't complained at all at the huge burdens placed upon them.

The traditional way to treat agarophonia is to get the woman to set up a hierarchy of fear – perhaps from posting a letter through to shopping in a supermarket – to learn relaxation techniques and then to begin to work her way up the hierarchy using relaxation as a way to control her fear. On the face of it, this seems to work well. However, nine times out of ten you get two-thirds of the way up the hierarchy, the woman is beginning to express enthusiasm about getting stronger, and suddenly everything starts to go wrong. Their husbands tell them that this is doing them no good at all; that they're sick, and shouldn't be stretching themselves like this; and so on. And the woman appears to agree.

It was very frustrating for a trainee. I felt such a failure. But then I went to a conference where a psychologist told the audience that he had begun to treat these women as having, not a fear of leaving the house, but a fear of ever returning. From then on it all started to make sense: these were women who were sharing with their husbands a fear that, if they were allowed out, they wouldn't want to come back. In other words, like the women described in the sections above, they were afraid that freedom might allow them to find someone else to replace a husband whose own anxieties over his potency were just as great as hers. When pressed, some women would tell me that their husbands seemed to be getting poorly now: that he'd had a panic attack himself recently, and she was worried about him and felt that none of this was doing either of them any good.

To illustrate this, Helen came to me after twelve years of

agarophobia. She'd been a top-notch secretary when she'd married but, after three years and no children, her husband's mother came to live with them and, when she became bedridden, Helen gave up her job to look after her. By shopping on his way home, her husband Dave helped out more and more so that his mother would not have to be left alone by Helen. When the mother died five years later Helen found she felt very reluctant to go shopping alone, but forced herself on one occasion and had a panic attack in the supermarket. From then on, her fear of repeating this grew, and Dave helped out more and more until eventually she was unable to leave the house.

Various health workers had seen her over the years: every now and then her doctor would send someone else to her to try to help, but everyone got only so far and no further. When I saw her, I'd begun to notice the patterns and to read the new ideas which suggested that agorophobia might be a marital problem. Sure enough, as she began to do well and to meet the tasks she and I had set together, there was a sudden about-face, and she became very weepy during the sessions and said she felt I was pushing her too hard. I remember standing up for something, and glancing out of the window, and there below, with his gaze fixed on the window of my office, was Dave.

'Does Dave always wait outside for you?' I asked. She said at first he'd sat in his car, or gone for a half at the pub, but now he preferred to stand there. 'He's having some trouble with his nerves,' she explained.

We began to explore the marriage, including its sexual side. There was no doubt that Dave was an angel when it came to housekeeping, but in the bedroom things had never been much good, and they hadn't made love for twelve years or more. She knew, but could admit only reluctantly, that this problem of hers was really one that belonged to both of them. She talked about how jealous and anxious he'd been when she worked, and gradually admitted that it was no coincidence that her recent improvement led to his renewed fears. Eventually, they agreed to see a male therapist and myself together for marital therapy, and at last we beat the barrier to change.

This fear that some men experience is by no means a new one, raised by the advent of feminism or any other recent movement. Back in Ancient Greece, Euripides told us: 'A woman should be good for everything at home, but abroad good for nothing.' And Bonaparte himself, conqueror of nations, said: 'The husband must possess the absolute power and right to say to his wife: "Madam, you shall not go out, you shall not go to the theatre, you shall not receive such and such a person; for the children you will bear shall be mine."' Perhaps he worried about saying 'Not tonight, Josephine' just once too often!

And it's not just agarophobia that results from this protection of a husband's sexual pride by both partners. Women who suffer from hypochondriasis, or illness phobia, are often in a similar position. I have seen many of them over the years who have submitted their poor bodies to terrible tests thinking they have some illness or other. A psychoanalyst suggested I ask them about their sex lives and again I discovered that there had been no sex for a very long time – ten, fifteen, even twenty years. This was put down to the woman's physical problems but, getting them to look at dates more accurately, they would admit eventually that sex stopped some time before her pains began. Had they talked about it? Never. Recent research has backed this up. The psychological and physical health of women in a dissatisfied marriage is considerably worse than the man's; in a satisfied marriage it's equal. It isn't that women need sex to be healthy – nuns are often cheerful and long-lived – but living a lie is bad for your health, especially when your being ill seems an essential part of the marriage.

The woman's problems – whether psychological or physical – had developed as an explanation for what was going wrong in the relationship. Together they draped a veil over the fact that his symbol of manliness was less than rocklike, and instead she took the problems, the sickness, onto her own shoulders. Of course, in doing this, she stopped him ever seeking help, or learning new ways to make love that didn't involve one narrow form of intercourse; and she destroyed her own life by trapping herself in a gilded cage, or by subjecting her body to various tortures and her mind to torment.

Chapter 10

Mid-life Crises

I am worn out with dreams;
A weather-worn, marble triton
Among the streams;

W. B. Yeats, *Men Improve*
with the Years

S OME YEARS ago I worked in a psychotherapy clinic
funded by the Medical Research Council to look at what
helped people who had breakdowns in some way con-
nected to their work. Our clients were in managerial or
professional jobs, so they tended to be high up in the health
service, the arts, industry, civil service and so on. Of those we
saw, two-thirds were men, and all of them were depressed.
Despite this, they were all still working, with very few even
taking time off, though the quality of their work must have
suffered quite a bit since depression affects your decision-
making and concentration quite profoundly.

One of the most striking things immediately apparent was
that the men's average age was right on forty, while the
women's was precisely fifty. Although there was, of course,
some variation around these averages, the vast majority were
bunched right up close to the decade birthday. These were men
and women who were highly successful in terms of their
careers and none had had any serious psychological problems
before. What we were seeing clearly was a crisis situation and,

because of the age it happened in the men, what it was to do with for them undoubtedly concerned their mid-life. We realized that, although the crisis was happening around ten years later in women, it had remarkably similar elements to it.

What we saw first of all was their depression – their tears, feelings of hopelessness, isolation from everyone including their wives or husbands, indecision about everything. Some had separated from their partners before they came to therapy; some were drinking much more heavily. Almost all of them said they had no idea at all what started it, but there was often a life event like a parent's death or serious illness or dementia, a disappointment at work, a car crash, and so on, that came shortly before the depression began.

Within therapy a striking difference that emerged was that the men often described a longing to run away, to escape from everything in their lives – marriage, children, jobs, mortgages, possessions. None of the women mentioned this urge. I have never heard a woman patient talk about escape in these terms, though, like men, they might say they sometimes wish they could go to sleep and never wake up – which I always take to mean they want to die. Of course, women do leave their husbands and even their children too, but I don't see it as the result of a fantasy as it often is with men. Men describe almost literally riding off into the sunset (using a horse or motorcycle or yacht), whereas women usually feel they're going to have to set up house elsewhere, often just round the corner so the kids can see their dad. What I know many women do fantasise about is that the men will leave them. Because they are not brought up to act, and certainly not to abandon someone, very many women sit around hoping and waiting for the man to do it for them! He is, after all, more practised at that sort of thing. For some this comes out as fantasies of his death – either by actively longing for it or by worrying and imagining frequently and in full technicolor when he's late that it's because he's involved in a terrible car crash. Others report being able to get the man to go, even for brief periods, by precipitating the right kind of row. Anything rather than do the dirty deed themselves.

Two men that I was to see in therapy did a bunk right before the first session. One vanished completely, and I later had a postcard from India apologizing for his not turning up; the other one, Roger, took his sailing boat and set off to sail round Britain. His wife and boss tracked him down at Scarborough, and he turned up next week to explain. He said the urge to go had got so great he didn't know what to do about it, but also (I suggested) he didn't really *want* to do anything about it. Hence the rushed departure just before we'd first agreed to meet.

The main theme throughout his therapy was to do with responsibility. He was in charge of production at a huge chemical plant, on call twenty-four hours a day, seven days a week. Despite this real burden, he still wasn't delegating even when he could. Worse still, he seemed to assume responsibility for me – asking me how I was, suggesting I looked tired, complimenting me on my hair. When I pointed out how inappropriate this was and asked whether he took this type of responsibility for the happiness of people at work, and perhaps also his wife, he realized this was true. Roger had kept his wife totally dependent on him because of his need to take care of everything. He didn't seem to know any behaviour between doing this and doing absolutely nothing by running away. Looking back to his childhood he could explain this by his relationship to his mother. She had been depressed and he had felt guilty that he couldn't make her happy. His early life was so miserable that he often dreamed of doing a bunk, but instead he stayed like a good little boy. He told me:

> I love my wife but I can't stand to be with her. When I'm away from her I long to be home, and when I'm home I can't wait to get away. I really want her, but I can't even make love to her. I don't know what's happening to me.

The dichotomy of either running away or being 'the good husband' can be seen in many of the letters I get from women whose husbands of twenty years have suddenly decided they have to be alone. For example:

> I've been married for thirty-two years. He changed in his behaviour and his mind last December and walked

out in April. He's gone to a bedsit. He says the last twenty-five years have been hell, but that he loves me. But then he says he can't live with me. I am devastated. It would have been better if he'd died.

And:

My loving husband of twenty-nine years marriage left home almost without warning and definitely without staying to say farewell – just a note. In the past difficult twenty months he has never given a definite reason, but just keeps repeating I don't love you enough to live with you anymore. And yet he heaps praises on me, agrees I'm kind, that I'm the best friend he ever had . . .

It seemed to me that this chaos of feelings and behaviour is not such a new thing for men. The toing and froing that they experience happens to them first as toddlers when they start their independence from their mothers. It happens again in their adolescence, when they 'leave' both parents – wanting them but then not wanting them, needing them and rejecting them. Significantly both adolescence and mid-life are marked by an increase in male suicide: when you leave someone you are also abandoned, and loss is related to suicide and depression. Significant, too, that in each of these three crises, or turning points, the boy or man will often head towards other men. It may not always be obvious in the mid-life crisis, but it's usually there, nevertheless, whether it's a football team or a men's group. Elaine told me:

Julian was forced to give up professional football because of arthritis. Our lives as a couple had revolved around matches for years. He changed overnight, so I didn't know him. He thought he'd missed out on his youth and blamed me (though actually it was football). He wanted to start going out with 'the boys' when we had always done things together. 'The boys' were much younger than him, but they looked up to him.

Marlena said:

He is forty-four and has been married for half his life – twenty-two years. His values seem to have changed. He bought an MGB roadster, he wants to be out at the pub or clubs or discos, with the boys. He talks about how nice and pretty other women are. He stays out till two and three am and then wonders why I'm upset. He says, 'You're behaving like my mother.'

Yes, well; that's not really surprising, is it? When patterns repeat like this, when old strings are being pulled, you can be pretty sure that there is something that's stuck psychologically, something you might now be able to let go of.

Who Left Whom?

BECAUSE OF the difficult choice that the little boy has to make in separating so early from his mother, chances are he places the blame for this onto her: that way the guilt will feel more tolerable. He may project onto her the abandoning act (as if she left him, rather than he left her) or he may feel that she was smothering him and so he was forced to join the un-smothering world of men. Many men then grow up to fear that women will either s-mother them or abandon them; there is no in-between. They cannot see them simply as equal partners. Others control the fear by being either smothering or abandoning themselves, like Roger, above, or like the younger man in this letter:

From the beginning I was rather uncomfortable in the relationship as I felt that I 'looked after' Joan, and was the stronger one. As she was Australian, I was her only contact really and so I gradually became stifled, almost claustrophobic, and I just did not feel attracted to her any more. She was trying even harder to make me love her by almost mothering me. I just withdrew more. Sex became very unloving, ungratifying and rare.

It's a long letter. It goes on to tell me that Joan returned to Australia (not surprisingly) and it's clear from her letters that she's feeling strong, developing her career and making a good life for herself. Whereupon he suddenly realizes that he loves her more than life itself, and rushes over to be with her. He proposes and with some real reluctance she accepts and comes back to England, and the relationship dips almost instantly back to square one.

This behaviour – of getting too close and then running away – is a source of complaint for many young women nowadays. But nevertheless most men do actually settle down to marriage eventually. They take the plunge, as they say, even if it's only a reaction to the male version of being left on some shelf when it seems that all their mates are blowing bubbles at their bonny new babies. Because of this, they do actually slip into the responsibility mode, and most of them take quite a bit (if not all) of the economic burden once babies are born. Because that's what men do and because society has ensured it happens like that by paying men more than women. Because men's boundaries are strong and it's either all or nothing, in-betweens are difficult for them. And then they see the neon signs of mid-life, the implications of the downhill slope, pinnacles passed, and all that. And that's when they think most strongly about escape.

Losing Things

THE DEPRESSION and risk of suicide that is often part of this crisis is marked by the urge to escape, to be impulsive, to give up (or, in young men, not to take on) the extremely onerous burdens of being a man. Why it happens particularly around forty in men and fifty in women is, however, primarily to do with loss. For men, much of what they lose concerns dreams and aspirations; for women, most of the losses are more tangible.

It's worth spelling out what men and women tell me

they feel they're losing, because to some extent their own experiences involve the same sadnesses we all face when aspects of our lives we cherished are suddenly but clearly gone for ever.

• **Losing your looks.** At around forty, give or take a year or two according to their genes, many men begin to lose their hair. Don't scoff, you women readers. This is just as tragic for most men as is your own sagging chinline or widening frame. I have had men in tears about their baldness, just as I have had women weep for the beauty they feel has disappeared. They plot and plan over hair transplants just as much as you raise your cheeks with your palms and wonder about a facelift. All the other features of growing older have somehow been discounted by men – grey hair, paunches, wrinkles are all taken care of in the media image of power. But somehow baldness isn't. They try to say it's a sign of virility (what else?), but you can tell by their nervous laughs that they don't believe it.

• **Losing your aspirations.** Around this time in most men's careers it becomes clear whether or not they're going to 'make it' in the types of ways our society allows men. This is the time that many men realize they are not going to sit in the managing director's chair, be the greatest brain surgeon, drive the engine, or reach whatever career pinnacle they dreamt about for years. This loss of a dream happens much more in men than in women because, as we've seen, progress in jobs has become for many of them a symbol of sexuality. Power is sexy – every woman's magazine has told you that – and now they realize that power as they expected it simply isn't going to happen. Nowadays, it may well not even be a question of getting to the top, but more of having a job at all. The early-retirement brigade are prime suspects for the mid-life crisis.

Most women don't have dreams like this: promotions are still frequently put down to luck rather than achievement, and few of them have any real career plans mapped out. This is often seen in organizations as a bad thing but one good result of it is that, where there are few dreams, there are also fewer disappointments.

• **The waning of sexual powers.** Actually, sexual athleticism in men begins to deteriorate much, much earlier than forty. It starts to drop off from around the age of twenty, but we're generally unaware of this because marriage and children mean there are outside difficulties that can explain any slowing down in sexual activity. Unfortunately, around the age of forty, when you can put a lock on your bedroom door and tell your teenagers you're having an early night, many women are starting to become much more confident lovers, more able to have orgasms, for example – and this only goes to highlight any problems the man might have. And because he's learnt to externalize blame, and because sexuality (defined as it is only in terms of an erect penis) is so very important in being a man, then of course it must be something his wife is doing, or not doing. But he just might not be too sure that this is true.

It's not surprising that at the moment, various practitioners, medical and otherwise, are reaping the rewards of all this doubt by proposing the idea of a male menopause, treated with HRT in the form of testosterone. The medicalization of the female menopause has prompted the oestrogen-progesterone supplements and the ecstatic praise of its gurus who swear they wouldn't live this glamorous life without it, and so it's inevitable that men would want some of the goodies too. If life can be changed by a pill, then let's have some fast. But there's no clear evidence that testosterone has an effect even on sexual problems, so the chances are slight indeed of its altering you in a way that makes you feel cheerful, loved by your wife and family, and no longer caring whether or not you make it to the top (or even if you have a job or not). But if you believe a hair transplant makes you look more attractive, I guess you'll believe anything.

• **Losing the dream family.** Much of the research which looks at the aspirations of young boys and girls shows that they remain quite dismally traditional in their ideas about their futures. Both see themselves as getting married, and having children, and the picture they paint of this is quite roses round the door, hubby bringing home the bacon, dinner on the table, pretty little children, and so on. Even though their own experiences of family life are often very different. Women lose this dream pretty smartly as soon as they have their first baby – even, it seems, quite soon after the wedding bells have tolled. They quickly learn that children are not the clean, polite, loving little angels of the picture-books, that looking after a family is not by any means an easy or always a joyful experience, and marriage itself is difficult and usually unromantic.

Even today, with faint visions of equality on some people's horizons, most men are protected from this reality of family life all through the years when the children are young. Even now, it's father who comes home to the cleaned-up kids, the homework done, the meal ready. He rarely has to find their gym kits in the morning or stay home for them when they're ill. And then they are in their teens and all of a sudden they have stopped caring about behaving when dad comes home, stopped cleaning up for their fathers (themselves or their mess), treating him with respect, and so on. What is worse, when he is around forty, they are usually bursting with adolescent aggravation, full of rampant sexuality (and rubbing his nose in it at every opportunity), dripping with ideals very similar to those he lost so many years ago. They're the Young Turks ready to take over whenever he cares to leave. Nothing reminds him of what he's lost so much as the sight and sounds of young people on the edge of being adults. Nothing perhaps except his wife who is aging alongside him like some constant unflattering mirror, reflecting his own decline.

• **The loss of a parent.** When men are around the age of forty and women around the age of fifty, it is quite common for the same sex parent to die. The difference in ages comes because men father children at a slightly older age than women give birth, and also men die slightly younger than women do. Even where parents do not die, some dement, which has a similar effect as death or maybe worse; while those that survive are recognizably elderly by now. In other words, men in some way lose their fathers at around forty, and women lose their mothers about ten years later.

What this does for men in particular is to make them suddenly aware of their mortality. Just at a time when they are realizing the end of many of their early dreams, they are catching a glimpse of the certainty of death. The power of being a man is evaporating before their eyes: it didn't get them what they thought it would, and it won't protect them in the end.

Intimations of mortality are, however, not at all new to most women, perhaps partly because of childbirth, but also because of the more gradual waning of her youth and beauty in terms of what society sees as acceptable. So from much younger than men, women are acutely aware of aging, and all the articles in the world on how great it is to be forty, don't help the first time you realize you are no longer being seen as a person. Nevertheless, the loss of youth still hits women quite hard at around fifty, linked undoubtedly to the loss of her ability to continue to have children. It will be interesting to see just what effect the possibility of continued procreation has on the self-esteem of middle-aged women in the future. (Certainly the age that we're told it's still OK to be a woman – dubious thanks to the likes of Jane Fonda and Tina Turner – seems to be carried on forward just ahead of me, like a tattered pennant. Soon, I have no doubt, all these female Dorian Grays will be telling me it's great to be sixty, and demonstrating it elegantly with the splits.)

Women suffer one loss more strongly than men. Their children leave home and, if they have put most of their life's energies into looking after them, then this can leave them with a great sense of emptiness, popularly called the 'empty nest syndrome'. As more and more women have careers of their own, this is likely to fade, and I now get just as many letters from mothers who want their sons and daughters to go so that they can finally start enjoying themselves with somewhat gayer abandon, as I do from those who mourn their loss for long periods. And women also suffer one loss more frequently than men: the husband may well have left home too. The ten years between his mid-life crisis and hers is a pretty rocky decade for marriages.

What He Did Next

T HE HUSBAND'S reactions to the losses that he is experiencing may take a number of forms:

1. Depression

He may become clinically depressed. Certainly many of the men I've seen in therapy come into this category and so do a number of those whose wives write to me to find out how to help. Apart from sometimes showing the more obvious signs of tears and despair, depression is also marked by symptoms such as:

> Early waking, sometimes with fears and forebodings
> Loss of libido
> Loss of appetite
> Guilt
> Thoughts about being useless, or everything being
>   hopeless
> Anger and irritability
> Thoughts of death and dying, including suicide

If you know someone that you think may be contemplating suicide, don't hang about being polite. For a start, ask him (or her) if that's what they mean when they said 'I just want to get away from everything', or 'I don't want to wake up'. If they don't actually mean that they want to die, then that's fine – you won't be encouraging them by mentioning it. But if they do, then it's much better to let them talk about it (rather than you just talk them out of it), and to let their doctor know as soon as you can so that they can be referred for help.

Most men suffering the mid-life crisis aren't actually suicidal; they're just somewhat depressed. I realize it seems little comfort to be told that depression is a perfectly normal reaction to loss, or that it is probably the most useful form of the mid-life crisis, but that's the truth. Depression involves a withdrawing from life in some way, which is usually seen as a symptom, but can equally be part of the mind or body's natural means to cure. To do this, it needs to be used as a time to reflect on what has been, what has gone, and what can be done about it to make the rest of one's life more conducive to contentment. When men stop chasing dangling carrots, when they cease constructing their phallic monuments, they are bound to feel somewhat at a loss for a while in terms of knowing what they should do next. It might take a couple of years at least to sort out what they want, but it's time well spent. Following the mid-life, many will be working out how to live life without the rules of the club: to learn, for example that being masculine doesn't always mean to dominate, to be ceaselessly sexual, to win. Their props, sometimes even a partner who may have been the greatest prop of all, perhaps are gone, and it's difficult to learn to walk without them. Even if she's still there, as most will be, it still takes time to learn how to walk beside her rather than trample on her or follow with her some path that now feels wrong.

2. Alcohol

Drinking is macho – it's what men do – and because of the competitive nature of so much of male activity, drinking more than other men, or at least as much, continues to be one of the badges of the masculinity club. Small wonder then that many men begin to block out the pain of the experience of mid-life with alcohol. This is the time when those who have regularly used alcohol to deal with distressing or anxious events may now start to use it much more heavily, and in a manner that can lead to all the dismal effects of alcoholism. If you are feeling anxious that some of the hallmarks of being a man are deserting you, drinking heavily is one that anyone can do – a legitimate mark of masculinity and a drug that stops you thinking about what you've lost.

Although an increasing proportion of alcoholics are women, they are much more likely to be secret drinkers; male alcoholics do a lot of public drinking, even if they also have a bottle of whisky in their desk drawer, and hide their Special Brew cans behind the paint tins in the cellar. Public heavy drinking is part of what it means to be a man, and it's very difficult to abstain and still feel legitimately masculine. A friend of mine had been sober for six months when he came across the usual pub bore who kept trying to force him to accept a pint. The urgency of the pressure really said more about the man than it did about anything else, but my friend, relatively unaggressive usually, was nearly apoplectic when he told me about it. After such difficulty and hard work in stopping drinking, I was astounded to hear him say things like: 'I could drink him under the table any night of the week. Any time he wants me to take him on he's only got to say.' I wasn't surprised to hear he was back on the booze very shortly afterwards. Being sober is very different to simply not drinking.

People often take a very long time to acknowledge and begin to tackle a drinking problem. In a recent report of male doctors who are reformed alcoholics, the average length of time that they knew, looking back, that their drinking was out of control was around twenty years – a terribly long period of strain on marriages and families in general. It's difficult for a wife to know that her husband has slipped over some mysterious divide from heavy drinking into alcoholism, but not as difficult as it needs to be if only they could find the courage to put a name to what's going wrong. Often, over quite a long period of time, she will appear to be the party pooper, always trying to stop hubby from being the life and soul. But also, because she makes internal attributions – blames herself when things go wrong – she is quite likely to do this over his drinking as well. Especially as, chances are, he's telling her that if only she wasn't so X, Y or Z, he wouldn't drink so much.

Male friends are really no help at all because they too are in the club and admitting that their buddy is not handling his alcohol too well may mean that they have a problem too. There's no real reason for the man to recognize it – until it gets him into dire trouble, it seems to serve him well. Male friends don't comment because they don't want to recognize it in themselves; and women ignore it because they have this deep-seated desire not to question anything that contributes to a man's masculinity. Not to rock the boat in any way.

As a simple way to discover if there's a drinking problem,

I like the 4 L's test, at least for starters. It simply asks if alcohol is having an effect on:

Love   Is marriage or friendship suffering? Has a spouse or friend ever mentioned your drinking might be a problem?

Labour Has there been a warning, however mild, at work?

Lucre   Is the cost of alcohol affecting the bank balance significantly?

Law   Has drinking brought you into contact with the law? Have you lost your licence, etc.

If you can answer yes to any of these, then it is quite likely that your drinking is getting or already is out of hand. If it's around the mid–life period then you would be much better off stopping the fuzz of alcohol in order to look at yourself in focus at last. No, it isn't always pleasant, but it's better than being dead or killing off all the joy around you. In the end, most people who learn to drink normally or, more commonly, to abstain through Alcoholics Anonymous, actually report a growing joy within themselves as they begin to deal with the issues that lie behind the booze. Here's one man's comments on what changed for him when he stopped drinking and began to face things at last through AA.

The first change for me was just beginning to talk openly about myself and what I'd done. This was made easier by the stories that others were telling. I had to stop lying to myself quite quickly because I heard them saying what they used to do and the lies they used to tell, and I'd done just the same. I'd never heard a man talking about being frightened of things like his wife's career blossoming, but there was a man admitting it and sounding fine. It was good too to be equal with women in the group in terms of sharing the same distress, the same fears about things. It had never

191

occurred to me that we could be alike in any way. But I guess the most important thing of all was to stop blaming women – well, my ex-wife to be specific – for everything bad that had happened to me. While she was still around I blamed her for my drinking, but when she left that was a bit more difficult, so I had to blame her for leaving me an addict. What I learned most was that in saying I was to blame, I got the power to change things. That sounds so easy, but actually it was a revelation.

Alcoholics can change and can enjoy their lives much better after that, but it won't be their partners that changed them. As a partner (whether male or female), you need to realize that you've done nothing to help so far. That's not to say you're to blame – the very opposite – but that, despite all your efforts to make things all right, you've failed to change a thing. Because of this you have to let the alcoholic go; you have to say: 'It's your problem, I give up.' That's often the moment that they start to take responsibility for themselves. This happens very quickly when the drinker is female, but tends to go on for years when it's a man: husbands leave their alcoholic wives much more frequently and swiftly than vice versa because a wife fears to be the one to abandon, and often thinks the problem is down to her. Paradoxical as it may sound, realizing that she can't control everything is a very important step in ultimately making things better.

3. Affairs

Some affairs are simply an escape from the reality of one's situation. However, in the mid-life period the escape is usually to someone younger. It is an escape from growing old and dying. The man, or at least his unconscious, reasons that by taking a younger wife he gets the chance to give middle age the slip: he can even start a new family, a new fantasy of the pretty woman dependent upon him, snuggled into his manly breast. He starts to shop at Next and Gap, has his hair done at Sassoons or visits those who promise miracles by way of transplants and toupees; he even buys a sports car. He is young, devil-may-care. He says things like: 'It's my chance of happiness; I can't let it go.' His wife wonders who on earth the stranger is.

One of the differences between affairs at this time and at other times is that this is more serious. It's not a fling to make a point, to gain retribution or equal any scores. This is done with the intention of blocking out the pain of lost dreams by going back to sleep as deeply as possible. This is about forgetting, and he can't wait to do it. Because of this, a wife usually finds out about the affair much more frequently and quickly than she does where it's simply lust. If he doesn't tell her outright, he certainly lets her know in other ways. I am sure that it's very rare indeed that a partner discovers infidelity unless the wanderer (happy or otherwise) actually wants her or him to know. So in this situation it becomes essential that his wife knows, either because he wants to escape middle-age as soon as he can, or because in some strange way it's as if he almost wants her blessing.

There are different ways of giving blessings. You can say, 'Right fine, go. You live your life and I'll get on with enjoying mine', which seems perfectly reasonable to me and is probably the best way to get him running back. Or you can do everything to try and understand and make things all right for him, like this woman is doing:

> My husband has been playing squash with a young lady for the past few years, but now says that he has fallen in love with her. She is twenty-eight and he is forty-five. He has gone to stay with his parents, but comes here and has a meal and makes love – only if he wants to. I am trying so hard to be understanding that when a catalogue for clothes was posted to me, he said she had a birthday coming up, and we both chose a blouse for her. He seemed pleased about that. I want him back so much.

Of course, that is simply rewarding bad behaviour which – as any psychologist or dog trainer will tell you – is likely to be followed by more and more of the same. This is a time when you really have to make some very firm boundaries. As a wife, you don't need to condone anything: in the end you have to say how much you will tolerate in terms of what's the best for you and your children, and then stick to it.

But I admit that's easier to say sometimes than to do. Quite often the husband is in true turmoil. He's using every strategy at once: trying to run off with someone else, drinking too much, still loving his wife, and feeling so depressed that the only way out seems like suicide.

Although this is very distressing for all parties, in the end the woman has to set limits. She still has to say that he must sort things out for himself, that she is not the one who can make it all better, that he must take responsibility for the pain he's causing to everyone, that children are not resilient, and that he can't just come and go as he pleases but must choose. Of course, it's particularly difficult for her to say this because of her reawakened fear of abandonment – a hell of a marriage is better than a heaven of solitude, she thinks – and her tendency to blame herself (or possibly the other woman, as a representative of herself) makes her take responsibility for making things OK again. 'What can I do to help him?' is the most frequent question I get, asked plaintively after a long description of appalling behaviour on his part. Just as with alcoholism and depression, you won't in the end be able to help or change him: you can only encourage him to seek help elsewhere if things seem bad enough. If they don't, then chances are it will all turn out OK because he sorts it out for himself. The worst scenario, I think, is when the wife does everything she can to make things better; the husband returns because he was ambivalent and frightened anyway; and they go on as before but more so, in that now she becomes totally obsessed with making it all right and not rocking the boat in any way at all. The smothering that is inevitable from such behaviour simply makes him more abusive or more likely to leave again, especially as her cottonwool insulation has meant he hasn't faced any of the things that had first prompted him to go.

What to do About Mid-life

WELL, ONE could say there's nothing you can actually do about it except face it. That's true, but if you're going to stay together and to make something better from it, then there is no way that one partner can change without the other changing too. Part of the episode is to do with the collusive nature of the problems, so we need to look at how each partner has to tackle the crisis.

As a man who recognizes some of the points above are contributing to the anguish that you're feeling, here are a few points to help you through:

- Recognize what you're running away from, and stop still for a time. This takes courage, of course, and it might involve you leaving home to live alone for a while, which can be difficult.

- If you have any remote inkling that you just might have a drinking problem, go to an AA meeting. If the accounts you hear strike home at all, then chances are you have, and you should tackle it as fast as possible before it destroys you and your family.

- Don't be tempted to start a new relationship (and especially not a new family) until you fully appreciate what has made the last one fail. Don't look for reasons in your wife, but only in yourself.

- Explain to your children as well and as honestly as you can what is happening to you. Then it can be a learning experience for them as well. Expect them to feel angry with you – that's their business.

- Don't seek too much consolation with male friends. Chances are you're all around the same age, and all in the men's club together. This means you'll explain everything using the old cliché reasons concerning your wife and your life. That won't make you feel any better at all in the long run.

- If you're depressed, get help for it. Anti–depressant medication might be helpful in the short run, but make sure you also get some psychotherapy or counselling from someone that has been recommended to you. Although it's often painful at first, most men come to realize it's actually exciting in the vistas that get opened up.

As a woman whose partner's behaviour seems very like that described above, here are some of the things which you must do if you want things to change:

- Don't argue with him over his feelings. Don't try to cheer him up. Just listen to him and try to understand.

- Don't be a prop, except to be there and listen when you say you will. Propped objects never stand straight.

- Decide what your limits are. This is tricky for women to do, but you've got to draw a line somewhere in terms of what you're going to put up with, and for how long. If it's too hard to do alone, then get help.

- Make any agreement to giving him a second chance conditional on counselling – perhaps marital initially.

- Start to develop yourself – recapture old interests, and form new ones; make long-term plans just for you; get all the training you can; take yourself off for a holiday alone or with a girlfriend. All this increasing independence will stand you in good stead for the future, whether it's with him or not.

- Don't try to make things the same as they once
  were. Realize that you might have thought it was all
  fine, but in the end it didn't work. If you try to
  smooth everything away, chances are it will happen
  all over again. This is the time for revolution, not
  the status quo.

Finally, you both need to recognize that change is at best uncomfortable and sometimes really painful, so it's not surprising that most of us fear it. Nevertheless, it's never so bad as the pain you're suffering now. Living within a miserable marriage that is fulfilling neither of you is like walking in shoes four sizes too small: you can do it, but it will gradually cripple you. The word 'crisis' comes from the Greek meaning a turning point, and that's what it is – a chance to make things better.

This won't happen by one or both of you flying into the arms of someone else – you'll simply take your despair along with you like a pilgrim's burden. The change for the better can usually take place within the marriage itself, but it means giving up old straitjackets for new freedoms and it's this that frightens people. As a man you are giving up the trappings that have built up your sense of masculinity (alcohol, girl-friends, being top dog at work) and discovering a new way of being a man that doesn't depend upon being one up on women, or on men. As a woman you are learning not to try to be in control of everyone, even if it just seems that you're being kind and helpful; you are setting boundaries which you are brave enough to acknowledge might mean you'll be alone, and you are developing the ability to be a separate person that you care about. This way, the second half of your lives, whether together or apart, will usually be much better than the first.

_____ *Chapter 11* _____

Preferring Other Things

Someone once remarked that in adolescence pornography is a substitute for sex, whereas in adulthood sex is a substitute for pornography.

Edmund White, *New Times* magazine, 1979

WITHIN A marriage, sexual satisfaction can be taken as a barometer of other aspects of the relationship. It can give a clue as to how much passion there is around, it's true, but much more usefully it tells us how well people are communicating, how much they care about each other, whether there is anger, love, emptiness, etc. This is absolutely not to take sexual satisfaction as meaning that both parties have orgasms on demand and with great frequency; they may have no sex at all and still be satisfied so long as they both agree and feel comfortable with that situation. It's the mutuality of their sex-life or lack of it that on the whole suggests things are good enough within this marriage.

And that's usually how it is. But at least a third of first marriages, and even more of second ones, end in divorce, and a large proportion of the others live with unhappiness which often has something sexual at its heart. Whereas the next chapter looks at relationships where the capacity for sex itself is less than one or both partners want, this chapter looks at why one partner in a marriage turns to other things, or to other people, in order to try to get what they think they want.

Third Party Present

LOVE TRIANGLES exist right through our lives. As children we form different types of alliances with different parents. So, for example, boys might be attracted to their mothers and create the Oedipal triangle against dad, but they might also side with dad and consolidate male power against mum from early on. Triangles can exist between you, a parent and a brother or sister you see as preferred. Then when you become adult, there are triangles caused by your own children and your partner, or by your partner's job, by his or her lover, or still by a mother or a father. If you are out of a permanent relationship yourself, you might continually find yourself the third point of the triangle in someone else's marriage. For example, Tricia came for help and described two problems, both of which showed just how important these triangles can be:

> For the last three years I've been having an affair with a freelance photographer whom I commission to do quite a lot of work for the magazine I work on. I love him, but worry that he may be continuing our relationship because it's 'good for business'. I don't do anything wrong, but I guess I would give the job to him if all else was equal, and I do worry what my boss would say if she found out. He's married, of course, and has children. He says he loves me and wants to leave them and marry me, and half the time I believe this, but then I have heard it from men before.
>
> My other problem is my mother. We seem to have a lot of resentment that goes right back. Now I resent her because I feel she doesn't like me and prefers my brother whom she still goes on holiday with. She spends a lot of time and money on him. My parents rowed a lot when I was young and my father went off

with his secretary which my mother has never got over. When I see my father now, I don't tell my mother because it would upset her so much. I feel a pretty unlovable person and I'm very miserable. I feel there's something in me that drives people away.

Tricia's triangles, probably beginning with herself and her parents, have gone on throughout her life, and all of them are linked to betrayal. She feels betrayed herself and she betrays others – her lover's wife, her mother, her work. When we explored her early years, she described how she was the apple of her father's eye. Her mother seemed to resent this, but also she was so caught up with her son, that Tricia felt her father was the only one to give her love. Relations between mother and daughter grew more and more distant. Then her father left with his secretary, and the betrayal felt by Tricia was perhaps just as great as that felt by her mother. But she also felt guilty that she had somehow let her mother down in never supporting her. Since she was in her early twenties she had always found herself in relations with married men. Over time this seemed to be almost a way of punishing herself for 'betraying' her mother – setting herself up to hurt the wife, and then being hurt herself when finally she was dropped.

Men and women who find themselves repeatedly the third point of the triangle need to question just what triangles have existed in their lives, and also how much they fear ultimate commitment because of the possibility of betrayal, either of them or by them.

But what is going on in the marriage itself? What do affairs mean to the partners? Why do they occur? It's probably true that there are as many reasons for someone straying from a permanent relationship as there are married couples, but some overriding causes can be seen, in terms of three basic emotions: anger, guilt and fear.

Anger

A LOT OF affairs are to do with one party being angry with the other, even if they don't admit it or even acknowledge it to themselves. What makes you angry depends very much on what strings the current situation pulls that tweak earlier childhood grievances. So some people get angry because their partners aren't giving them as much as they expected – less attention, less admiration, less communication. But others seem to resent attention and get annoyed at what they see as too much smothering mothering, clinging or controlling, or too much responsibility.

For a while at least, a lover can be all things to all men (or women). She or he may provide the recognition and admiration that seems to be lacking in the marriage, can perhaps slip them back into those lovely honeymoon days of re-parenting. And the lover appears to have independence and strength, usually living alone and self-sufficient – a great relief from the burdens of responsibility. Of course, if and when the attention reduces or becomes overpoweringly intrusive, or if the independence wanes and there are tears that you're not there enough, then you can simply walk away, back to the possibly welcomed humdrum of home.

But anger can belong to the present as well as the past. At the most basic level of human interactions (one that most of us fall back into at the drop of a duelling glove), we retaliate angrily to wrongs seen as done to us, often in as similar a way as possible to the original hurtful act. An eye for an eye. A tooth for a tooth. An affair for an affair. Many affairs are acts of revenge, not just because the person who's angry decides to give the partner the same medicine as they were given, but sometimes because the offending partner may actually encourage this to relieve his or her guilt, particularly if their affair is still continuing. Kate told me:

> When Tom was having an affair with Sandra, he kept saying to me that there was something wrong with me because I didn't want one too; he hinted that I was

under-sexed. So eventually I went off with Mike, and it was very nice. Tom didn't get jealous but we both agreed to stop our affairs. Then I met John who was altogether more glamorous than Mike had been, quite a well-known writer in fact, and this time Tom got wildly jealous. This tipped the scales in my direction. It took quite a few affairs by both of us before we decided that there might be other ways to make things more balanced! We couldn't keep on paying each other back like this.

But sometimes you have to search more carefully for subtler clues than this in order to find the source of the anger. Sometimes these reasons are hidden within the society norms for marriage. So men might get angry for the responsibility they feel they have to shoulder; women might get angry for having to play second fiddle in careers; men might feel put out because of the birth of a child. All such ordinary events that we feel we have no right to be cross about them, and because of that we often never even realize we are cross, but merely act out our anger without too much thought.

Perhaps one partner has moved the other one to a different part of the country or to another country altogether, for example. Even where that seems quite appropriate it can cause enormous resentment which shows itself in various ways, including affairs. Luke and Abi had moved to Singapore when Luke was promoted to running his company's office there. Abi had given up her teaching post, put the boys into boarding school, and left her elderly father – all without apparent complaint. But after a few months she began drinking quite heavily, and then started an affair with a young Singalese who was a clerk in her husband's office. The young man was in a dreadful position, especially as she made things pretty obvious whenever she came to the office. When he ended it, she walked up to his desk drunk and started to hit him with her bag, screaming at him for his betrayal.

The whole business was put down to a nervous breakdown brought on by the strange environment and an excess of alcohol, but actually she had attacked her husband where it hurt him most – in his foreign office where he was furthering his career at the expense of her life. It was only within therapy, first individual and then with both of them, that she could start to explore the betrayal and anger she had felt at being so casually asked to leave so much behind – an anger which was completely understandable, but which she didn't feel able to even acknowledge because it seemed to her wrong. Much of their therapy consisted of learning new ways to communicate feelings, such as those discussed in chapter seven.

An affair that's to do with retaliation is always part of the marital relationship itself – I'm having sex with him or her because I'm angry with you – so its remedies will similarly lie again within the marriage.

But even if there are countless reasons for anger within your marriage now, don't forget to see if your feelings correspond in any way with those you had when you were young. We transfer our feelings about early relationships onto present ones, both at home and at work. For example, research has demonstrated this transference of feelings and expectations in a group of doctors, followed up over a number of years. If they reported their fathers as critical, difficult to please and unsupportive, years later they were more likely to see their bosses as causing them similar problems. And it's even more likely that we will transfer past feelings onto our partners than we do onto those at work. But it doesn't matter whether anger has a base in the present or in the past, just feeling it is enough to prompt the retaliation of an affair.

Guilt

MEN AND women also have affairs because there is something about their relationship with their partners that makes them feel guilty, and this doesn't happen so much when they go outside to play. Strange I agree, but there you are! As I described in detail in chapter seven, in the eyes of a new husband, marrying can turn a wife from Wicked Woman to Good Fairy or even Angel, and so guilt instantly takes away their sexual attractiveness as they change from lover into mother. This happens to some men not just when they marry, but especially when their wives get pregnant. Although seeking other women at that time is usually put down to the unattractiveness of the wife, or because she is no longer so keen on sex, for many men it's simply that she's becoming a mother, and you don't have sex with mums. As we describe in the next chapter, some men lose all interest or can become temporarily impotent because of this, but others simply turn their attentions elsewhere – to an affair with another woman, to prostitutes (just to make the contrast really clear), to pornography, and so on.

Anger and guilt are intimately linked. Some guilt is perfectly justified – it plays a useful and normal role in society – and if we accept that we have done something wrong in the present and try to make amends and then forgive ourselves, the effects of guilt will lessen and it won't be translated into anger. However, if we find the guilt so uncomfortable that we are unable to shoulder it and so blame everyone and everything around us, then anger will be the result.

Fear

PEOPLE OFTEN have affairs because they are afraid of something that is happening to them. For example, in the last chapter I described how men (and occasionally women) may go off with someone else because they have realized that youth has ended and that life itself is finite. The fear that this arouses prompts them into a denial of their impermanence by pairing up with someone who is usually somewhat younger than them.

Other people are deeply frightened of commitment and responsibility, and yet long for love and so still end up married. Sometimes they can cope with this until a first child is born, but then they may have an affair, as if this dilutes their commitment in some way. This conflict between being close and fearing closeness can go on for years and sometimes I see a man on his third young family: he looks for something he felt was missing for him in his early family, but then it fails to provide that magic ingredient that he thinks would make life swell, and he moves on to the next adoring woman. Sometimes affairs happen because a man or woman feels unlovable and so needs constant reaffirmation that they are loved, both by the lover and by the subsequent forgiveness of the partner when he or she finds out. This is unlikely to be a one-off affair, but more of a pattern that will last until they can accept that they were not loved as they should have been when they were young. This can be very sad to recognize, but it can also cut the strings and let them start to accept the ordinary love that's now on offer.

Then there are the Don Juans of this world: they may not look afraid, but they are most commonly men who are very frightened that their sexual prowess is not as good as they feel it should be, or even that it might be men who attract them most. Here's one who, as far as his wife can tell, simply flirts:

> He flirts with everyone we come in contact with – man, woman or child – even those we meet in the street or on public transport. It seems like a sort of tic that he is unable to control. And of course, he does it nonstop with our women friends, and their husbands seem to put up with it. He uses women like public lavatories, and probably thinks of them that way. He's even flirted with our doctor so that, when I went to her to say how unhappy I was, she basically told me I was lucky.

Like many of these charming men, her husband lies constantly – not just to get out of situations or to shift blame, but almost for the sake of it. A friend of mine had a lover for a couple of years who would whisk her off to Paris or Vancouver Island at almost a whim. But she had to pay dearly by putting up with the lies that he used in order to make himself feel in control of everything, just for the power of manipulation itself. He had other women constantly, and so some deviousness might be thought inevitable, but it was more than this. For example, one day, when she was in Leeds and he was supposed to be in London, he rang her saying he was in Liverpool, visiting a colleague. He described the view of the Mersey from the window, and how it was a much nicer city than he'd thought. She rang back, having forgotten to tell him something, and of course, he wasn't there at all. He was in Leicester. A totally pointless lie unless you want to confuse, control, and hurt a woman – even though she might never have known. Like most Don Juans, he is clearly someone who hates women because he both fears them and wants them. Such men go out of their way to get their heterosexual abilities confirmed as often as they can, suggesting that they might have quite strong doubts about just how heterosexual they really are, but also that being heterosexual matters dreadfully.

A Gay Affair

W HEN A husband or wife goes off with someone of the same sex, it feels to the partner left behind that the issues involved are much more dreadful than if they had left them for a heterosexual affair. Men's horror of this comes from the feeling that their very masculinity has been mocked; women talk about it more in terms of the shame of their husband being gay, and the implication that he isn't a real man after all. For example:

> My husband of fifteen years has just told me that he's a homosexual and for the last five years he has been involved with a man that he loves. He sees him about once a week and has been away with him to conferences and even on holiday. I never suspected anything and it has come as a ghastly shock. My husband wants to continue this relationship but for us to stay as we are. He has moved into the spare bedroom. I agreed that we must do this, partly because I am afraid to think of myself alone, but also because he is a solicitor in our town and I can't bear to have people talking. It would ruin him.

So what is she going to do? Put up with living a lie in the spare room for the rest of her life? The trouble is that when a husband declares himself to be having an affair with a man, his wife treats this in different ways to how she would if it were another woman: rather than feeling anger, she feels shame, for example. But it's just the same – he has someone else and all three of them have to decide what they are going to do about it. The difference is that gay men are very unlikely to change their mind and decide to be happily heterosexual again after all (though I know two who have recently done so), whereas other men's affairs may very well be one-off protests, or done for any of the reasons we discussed earlier.

So if your partner has turned out to be actively homosexual, you need to decide what you want out of the relationship and whether you still have enough to make it work. If you feel that this is possible, you need to draw up some new terms about boundaries so that he or she knows clearly when they step past the limits of your tolerance. And then you see if that works for both of you, knowing that you can make real changes if it doesn't. But you do all that when your partner's lover is heterosexual too. Realizing that it's at heart no different can sometimes take away the feelings of shame and let you feel justifiably jealous and angry instead. Shame can make you live a lie, while anger often leads to action.

Recovering from the Blow

WHEN OUR partners have affairs, and we find out, we are knocked for six. Whether men or women, we have been rejected. Whether for failing to be man enough, or for failing to be lovable enough, our partner has abandoned us for someone else. All the baby fears of being left alone come to the fore. All the pain of jealous rage makes us want to hit things, throw things, stamp and scratch, just as if we were toddlers once again. We don't think we can possibly survive – because we couldn't have survived when we were young and that is where we are now once more.

Betrayal is as old as mankind. It's a constant theme of the Bible, of myth, of Shakespeare, of literature right up to today. Its universality means that it must be very important, very difficult for all of us to work through. If you have been betrayed as a child – if a mother or father left you, for example

– then a partner's affair will feel worse than ever. But remarkably, most of us do manage to get through these traumas and sometimes both as a couple and as individuals we mature because of them. Time really does make a difference, and there are other things you can do to ease the way towards forgiveness or letting go.

- It's awful for both of you, but your morbid curiosity about exactly what happened is quite normal, so don't think you're going mad because you insist on your partner going into every gory detail of the ups and downs and ins and outs of the affair – both the social and the sexual side. It's perfectly normal, but after a while it really doesn't help. At a certain point you have to realize that you won't ever know the exact truth (because it doesn't exist), and that you're ready to stop hurting yourself and him with your anger, and to put it all behind you. Some of the exercises in chapter seven will help you here.

- Both of you must stop each other ladling out blame for what's happened. It won't do any good at all – not even to the one who's blaming because it will keep you a victim. The thing has happened, and you both have to see what you're going to do about it. Start your marriage again from this point on.

- Don't issue an ultimatum – 'If you see her/him again, that will be it!' It doesn't work in war (except to create war), and it won't help in adultery. While you can set your own limits – and you should – about what in future you will tolerate and when you will decide that enough's enough, keep this to yourself. Threats never make a good basis for a renewed marriage.

- Teach yourself to trust again: it won't happen overnight. Marital therapist Gayla Margolin suggests the following exercise:

[Each week] each of you says to the other, 'I've been faithful this week,' or 'I haven't'. The other person responds, 'I know you've been faithful'. or, 'I know you haven't'. Each of you makes two types of statements. If one says, 'I haven't been faithful,' and the other says, 'I know you haven't', all that takes place is what would occur anyway, but it would happen weeks in the future after many accusations, recriminations, and hurt feelings. The most destructive situation is for one to say, 'I've been faithful', and for the other to think, 'No, you haven't', but not to say that. It is just as hard to say, 'I don't think you've been faithful,' as to say, 'I haven't been faithful.' Either one is a shattering statement. But the only way to develop trust is to be very straightforward on both sides.

- Decide that, whatever happens, you won't be the same again. Start from today to become a separate person, to develop yourself in all the ways you want – maybe some plans you let go of years ago. Work towards financial independence as well – it really doesn't hurt a good relationship at all, and if it isn't good, then there are other remedies beyond poverty and dependence!

- If this affair is actually just one incident in a chain of abuse, then do ask yourself why you are staying with this person. Is it just because the thought of being alone is worse than the pain of being together? The trouble is, the longer you stay, the more helpless you become, and the effort to escape seems insurmountable. Do use friends and perhaps a counsellor or doctor to help you to have the courage to make the right decision.

Musical Chairs

O F COURSE, not all affairs are temporary preoccupations designed to fulfil some narrow purpose or act out a particular emotion. Some are seen as real escape routes from an unhappy marriage which the man or woman doesn't dare to leave until they know they have someone else. In this case it may be a deep fear of being alone that actually prompts the need for the affair. People who have passed from their parents' home into their marital home have never experienced life on their own and for them the thought of stepping out of even an abusive situation is more frightening than staying put with what they know. Karen told me:

> My marriage had been awful from the word go. In fact, it was pretty dreadful beforehand, but I didn't know how to get out of it. After a couple of years of abuse and misery I got a new job and Luke, my boss, said to me the first week I was there, and right out of the blue: 'Are you happily married?' I turned to jelly because the question was so direct that I knew at once the only answer was no. I also knew that what he was saying was 'Come to me, I'll make it better.' I mumbled something about 'I think so' but I sounded very unconvinced and the next day we started an affair and the day after that I left Harry.
>
> Looking back, that wasn't really the way to do it, but I was so crushed by Harry that I had no strength left to go it alone. Luke and I talked about marriage and we had some fun for a little while, and then it just faded away. Well, he left me, but that was OK eventually because it meant I had time alone at last to sort myself out. That's taken a long time, but Luke helped me on my way.

Whatever their cause, affairs are a symptom that something is going wrong in the marriage. At the very least they mean that communication has broken down. They can bring about considerable distress, and lost trust can take years to re-develop, so I would always advise talking instead of wandering. However, if they do happen, then despite the hurt, most couples manage to do something to make things better in the future, even if this simply involves living slightly more separate lives which allow each one to become more of an individual. Unless you are in a really unhappy or abusive marriage, do try to use an affair as an indication that something needs changing, rather than rushing to the divorce courts in a huff. Many people say later how much they regret having done this, even though it might seem the only solution at the time.

Couples share secrets which they keep from the world, and individual partners have secrets from each other. That's not necessarily a bad thing, so long as no one is hurt. Do realize therefore that, if you've discovered your partner's infidelity, chances are it's because he or she wanted you to. This might be because the whole thing had outlived its usefulness and was giving too much trouble, or because you need to realize how angry he or she really is, or because your partner wants to work things out differently. Or all three. You're perfectly entitled to feel betrayed and furious, and chances are it won't go fast, but, unless it's part of a pattern of abuse, do use it as an opportunity for change.

Some Mothers and Others

O F COURSE, the third party might not be a lover at all, but might be your mother-in-law. For example:

The other woman in my husband's life is his overbearing, utterly annoying, scheming and spiteful mother, who is very clever at manipulating and emotional blackmail. I don't want a weak husband, withdrawn, pandering to his mother. I want to be the woman in his life, the one he looks to. I just want him to tell me I'm wonderful occasionally, and to take the initiative in bed. I guess I am very jealous and I'm turning into a bitch. Should I buy him presents? Try to make the house tidier? Do I have to wait till death takes its natural course?

Well, the reward of a tidy house might not be what he wants most! Maybe she should ask him what he needs from her, and she can tell him what she wants from him: they could try to make things better rather than her getting angrier and bitchier, and him withdrawing more and more. They'll get nowhere together like that. Instead each of them could write out what they want from the other, and then negotiate on what they're prepared to give in exchange. Certainly one of the things that I would want from him would be that we would present a united front in all dealings with mum. It did strike me, however, reading this letter, that although the writer seemed strong, she was actually quite dependent, expecting him to fulful many aspects of her life. I suspected that his mother was this way too, and that this was a man, not just torn between the two of them, but also withdrawing from them both as much as he could.

Fathers-in-law are usually seen as less of a problem: although they can be enormously obstructive in letting their daughters marry and continue to be very competitive with her new husband, they are not seen as so interfering as mothers. Perhaps this is because, for men, competition is perceived as perfectly normal and they have lots of acceptable ways (like the golf course) to channel it. Nevertheless, I recently witnessed a drunken father at his daughter's wedding, grabbing at her buttocks in a way that made me think it would be just as hard for him to truly 'give away' his daughter as it is for some mothers to give away a son.

But also for some women, rejection is such a fear that they need to keep everyone, including sons, under their wings if at all possible. This is especially the case if the mother's husband has left, or seems absent even though he's still around. Dealing with the parent as a couple along lines you agree together is just as important as doing this with a child.

Using Pornography

PORNOGRAPHY DEMONSTRATES the differences between men and women. It not only shows the physical differences as explicitly as possible (just in case you didn't attend that class at school), but it also adds to these with suspenders and g-strings and funny bras, as well as demonstrating in all but the few, that women are done to by men – that men have power over women. The differences that are spelled out with neon lit dildos, are there to reassure us on any doubts or anxieties we might have had that the sexes are really not so different after all.

Men are not alone in using pornography to arouse themselves sexually; many women do it too. Recently I was lying in bed with a cold, red-nosed and snuffling and trying to answer some mail when I looked out of the window down into the lounge of the house opposite. I don't know the occupants, but it was ten o'clock in the morning, the sun was shining, and there was a woman standing with a feather duster (honestly) watching a hard porn video in an extraordinarily casual way. The image of me watching her watching pornography might inspire a Greenaway film but at a more mundane level it lets us realize how, even in the best-ordered, best-dusted homes, pornography is not unheard of.

Nevertheless, most of it is designed to make women objects and playthings for men: something which is clearly as sexually arousing to some women as it is to male partners. In a very honest chapter in the book *Sex and Love*, feminist writer Lynne Segal describes how she avoids all pornography, but still has fantasies during sex which are just as pornographic as the glossy pages themselves. Whether it's actually pornography or simply fantasy, or even romantic pulp fiction, it's always to do with power: he has power over me, and I have the power to give him what he wants and make him happy. Unfortunately, power is rarely used in such an interactive way! Here's John Scholtenberg saying why he hates pornography:

> Pornography also eroticizes male supremacy. It makes dominance and subordination feel like sex; it makes

213

> hierarchy feel like sex; it makes force and violence feel like sex; it makes . . . inequality feel like sex . . . It makes reciprocity make you go limp. It makes mutuality leave you cold.

The difference between men and women using pornography is that few women use it in preference to the Real Thing, although they might like it as an adjunct. However, a proportion of men seem to find the way it distances them from women satisfactory in itself: they would prefer to masturbate to an image of men's power over women, than to confront their feelings towards women in the real world, and it's this that upsets their partners.

> I have been married for a year, but we lived together for the previous three. Both of us have been married before. Our sex life was always good until the last nine months, when it seemed to tail off. He had a new teaching job and we sort of silently accepted that this was the cause, that he was just too tired. But last week I woke up and found he wasn't in bed, and I went downstairs and he was sitting in the armchair masturbating and gazing at some horrible porn. We've talked about it, and he's thrown it all away, but he says it happened the first time he married too. He says he doesn't know why.

When you only get a letter from someone, and no chance to ask more questions, it's not always possible to say why things have happened. But it is extraordinary the way that people very frequently provide all or most of the clues. Here at least I could make some guesses that what was happening was not so different to some of the reasons for affairs discussed above: chances are that on marriage she changed from Wicked Woman to White Angel, and with that desire vanished. Instead of having an affair, he was turning to pornography, as he'd done once before.

But many other things might be happening. All the causes of affairs I discussed earlier – anger, envy, fear – can all make someone turn towards pornography just as it might make them turn to another woman. Especially anger. He might put it down to her lack of ability to arouse him – if she'd just do this or that he wouldn't have to turn to porn – just as he might blame her when he saw other women or prostitutes. Men (in particular those in permanent relationships) usually feel just as much guilt over using pornography in this way as they do over having affairs: it leaves them depressed, shamed and unhappy.

The main difference between this and actual affairs is that using pornography lets the man feel total power and control over his sexuality in ways that can't happen in normal intercourse. To have good sex you have to be able to surrender control and allow yourself to depend on someone else for a while, and so pornography might also be used by those who find letting go in this way particularly difficult.

As Scholtenberg pointed out, using pornography for masturbation can be almost addictive for people, so they stop wanting real sex which is complicated because it involves real people – so much easier just to relate to a few well-thumbed pages, for example. If for no other reason, this is why it will spoil a relationship and make intercourse with someone you love more and more difficult. Like an addiction, you can only stop by stopping. You throw away the porn and you start to learn again to relate to another human being. Where it's difficult, you work harder. It's not always easy to give up something that is there to some extent throughout the media – it's a bit like adding a dribble of alcohol to the drinking water and expecting an alcoholic to be able to abstain – but the promise is that eventually you'll enjoy making love so much more.

Violent, Obsessional Sex

MANY WOMEN are physically abused by men. As Marilyn French points out in *The War Against Women*, every day in the United States four women are beaten to death by men, and less fatal attacks take place every twelve seconds. And men sexually abuse women too; often under the sacrament of marriage. Some women don't seem too sure that what is happening to them is wrong: 'Is this OK?' they ask.

Olga's husband insisted she have an abortion when she found she was pregnant. She could have refused, but she didn't. He was physically cruel to her when she returned, and she had a severe infection and then a hysterectomy. He insisted on oral sex for some time after that. He started an affair with another woman and eventually left Olga but lived with the new woman just around the corner. He became consumed with wanting two women at once – first Olga and a prostitute, then Olga and his new woman. He used 'vile things' on both of them. He is much younger than all his women. Olga ends her letter: 'He hates children and his mother. He's never seen his father. Are we all mother figures? Is he a misogynist?' Well, Olga, I think the answer to that has to be yes. Yes to both questions.

We hear a lot about consenting males in private, but what about consenting women? Olga, and many like her, show us how difficult the concept of consent really is. Medical ethics as a subject takes up many shelves in every library, and much of what it discusses is the consent of patients and how it can possibly be true consent when the doctor who requires it is in a position of power. And men are so often in a position of power over women, especially within marriage, that the concept of women's consent to some of the sexual acts they endure is quite ludicrous. And yet judges even perceive consent in the behaviour of eight-year-old girls. And you can see why:

1. It's very convenient to see willingness: it gets you what you want with a minimum of guilt.

2. The woman/girl frequently appears to go along with it. Let's face it, Olga could have (and obviously should have) ended her relationship at any of a number of points rather than let him be the one who makes all the decisions.

3. Society (men and women) finds it easier and more comfortable to support the status quo, to be able to delineate clear differences: men abuse and women

take it. Worse still: because women don't leave (the
room, the marriage, whatever) some men think that
whatever they do, women seem to like it.

How neat! Women's need to bind a relationship, to avoid
abandonment, remains paramount and lets men get away with
murder. Olga ends her letter: 'Am I stupid to think that in the
future there could ever be a chance for us if all this gets sorted
out?' Her fear is rejection; his is rejection for not being a Real
(cruel, abusive, threatening) Man: they were made for each
other. Although Olga's case might seem unusually extreme,
anyone who deals with the intimate details of people's lives
together knows that it is far from rare. And it happens in the
most orderly of homes in people who are young, middle-aged
and even elderly.

Barry had taken early retirement while Sylvia still worked
part-time. Although it had seemed a good idea to stop work,
he now found himself resenting Sylvia's activity. Making love
had changed: now she felt herself almost attacked, and,
although he knew she had suffered from a prolapse, he was
aggressive and sex was painful. He had also become dreadfully
mean. They had had a good marriage up till now, and there
were enough positive feelings left for them both to be able to
acknowledge that things were wrong, and to decide to get help
in changing. Most of this centred around Barry's new feelings
of powerlessness at leaving work. He knew he was hurting
Sylvia, and his guilt made him feel even more angry towards
her. Just opening up these feelings was enough for them to
work out new ways of being together that were more open
and satisfying for them both.

But not all women can so easily see that it might be the
men who have the problems. Many of them continue to take
it on themselves. And all men in relationships such as these do
their best to place the blame where it feels most comfortable –
on their partners. So nothing changes:

I have been married for thirty-two years. For the past
twenty years our sex life has been a disaster. The
problem is he won't discuss it and all he ever says is
'You want to analyse everything', or 'Sort yourself

out!' The main problem is that he wanted to do things to me which were painful and against the law. He said this was for 'experimentation'. He says I'm frigid, and that we should add spice to our sex life.

Twenty years! If you told someone they had a twenty-year sentence and would share a cell with a sadist but the door was open if you wanted to leave . . . Well, what do you think you'd do? This immobility of women comes back to the learned helplessness I described in chapter two: the harnessed dogs who were shocked so many times that, when escape was made possible, they could no longer take advantage of it. It's worsened by being told you're frigid – that helps you to think you'll be no good for any other man either, should you ever dare to leave. But this life sentence is not just terrible for the prisoner; the prison guard stays there too. Until she clearly says enough's enough, he is as much a captive in his unhappiness as she is. If he thinks that just having anal intercourse will suddenly make the sun shine he's wrong, wrong, wrong. While he seeks a solution to his misery through her rather than through himself, he will continue on the wrong road for ever.

Hobbies, Sport and Too Much Work

IT's ALL right. I'm not going to say that every male train-spotter or rugby-player or potting shed occupant is really avoiding the bedroom. Though they may be. These pastimes are so much less harmful than any we've discussed before that I feel a little apologetic putting them in the same chapter. But any activity that takes up vast amounts of a man's time needs to be considered as a possible avoidance strategy for something else – maybe just relating to others, maybe that activity which creates the most anxiety, where his maleness might most be questioned. And work has to be included too. Sometimes it's used as a good excuse – 'I'm too tired tonight from earning all that money in order to look after you and the kiddies.' Well, fine once or twice, but if it continues then it's time to ask what's wrong and what can be changed. Of course no one enjoys making love so much when they're tired, but at least ask yourselves is this all really necessary? Can we find time at the weekends? Can you get away together that much more often? If you can, but you're still not doing it, then it's a good idea to ask yourselves why not.

As we are driven into a land where half the people don't work at all (and so feel powerless), while the other half work all hours (and so feel exhausted), it is small wonder that impotence happens and that it's increasing. What's more, as we shall see in the next chapter, if it happens once, the anxiety and fear this causes makes it much more likely to happen again and again.

Enough's Enough

MARRIAGES CAN survive all sorts of dreadful upheavals and unpleasant behaviours once they are talked about honestly and the decision is made to change. Indeed, many couples blossom when they have worked through difficult patches of all kinds. However, it's just as important to be able to know when things have gone on too long, and that your hopes of your partner's changing are simply unrealistic. In all these cases, of one partner apparently preferring someone or something else, the main thing to decide is what you want and what your limits really are. That's not always easy, and it might be that you need considerable support to help you do this. If you find it really difficult to decide what's right for you, ask yourself:

• Are you settling for less than you deserve?

• Are both of you wanting and trying to save the marriage, or just you?

- Are you really saying that life on your own is worse than this? How do you know? Look around you and gather up some evidence.

- Do you think people would look down on you if you left an abusive marriage? Who are you keeping up the front for?

- Why aren't you getting help in all this? Are you worried that a counsellor, for example, will point out truths you think would be too difficult to hear?

I always want couples to save their marriages – it's a good experience for them and for their children to learn that there are ways to work things out, difficult though the process may be. But sometimes you do have to question what it is you're trying to save, and how mutual is the desire to do so. In the end it may be that one or both of you have to acknowledge that enough's enough.

Chapter 12

All Gone Sex

And priests in black gowns were walking their rounds,
And binding with briars my joys and desires.

William Blake *Garden of Love*

BECAUSE SO many facets of masculinity and male power dance around the erect penis, the fact that some men for all or part of their lives don't have great appetites for sex or can't perform sex in any narrowly defined way, causes great distress to them and their partners alike. Men's view of themselves as masculine depends at its core on their heterosexuality, whereas in women their perceptions of themselves as womanly rest on a wider range of attributes and behaviours.

It says a lot that our word for men failing to be able to consummate a relationship sexually is 'impotent' or powerless. When a man says he's impotent, he's not just saying he finds it hard to get an erection, and the woman who hears him hears more than the message that sex may now be difficult. Although both inside and outside the home men have built their worlds with all sorts of protection and props for real or threatened impotence (as described in chapter nine and chapter eleven) they still feel the need to maintain the notion that in the bedroom they are king. This fiction is constructed and lived out in his dealings with other men, but also in many instances even with his wife, despite all the evidence to the contrary that they both try to ignore.

Because women want to believe it too. Most of the myths with which we have grown up and the stereotypes that we adhere to tell us that men are sexually active, eager to perform at the drop of a hat (or even with their hats still on) and, if anything, need restraining rather than any encouragement. The reality is often very different and when this occurs many women will either blame themselves or go to the other extreme and see this as a major failure in masculinity. Blame in any form, at either extreme, is only likely to perpetuate the problem.

It's clear from all that we've said in the last few chapters that many women do still believe that they have the key to making things work or not; but I suspect that this will decrease as the facts about impotence are better understood. When blame is directed at the man, then the threat of rejection rears its head in the one way it really matters – he may be abandoned for not being a man. Then what might have been just a temporary decline can become a permanent droop.

As I said in chapter one, perceptions about sex changed radically when Masters and Johnson suggested that women might have a chance of orgasm equal to men. Once that began to filter down from scientific journals to women's magazines, the possibility that men might not always be good at producing orgasms in women caused a slow puncture in power relations which has only just become apparent. No one knows how prevalent impotence is, but we do know that it's much more widespread than we had ever realized. We don't know if it's increasing, but we do know that it's become a much greater concern. At least this subject is at last discussed rather than seen only as the woman's failure to create sufficient desire.

In the mid-eighties Elliott published a survey of the psychological literature on sexual problems and found that the word 'frigidity' – very popular in the post-war period – had now almost vanished from the titles, while the use of the word 'impotence' had risen dramatically. Similarly, a study reported in *Family Practitioner* magazine found that one in five people were dissatisfied with sex, and top of the complaints was a lack of desire – prominent in men as well as women. In other words, just as with infertility where man's role has increasingly been recognized, sexual problems are changing from being seen as due to women's distaste or horror of intercourse to men's lack of desire or inability to perform successfully. Shifting the focus is not the same as shifting the blame: although it might seem tough on men to redirect the problem in this way, in the end, like all the issues we've discussed, things can only be improved when you focus on the real difficulty, rather than coyly shifting the lens to point elsewhere just for the sake of protecting male pride. The important thing now is to make sure that men's lack of desire, where it exists, is not put down to women, and its cure is not seen by both partners as being up to the woman to deliver.

What is it that makes men impotent, and what, if anything, can be done about it? Well, the physiological causes are myriad – there are various conditions like diabetes, head and spinal injuries, multiple sclerosis, and many more which can create difficulties. But how serious these are in terms of joy and desire will usually depend on the attitudes of those with the illness and their partners. All causes have some psychological side to them, and the majority are created almost entirely by the mind, so it's these that we'll discuss in detail.

Hell and Damnation

I have been living with my partner for the past two years and we get on well together and love each other. Our only problem is that he has a real aversion to most forms of sex. He feels that it is dirty and cannot stand the idea of kissing, penetration, or masturbation. Although he gets aroused, our sex life is, to say the least, pretty limited. I have a friend whose husband had the same problems and in the end they separated. I really don't want that to happen to us. No one seems to be able to help us and it's hard to even find someone to talk to.

If you think that sex is dirty or wicked, whether you're a man or a woman, then you're not likely to enjoy it much, and sometimes this will go so far as to cause actual impotence or at least an inability to carry out the sexual act. If a parent has made that clear either directly – for example, by raising the fear of the devil – or indirectly, by expressing disgust at what she or he sees in the nappy, or at the child's handling its genitals or masturbating, then the boy or girl will learn quickly that that part of the anatomy might get excited, but it can't be touched. This may be translated in later years to the idea that the messiness of sex is disgusting.

But even where this hasn't happened, the image of mother can affect the ability of men to have sex. The scenario that I've described in chapters eight and eleven about how sex can stop or become much less satisfying upon marriage, is relatively common and is particularly distressing when it's been good before the wedding ring was slipped on his finger. When this happens, some men turn to other women or pornography to prove that their masculinity is still intact, while others simply slip into silent despair. To themselves they may attribute the problem to some deficit of their wives – like the man who told his new young bride that her breasts were too small, or those in chapter nine who were turned lovingly into hypochondriacs or agorophobics in order to lay the cause of the problem in her rather than in him. Other men look to physical illness as a reason, and search for a medical cure, refusing to acknowledge that there might be something they could do about their psyches that might make things better. But for others, like Lorraine and Gordon, there is just an awful silence about the change that's taken place:

> I thought I must be pretty unique to have a husband who appears to have no desire for sex: I'm really relieved to discover other women have the same problem. Before our marriage, Gordon and I had a good sex life together. In the months leading up to our marriage, things seemed to tail off a bit but I put this down to pre-wedding nerves. In the few months after the wedding we made love probably no more than four times, then things stopped altogether. I tried wearing sexier

underwear and all that, but it only seemed to make things worse. We've been married now for six years. One of the most upsetting aspects for me is that not only has Gordon no interest in sex, but he avoids any sort of physical contact with me – so he never kisses or cuddles me and won't even snuggle up to me in bed. If I hug him I can feel him physically tense and he will find some excuse to push me away. Whenever I broach the subject, he just refuses to talk about it and I can't go to our GP because he and my husband are friends.

Gordon's reluctance to deal with what has happened to the relationship between him and Lorraine is creating real unhappiness for both of them. Not only are they having no intercourse, but also any physical connection or comfort is being denied, probably because Gordon fears arousal by his wife (although he enjoyed it as her lover), and worries that she may make demands upon him if she gets excited.

You might think that couples separate quite quickly when they find themselves in this situation which goes against all our ideas of what true marriage is about. But frequently they don't. Ruth has been married for twenty-two years, and is only now beginning to feel that enough is enough:

> I love my husband dearly but have taken enough of being put down and rejected. I get no sex, no love. I am my husband's housekeeper and his mother. There are times when I could go into Safeways and ask any man to hold me in his arms. I just want to know what it feels like. I know too that my husband is as desperately lonely as I am, that he too is very unhappy and that his ego is in tatters.

Unless impotence – whether caused by a lack of desire or an inability to get an erection – is accepted as a fact within the marriage, a problematic reality to be dealt with by both partners together, just as they would deal with any other joint domestic problem, then not only physical intercourse stops, but verbal intercourse – communication – comes to a grinding halt as well. Then the pair get truly locked into a frozen life together, or separate still stinging with bewilderment and blame.

It can happen to women too, but the evidence for a lack of desire in them is not so anatomically obvious as it is in men, and anyway it fits with the folklore that wives are not as sexually active as mistresses. In addition, a man can excuse his own sudden lack of functioning, if it happens, for exactly the same reason – he finds his wife unexciting – and every other man will understand. Let's fact it, how many jokes have you heard about husbands' inability to perform? How many are there about dull sex with the mistress? But jokes about the wife are endless. In cultures where wives are not disparaged (the society of gentlemen), then there is still the equally useful and enduring myth that good women are not all that fond of sex.

Losing Power

WHEN PEOPLE are depressed they feel powerless, ineffectual – impotent. A loss of libido, whether to do with interest in or ability for sex, is one of the standard symptoms of depression. If doctors think you might be depressed, they will ask you if you're waking early, if you've lost your appetite, and if you no longer want sex. So do think about that as a possibility, if suddenly you feel that you don't care if you never make love again. Men are pretty hopeless at being able to label what they are feeling, especially when it is to do with being depressed, and so you might have to be quite astute in working out what's really happening to you.

Stress can have the same effect, so another check is to write down all the events that are happening to you or which have happened over the past year. The problem of not recognizing these is that a sudden experience of impotence is often a stressor in itself, and so adds to the burdens that are stopping the desire or abilities. Dealing with the background stress is more useful than treating impotence as the primary problem.

One cause of stress and depression that it would be nice for governments to be able to overlook, is unemployment. If there is anything that psychologists have proved without any question at all, it is that being unemployed creates psychological symptoms, rather than the other way around. These symptoms are often worse in men than in women, probably because of the stigma that still attaches to their unemployed state. Although in some parts of Britain there are more men without work than with, there is still a link between the power of having a job, and power within the bedroom.

The links between sexual potency, self-esteem and the psychological power that comes from rewarding work, can be seen in reverse when men become unemployed. When men lose their jobs, they sometimes seem to lose their ability to have sex as well. The effects of this – less cuddling, touching, sharing, talking – make the depression worse which makes the chances of impotence higher, and so on. Since men are more likely than women to externalize their anger rather than to direct it against themselves (though they do that too through suicide), it's also true that physical violence towards wives is greater in those who are unemployed than those with jobs. Small wonder that suicide in men increases alongside the unemployment rate, but more confusing that governments set health authorities targets to reduce the suicide rate while still blithely raising unemployment – 'A price worth paying'?

Of course, what men are feeling when they are unemployed is not dissimilar to what women feel within the traditional marriage – where they do not have their own earned income, for example. They too suffer a sense of powerlessness and have higher rates of depression. I see this as a very important factor in married women's apparent loss of libido. When a woman like this changes her life in some way – perhaps through therapy, or work, education, or something which gives her a sense of power once more – her sexual interest invariably returns, and she will be much more likely to enjoy it more fully than she has before.

The problem is that, within many marriages, this sense of power seems to be a shared item rather than an individual possession. Because of this, when one person gains power, the other loses. So as the woman begins to feel good about herself and to enjoy her sexuality, the man begins to feel crushed and unable to meet her needs. I recently had a play commissioned called 'Settling Scores'. It used the number of orgasms as a metaphor and a measure of power within a marriage: when he had more than she did he felt OK, superior, though somewhat complaining about her lack of sexual prowess. Then by chance she discovers multiple orgasms and so quickly begins having more than him. At first he goes to another woman to increase his score, but the strain tells as the demands rise, and finally his wife understands and so stops having orgasms again with him, but secretly takes young lovers. By the reaction of the audience, both men and women, there was considerable understanding of the point I was making. What has to be worked at in marriage is using your generosity to let the other partner develop and enjoy his or her own sense of power, without letting this affect your own.

Bundles of Joy

IN CHAPTER seven we talked about how babies do not always produce or prolong marital happiness as we might hope or expect. We discussed this in terms of how parenthood means less attention for someone, usually the husband, and how you need to be pretty strong as a couple to survive the new arrival with total satisfaction. But the other effect the baby sometimes has is to reduce sexual desire for both men and women.

Let's face it, with the birth of number one child, sex has become a more serious business. Now there is no doubt at all that it produces babies: there, growing steadily in your midst, is the result of all that bedroom activity. Breasts have changed from sexual objects to functional food dispensers; vaginas have now been pathways and perhaps are temporarily linked more to pain than to pleasure. Women can lose their interest in sex if they have suffered a lot of pain and fear during the birth; and men can see this as a rejection of their masculinity and turn elsewhere. But men can also lose their libido completely due to witnessing what they see as pain that they have inflicted on their partners. Although there is no formal research yet on this, midwives have told me that an increasing number of young couples report this to be a problem, something the midwives believe is because many more fathers are present at the birth.

Quite a lot of married life depends upon compromise, but sometimes this isn't possible, and sometimes it's good for one or other to actually get his own way or hers. When it comes to whether or not the father is to be present at the birth, this is going to be one of those no-compromise situations: if she wants it and you the father don't, then one of you is going to have to give in and both of you are going to have to deal with the consequences of this: not put up with them, just deal with them. So, potential mothers, forewarned is forearmed: recognize the possible effects of the man's presence at the birth, however slight they seem, and realize (because the man may not spell it out for fear of looking wimpish) that his fear is for you, not for himself. Being unable to stand the sight of so much of your blood is not squeamish or unmanly or a rejection of you, but just because of the difficulty he feels about his involvement in your pain. If you both decide that he's better not attending, then you need to recognize the possible anger and resentment the woman might feel if she's there alone. Expressing it is the best way of getting rid of it: it doesn't mean the man has to do anything about it – he can't – but that shouldn't stop the woman from saying how she feels.

None of this is to deny that many men find the birth of their children a real high; maybe even a sexual high that makes them want to do it all over again as soon as possible – but that doesn't make them any more or less a man than those who can't stand the thought. Perhaps they are the lucky ones who have never been made by a parent to feel responsible for the pain of someone close; they are able to let another adult choose a course of action without feeling that any negative consequences are somehow down to them.

Angry Feelings

ANGER IS a real curse on successful sex. As we've seen, it is a prompt to have affairs, to turn to other things like violent or degrading sex, but it also has a way of affecting both partners' abilities to enjoy any sort of intercourse. Anger can create any of the following problems:

- Apparent lack of any interest or desire.

- Premature ejaculation.

- Pain.

- Impotence.

Of course I'm not saying that anger is the only cause of any of these, and these last two conditions should be checked with your doctor. But the possibility of anger lurking around in the relationship is one that needs to be considered. These problems are all ways of making sure that sex doesn't happen or, if it does, that the other person doesn't like it much. Jean told me:

> Last year I found out that my husband was having an affair. I guess that really he wanted me to know because he left so many clues. Anyway, I didn't go off the deep end but we talked about it endlessly, he said how sorry he was, and I forgave him. I really believed that this could be a good thing, a new start and a freshening up of our marriage, but it isn't, because I have lost all interest in sex since then. I very much want to make it right because he is actually a wonderful man and it's making him very unhappy.

I suspect that what is keeping them stuck is that Jean has shown her distress and they have behaved in a beautifully civilized way, and then she thinks she has 'forgiven' him. But she hasn't. Forgiving involves leaving things behind you, and her anger is far from being left behind; instead it goes unmentioned. When you have been hurt in this way (in a way that touches the old fear of abandonment), then you won't just feel upset, you'll also be bloody angry. Unless you recognize this and express it to your partner (see chapter seven), you will continue to carry it round like a brick and use it to wound where you know it hurts most. This is absolutely not deliberate, nor is it usually even conscious, but it's certainly common.

Another way 'repressed anger' may be expressed is for a man (or very occasionally the woman) to orgasm within minutes or even seconds, or for the woman to suffer constriction of her vagina (vaginismus) so the man has to do without or to inflict pain on her if he really wants to go ahead. Even impotence itself can have anger at its root.

In order to turn things round, you first have to recognize what's wrong. Think about what you feel when you have sex. If you can recognize anger, aggression or resentment on the one hand, or even passivity and detachment – a blocking of feelings – on the other, then use some of the exercises in chapter seven in order to appreciate the cause of your anger and to release it safely.

Sometimes envy is at the root of what feels like anger. Envy is the hardest of all emotions for people to admit to, and so it can silently churn them up and destroy things in ways that are painful to both parties. Within a marriage envy can occur because the woman is actually envious of men as a whole, perhaps because she was brought up in a way that said that girls were not worth much, and being a boy gained much greater blessings. Sometimes this can happen with tomboys, for example, who (at least until a baby boy arrives) can take the place of a longed-for son. The inevitable envy that this arouses in the child can spill over into marriage and can destroy or mar sex as well as other aspects of the relationship. So the woman may make sure she never has an orgasm, thus making it clear that the husband is failing in a way that hurts most – his 'manliness'.

Men often suffer envy too: of their children for all the care and attention that they are getting; and of the pair of them, the kid and the mum, snug and secure and well looked after at home while he has to go out and earn for all three.

Dennis, whom I mentioned in chapter four, was clearly a 'New Man' who was desperately keen to make his relationship with his children different from the cold and distant relationship he had experienced with his own father. Watching him with his son, however, it seemed to me that he was acting this New Man role – that being a jolly easy-going and caring father didn't come at all naturally to him. And why should it? His destructive feelings towards his son, in particular, were not so surprising, especially as he had once suffered the arrival of a younger brother of his own, not to mention the problems he had each time his father reappeared after quitting the family yet again. New Men, who may do their best to be different from their unaffectionate, critical and absent fathers, may still find the presence of the cared for child difficult to bear because it awakens in them the child who wasn't cared for enough.

Envy is inevitable in this sort of situation, but it is also enormously destructive, not just towards the person envied but particularly to the one experiencing it. I suspect it actually affects your physical health far more than we can imagine. By far the biggest step towards cure is to acknowledge that that is what you are feeling. To do this, try substituting the word envy for anger: does it fit any better? When you recognize it, it gets much easier to handle. Here are some of the ways I suggest tackling it in my book *OK2 Talk Feelings* which went with a BBC series of the same name:

- Forgive yourself for feeling envious or jealous: that will take away a lot of the anger that's attached. Talk about it if you can.

- If you feel envy, check what it suggests is missing in your life: is it appreciation, or friendship or power? Set out to try to find other ways to make up for what seems to be not there.

- When you're feeling envious, try to recall when you've felt like this before. Write it down and then add to it over time. Is there a pattern? If so, decide to let go of the past.

- Is someone spoiling things for you because of their envy? If so, don't accept it or feel guilty or think that you should try to make it up to them. It's their problem to deal with, not yours.

Sex and Alcohol

HEAVY DRINKING by men is seen in many cultures as being an important ingredient in demonstrating their masculinity. It's an unfortunate irony that it so badly affects that part of their anatomy which they consider even more central to their masculine image. I can only imagine that alcohol must let them forget their fears in this regard, because it certainly doesn't enhance performance in any way at all, despite claims to the contrary. It's not that everyone who drinks heavily suffers from brewer's droop – they don't – but this doesn't mean that women find sexual intercourse with a man who's drunk a satisfying or enjoyable activity. Sex that takes place regularly while under the influence can also be an excuse for poor sex or even cruel sex.

People seem to have one particular weak organ where alcohol's concerned. Although constant heavy drinking eventually affects large areas of your body, first effects can be seen in liver damage or brain damage or feminization in men. Testes shrink to the size of peas, breasts are developed and penises no longer get erect. If some men drink in order to feel manly, it's a cruel joke that they end up looking very like women. We know less of these effects in women, but it's clearly linked to sterility at least.

Dealing with Sexual Problems

THE PROPORTION of sexual problems due to physical or to psychological causes is an area of debate, especially as the medicalization of male sexuality increases. Although no one seems to argue now that sexual problems are purely psychological in origin, most would agree that our psyches – especially a fear of failure – are as much responsible as is our physiology. Even where for purely physical reasons men can

233

no longer achieve or hold an erection, the problem for the couple is more to do with one or both partners seeing sexual enjoyment as linked purely to the 'performance' of the penis. Because we've imbued it with such power and importance, for men the crux of manliness, if it fails we see this as the man losing his very masculinity.

But it doesn't have to be that way. There are many, many other ways to make love other than the old in-out. Just because that's what you've always done, it doesn't mean you always have to. This could be the start of something much more interesting. This book is not a sex manual – there's plenty of those on the market – its message is much more that there is no one way for sexual pleasure. Man and woman were given the ability to invent and to imagine, and thank God for that. So celebrate these skills together. So long as you both are honest about what you are happy with, and this is respected, so long as what you do is done with love, then both of you should begin to experience new aspects of sensuality and sexuality rather than staying as restricted as many couples appear to be. One of the first things to do is to ask your-selves why you have sex at all. People list a wide variety of things:

The pleasure of being close
A way of showing love
Time out for each other
An attempt to conceive
The sensuality of skin
To relieve frustration
To make up a row
Because it's fun
Because it's free

Apart from conception (and even this can sometimes be got round) none of these need to be achieved by the everyday this-is-what-men-do type of sex. So work out how else you can do it. You might even decide that sex is simply not necessary, and the evidence shows that, so long as this is a truly mutual decision, it does not appear to make the marriage less satisfy-ing. If you do decide this – or even if you don't – then spend some time working out how to get the most from the non-sexual side of your time together.

Beyond giving yourself this freedom, there have been numerous ways formulated for tackling various difficulties. If you don't have any physical causes, having checked with your doctor, the most commonly used way of treating a lack of desire or an inability to have orgasms, or impotence, comes from Masters and Johnson's work. Their ideas were particularly important in seeing enjoyable sexuality as a function of couples, rather than the individual, and this helped to stop the man or the woman being seen as The Problem. Most difficulties are caused or worsened by the anxiety of having to perform, and so treatment focuses on a series of exercises, called sensate focusing, which are graded in their intimacy and which gradually allow you to enjoy increasing levels of arousal without actual intercourse. In the early days of treatment intercourse is actually banned: you are simply allowed to focus on pleasure and comfort through touch. This takes away the idea of performance. The final stage of the treatment concentrates on communicating needs, being able to say no, and teaching ways to resolve conflict. Even when you follow up people some years after therapy, success rates for this treatment stay high, especially for women with vaginismus and men with difficulty in getting erections.

For those with premature ejaculation, the general advice is to just keep going. Recognizing that the orgasm is not the total objective, nor the end of sex, takes the focus off the time issue – 'I/He came so fast' is no longer so important when sex continues beyond orgasm. Others recommend using thicker condoms (or even local anaesthetic under a condom) to reduce sensitivity. Techniques such as squeezing the frenulum of the penis (the fold between its head and the shaft) just as he's about to come, seem to be OK for some people, but they all end up emphasizing ejaculation as the be-all-and-end-all of sex.

But more important than the success rates in terms of actual experiences, is the finding that most couples when they de-emphasize the traditional sexual act say that their sexual relationships overall are more satisfying: they are less inhibited, enjoying each other more, more focused on what they are doing, with better communication, and so on.

Medical Solutions

A s women have become stronger and more able to say that sexual problems are not just down to them, there has been a growth in reports of medical conditions as causes, with a de-emphasis on the psychological. This medicalization of male sexuality still puts the problem outside the psyche of the man, so he can conveniently change nothing but his equipment, which is simply faulty. Cures for impotence are, of course, as old as history, as any slaughtered rhinoceros would have told you, but now we see them blessed with the surgical spirit of medical science, so business is booming and I'm sure that we've seen nothing yet.

The modern miracle cures involve rather more painful interventions than sipping pink water, however. For example, injections of vasoactive treatments like papaverine into the penis which produce erections lasting up to four hours; hormonal therapy, though the link between testosterone and sexual desire is by no means proven; or surgery, such as implanting inflatable prostheses, or vascular surgery to improve the blood supply to the penis. Trials to establish the long-term success of these interventions are still inadequate. It's no use basing a good outcome on a surgeon saying that his implant works well and has healed nicely; he also needs to follow the couple over at least a year to see how truly satisfied both parties are with that method of sexual intercourse.

Worse still, it seems to me, are the operations to lengthen penises. After centuries of tortures on the bodies of women – whether it's to bind their feet, increase or decrease their breasts, elongate their necks, pierce their nipples, or whatever – I don't want similar retaliation on the bodies of men. Honestly, you're just fine!

Although some men feel that such methods are the only way for them, the problem is that again they focus everyone's attention on the penis and its potency or the lack of it. Sexual problems in both men and women are never only physiological; there is always an element of psychology lurking behind any difficulty, even if it is only in terms of your attitudes to it, so do consider this before you rush into treatments that may make you into a Real Man again.

A Checklist for Desire

IF THINGS do not feel right to you sexually – if you lack desire, or cannot get or sustain an erection, if sex is uncomfortable or you come too soon – then use this checklist to think about the possible causes. Most of the points apply whether you're a man or a woman. If you use the list as a couple, then it will be much more useful because, chances are, if you haven't been discussing it already, your partner will have invented plenty of excuses of her or his own, and it will be nice to know what they are and put them right.

• **Have you had any recent stress, upset or illness? Has anyone in your family become seriously ill?** Sometimes a fear of heart disease makes people decide to stop sex at a certain age, like fifty: what a shame if you then go on to live till you're eighty! Sometimes an operation in the pelvic area (for example, hysterectomy or colonectomy) results in a lack of desire. Don't forget that stress is bound to affect wider aspects of your life, so tackle it as soon as you can. Switch to non-sexual activities like massage for a while until desire returns.

• **Have you lost your job, and so perhaps feel you're no longer potent?** Sometimes seeing something as failure makes you worried that you'll always fail, and this leads to perform-ance stress. Realize that linking jobs to masculinity was just a way to get the workers working harder! The aristocrats and royals don't seem to have this hangup, and you needn't either. Sex is something you can enjoy even more when you're not tired and have all the time in the world. And it's free.

• **What were attitudes towards sex in your family when you were young? Could these be affecting you now?** You could seek psychotherapy for this, but most people will find that working your way through a book like *The Joy of Sex* will

237

quite quickly let you see that no thunderbolts will hit you just because you and your partner enjoy yourselves in bed.

• **Were you abused as a child, or as an adult?** If so, don't expect so much of yourself. A lack of desire is very understandable, and you should ask your doctor for a referral to a counsellor who specializes in these problems.

• **Are you depressed?** If so, ask your doctor for treatment for the depression – perhaps tablets in the short term, perhaps psychotherapy if things don't improve or problems come again.

• **Are you angry or envious about anything,** especially something that your partner has done, or that he or she represents? Could your partner be angry with you perhaps? Acknowledging this and then tackling it should help considerably.

• **Are you frightened of losing control?** Do you have to feel very secure in order to surrender yourself to someone else? If so, then don't push yourself so hard, but learn to surrender gently, step by step.

• **Are you prevaricating over sex?** Sometimes one or both parties want sex but don't want sex. They feel desire, but they fear to lose control, or they're angry, or any of the other blocks to satisfaction. They put it off until they get so tired that it's unenjoyable or impossible. Think about whether this is happening to you and make a rule that, if you feel like making love, you'll ask there and then.

• **Are you drinking too much?** And how long is a ball of string! Test this out by seeing what happens when you stop drinking. On the other hand, and just to be truly perverse, alcoholics who stop drinking often find that their sex drive (if it had previously stayed high) stops too. Don't worry about this or think you need a drink to help you through. Your drive will return quite happily in time. Until it does, just enjoy rediscovering each other without the blur of alcohol.

• **For men, do you still have erections while you sleep, or do you wake up with one?** In that case, you can be pretty sure the problems aren't just physical.

As a couple whose relationship is loving, the main block to making the sexual side satisfying once again is communication. If you can talk about these problems together, and perhaps decide to change something together, then most of them will fade away. Not because you've suddenly turned into Tarzan (a great relief to all Janes), but because you have widened your horizons and so no longer see it as a problem.

Chapter 13

One Small Step

For every complex problem there is a simple solution . . . and it's wrong.

H. L. Mencken

THIS BOOK is full of grand theories, and I've offered only small steps on how to tackle what's wrong. If I thought I could do anything more fundamental, I'd worry that I was starting to suffer from delusions of omnipotence, and I'm not. What's more, it's not that things between men and women can't go on like this much longer, because I'm sure they can. Although we're experiencing the greatest threat to the status quo of gender relations that history has recorded, still I would not underestimate the power of people's need to maintain that status quo and therefore to pull some rabbit from the hat and perform a trick that shakes our lives back close to 'normal' once again.

We could, for example, have a war and make men of those who we think might be losing a grip of their masculinity. We could devise economic sanctions that make women's position outside of the home a virtual impossibility and so take away those new seeds of self-confidence that seem to be causing so many problems. We could use the media to decry what's happening to our children, and place the blame full-square on the move towards a sexual, economic and social liberation of women. All these ploys have been used before, and have been successful in temporarily enforcing the status quo.

But now (at the risk of sounding naive) I think things just might have gone a step too far for any of these strategies to work properly again. Now we really are in a mess, a collapse of much that some of us hold dear. Out of this mess we have the possibility of forming something new and something infinitely better: new ways for men to enjoy their maleness; new ways for the sexes to be together; and new ways for us to parent our children. Change takes courage, but courage conquers fear. Even the smallest act of rebellion to what has come before can bring about a revolution in what comes after. This final chapter sets out the beginnings of an agenda to think about change.

An Agenda for Men

I FEEL kind of shy, making suggestions to men about what you might do. I know I've been doing it all through the book, but I mean, who am I to know what you really feel about all this? Well, it's true I probably know much more accurately about the feelings of women, but I am also pretty confident about some of you as well.

Above all, I'm aware of the deep and destructive unhappiness in many of you. Sometimes the destruction goes against others, sometimes against yourselves. I know about this because I see and hear from a biased sample of unhappy men, but this doesn't negate the knowledge; it just may limit it.

If you are unhappy or anxious about what's happening to you; if your marriage (and maybe your previous one) doesn't seem fulfilling, sexually or otherwise; or your relationship with your children is distant or disappointing – then what have you got to lose in trying to change? Male suicide totters higher and higher, alongside alcoholism and violence. Those seem simple solutions for some, but why not give the others a go first? Yes, change takes courage, but so does admitting that things aren't good, so maybe you're already well on the way. I know you like competition, so I'm going to put your agenda in the form of dares:

241

- Dare to be different. Dare to play with the male stereotypes and stand them on their heads. Notice how uncomfortable you feel and don't push it away: try to understand it and stay with it and it will begin to fade.

- Dare to express your feelings to someone you trust.

- Dare to listen to what your partner's really saying. Have courage enough to get so close you fear you'll be smothered. Don't blame her – just tell her what it reminds you of and how you feel.

- Dare to be a scientist and investigate what you and those around you are feeling.

- Dare to get close to your children and let them know you don't always succeed and you're not always strong. Especially, have the grace to let your sons win now and then.

- Dare to let women be as good as you. Bite your lip when you hear yourself arguing for difference.

- Dare to admit that you too might need to work on some aspects of your sexual relationship. And realize that this doesn't mean you're not a real man.

- Dare to divorce your mother. I promise that you'll love her even more.

- Dare to admit that, sometimes in the wee small hours, even you are frightened that you might not be as manly as you portray. If you can tell someone, this will help.

- Dare to admit that you too are frightened of rejection.

- Dare to admit that you were wrong and take responsibility for changing what you don't like.

- Dare to do the exercises that run through the book.

This sounds rather like the agenda for the New Man, but it isn't. New Men didn't do very well because they tried to be just like women, and they're not, and we women eventually saw through it and then got angry that we were temporarily misled. It's much more to do with discovering yourselves – your male qualities of having boundaries, concentration, and action that came from the time you stepped across to be a man; and your female qualities of being able to be close, dependent, and nurturing, that some of you once had and might have thought you'd left behind for ever.

It's about not asking questions like how's my career going, and how many times have I had sex this week, and will I make the new secretary before Jones does, should I beat up Smith for the way he looked at my wife, and how can I make sure I get a BMW by August? And how can I show them? It's more about questions like: am I doing with my life what I want to do? Have my wife and I explored each other as we should, as only marriage allows? Am I being the kind of dad I wanted my father to be? Do I feel excitement from being, or only from winning? If I die tomorrow, what moments gave me real true joy? How can I put a few more into my life now, today?

You can wait for a crisis before starting to ask these questions and to explore the possibilities they hint at. You can do it because of how you feel when your dad dies, when your son gets ill, when your wife leaves you, or when your doctor says stop drinking or you're dead. Or you can do it now and maybe save them all a lot of pain, not least yourself. Trying it out, giving an inch here and there, won't turn you instantly into a wimp, a weed, a wet, or a woman! There is a mile of interesting territory between Tarzan and your worst fears of effeminacy.

An Agenda for Women

MANY WOMEN have taken giant steps in the last twenty years and, even more exciting, many young ones are regarding their options and their relationships in different ways to those of their mothers. On the surface things look like they're progressing for women, but how much further can they go if men won't change as well? Not too far I suspect. Part of the reason why change might be stymied is to do with men: on the whole the old regime worked for them quite well; the new one looks much more difficult, much less friendly. No wonder they yearn for the status quo.

But the other block to change still comes from women themselves. Partly to do with their urge to keep relationships intact, they try endlessly to make things OK, to stay responsible where questions of relating are concerned. This stops men learning how to change themselves. Partly also to do with so many of them still hankering, usually secretly and silently and maybe unconsciously, for men 'to be Men'. There remains that romantic yearning for the strong silent male, the Clint Eastwood type, the pained loner with the hint of half-buried violence.

It's not just ladies who read Mills and Boon who feel like this: I have watched the staunchest of feminists fall on their knees to please a man with a violent but politically OK past. The politics made him acceptable, but the violence – I have no doubt – made him attractive. They wanted their own anger carried by such an angry man but when, each time, it got out of hand they were appalled and disgusted, as if they'd been duped. What they hated, and what they blamed him for, was that he had put them in touch with their own abilities for violence.

We have to stop getting men to do our dirty work, to carry our anger, to behave badly so that we can attach ourselves to a problem we might cure. We have to stop giving out white feathers to our menfolk and to the boys in our care. An agenda for women might be:

- Learn to recognize and carry your own negative feelings, not just the loving helpful ones, but those of anger, envy, greed, jealousy, and so on. And then forgive yourself and learn how to deal with them.

- Learn to recognize what you do with blame: when you direct it towards yourself, and how that makes you feel; and when you direct it towards others, and the feelings of helplessness that can result.

- Learn that you can't make your relationship all right all on your own. Dare to hand over some of the responsibility to your partner. Be honest about what that feels like – scary maybe?

- And where it really is just his problem (for example, with addiction or sexual deviance), declare yourself defeated and hand over the lot. Notice how that makes you feel.

- Learn to recognize your partner's pain, and not to see it as something to do with you, or something you can fix with effort.

- Practise making boundaries: decide on what's enough, what's unacceptable, and stick to it. Get some help in doing this at first, especially if it seems too hard.

- Recognize that relationships are never perfect, but at best just good enough. Accept that you'll never be the perfect wife, daughter or mother (but just good enough) and this will reduce your guilt and make you more tolerant of others.

- Practise the exercises in the book: they might not always mend your marriage, but they may at least help you to live alone if this is necessary.

An Agenda for Couples

SOME THINGS you have to do as individuals, and some things you ought to do together if your marriage is going to be truly satisfying. However, it's impossible to change something in one partner without its affecting the other one, and this isn't always easy to predict. For example, when an extremely obese wife lost an enormous amount of weight, her husband felt disconnected and lonely; being unable now to joke about her fat, he needed to learn new ways to communicate. And when an alcoholic husband finally stopped drinking, his wife became depressed because the whole direction of her helpful activity now had no purpose, and she had to find a new one.

But there are also ways to develop together as a couple, many of them described throughout the book. Above all, you need to spend time in each other's company. This doesn't mean that you have to be intensely talking about your marriage, but it might mean that you're both reading and sharing your impressions, or gardening or walking. It's shared time that creates a shared experience, one that you can discuss, interpret for each other, or merely savour: a building block for marriage.

Alongside this togetherness comes separateness. One man said: 'If only we could have been more separate, more independent, we would have stayed together.' It's the separateness that the poet and philosopher Kahlil Gibran saw as essential in marriage and wrote about in *The Prophet*:

> Love one another, but make not a bond of love:
> Let it rather be a moving sea between the shores of
>   your souls.
> Fill each other's cup but drink not from one cup.
> Give one another of your bread but eat not from the
>   same loaf.

Although marriage urges us back to a childlike dependency, we aren't children any longer, and we have to learn an adult way of being with someone we love. If we don't then all the fear and anger at needing someone and yet not wanting to, will spoil the relationship. Marriage is an opportunity to heal those childhood conflicts: it can teach us that two adults who are developed as separate individuals can come together and depend upon each other if and when they need, knowing that they can survive without the other. We all get it wrong at times, and slip back to wanting more of this or that, but through marriage we can work it out again. One can be parent and one can be child, if and when the need arises. So long as the roles aren't constant and it's not always just one of you who plays mum and dad, then the whole process can only be therapeutic. So long as you are honest with your feelings about this, and don't blame the other one for caring for you in ways that make you think of mum – your problem, not your partner's – then your marriage can only grow better.

Learn to recognize when your marriage is getting too close, too oppressive; and when it's getting too remote, too cool, and work out ways, together or individually, to take a step back or a step nearer. The distance in a relationship changes all the time, but the more attentive you are to this, the shorter the road you'll need to travel to make it OK again. It's only when you leave it till you're clinging (or being clung to) suffocatingly that the reaction is to run a mile.

Unfortunately most couples seek help for an ailing marriage only when it's on its last legs. Up till then men deal with its problems through avoidance (work, alcohol, sport, etc), while women deal with them by taking the responsibility to change things all by themselves. Neither method is particularly good. If you've tried the various exercises in this book, and still things don't feel right, then get help – the sooner the better. Honestly, it's a sign of strength, not of weakness.

An Agenda for Parents

WE CAN make changes in ourselves, even though they may be small, and these will pass on as an inheritance for the benefit of our children. Without tackling ourselves, it's very hard to make sure that the messages reach them, even if we know what they should be. But it's over generations that these developments have to take place, not overnight. So every little thing we can do to make being a man or being a woman better for them, is really doing something for the world.

What some parents think they should do for their children is to make them fit to deal with the world as it is, and they do this quite consciously and with good intentions. The rest of us do it subtly and more often unconsciously. So we teach our girls to give in, to bottle up anger, to accept men's behaviour and the status quo. We teach boys to hit back, to control, to compete, to take it like a man. Even for those who try hard not to give such lessons, some of it will come across from almost every father and every mother in the land. And, of course, I include myself in that. Whatever we miss is more than compensated for by the gender lessons that take place in our schools, both from the children and from the teachers themselves.

I don't think that this is the best we can do for our children. I believe that if we looked at our own unhappiness, difficulties in relationships, bottled up anger that eats us up or spreads itself to those around us, then we would know that we want something better for our children, and this will mean letting them be male and female in ways that we won't permit in ourselves. It may feel like taking risks, but I promise that it won't turn them into homosexuals. If they want to be gay, they will be that even if you force your sons into the Marines and your daughters into the *Tatler*. But really, our deep fear for our children is not so much that our girls will put on trousers and join the army; it is much more that our boys will put on lipstick and bat their eyelashes.

Bringing Up Boys

IF YOUR boys behave in ways that don't seem quite manly, as you've been taught to define it, then use this as a means to explore the feelings it produces in you. Try to understand where these come from, rather than trying to convey to him

248

that behaving like that will get him rejected by the fraternity he's joined and, of course, by you. It's that fraternity, the men's club, that's wrong, not your lad: it's the silly passwords, rules, ceremonies and terror of the outsider that need changing, not the boys who flaunt its laws.

As a father you are going to be the model that he'll copy when he leaves his mum and steps across to the world of men. What this means is that first of all, you'll have to be there. If you're not, he's going to model himself on the fantasy men around him, on action man, on Rambo, on the super-hero of his computer screen. And, presuming you are there for him, you then have to try your damnedest to be the sort of dad you wish you'd had yourself: he would have been kind, affectionate, companionable and easy to please. He would have been strong, but shown in ways that were never threatening or violent. He would have shown you how to do things, and taken you on fishing trips or walking. Not only do men agree with ease on what a good dad is like, the research backs it up that this is the sort of father that helps to produce the creative, contented and loving adult, whether male or female. It isn't a mystery.

You won't do all this perfectly, but you can try. Change will happen if we just do better than we were done by. What matters even more is that you don't fall into the trap of giving your son as good as you got – the 'It never did me any harm' form of cruelty, for example. It's this that perpetuates the unhappiness of the status quo.

As a mother, you need to make sure that you are not forcing your son into this same mould of masculinity that your father and your husband demonstrate to you. If it's not truly making all of you happy and good to be with, then why should it suit your son any better. It's so easy to tolerate 'typically masculine' behaviour from your husband just because your father gave it to your mother and to you, and then actually to encourage it in your son – just because you know no other way. But now you do, and at heart you always did.

Your task in helping a son to step across to masculinity is to let him go. To be there when he wants to step back, but then to let him go again. This is not so easy, because what you fear most is rejection, and so you really want to cling and stop him going. Letting him go doesn't just 'make a man of him'; much more importantly, it stops his fear of dependency, of feeling smothered by a woman which will mar his adult sexual relationships when he's older; it stops the guilt he feels towards you that will find its way out in anger towards your sex. Your task, as one of that sex, is to let him know that he's great, a potentially sexy man, but that you are not his partner and you never will be. That he can go, and you'll enjoy his accomplishments from the security of your own independence.

Bringing Up Daughters

THE AGENDA for women I've outlined above is also an agenda for the parents of daughters. Teach them that they can enjoy being a woman without having to act like a stereotype: they'll learn that easily if you model it for them yourselves. Teach them to set limits for what they should put up with and to recognize when things have gone too far. Make sure, of course, that you are not more tolerant of boys' or men's behaviour than you are of girls' or women's: 'That's all right in a man, but . . .'

Above all, give them the ability to value their independence. This will not only allow them to live better on their own, but it will paradoxically improve their relationships with men, taking away the fear of being smothered, as well as removing the woman's fear of having to tolerate everything just in case she is abandoned. Again, the best way to teach this as a mother is to model it yourself; as a father you need to show that independence is a virtue you appreciate, both in daughters and in wives. Finally, as a mother, you have to be able to let your daughter go – even gently push her from the nest – just as much as you do your boys. Unlike them, she has had no practice in stepping away, in separating, in creating that first boundary, and you have to make that all right for her, just as you did with your sons.

As a father, you have to let her know how much you appreciate her, but also make it clear that there is a barrier to this – that you and her mother (or stepmother) are a unit, distinct from her. Let her know that you're pleased that she's appreciated by other men, and that you are happy for her to enjoy more fully her relationship with another man. You think she's a great woman, but you're happy to give her away!

It's not at all easy to do any of these, let alone all of them, whether for daughters or for sons. In the conflicts that come during a distressing marriage, it's especially easy to forget your children's needs. Making an effort together to save a marriage, especially if you succeed, is a wonderful message for them to take into their adult lives. It tells them that marriage can be a struggle, but that difficulties can be overcome.

You'll do all this as imperfectly as anyone else, and that's all right. But trying consistently to detach yourselves from your own parenting and to do better by your own children is the only way we'll change ourselves and eventually change the world. We can each of us stir the cauldron of humanity in ways that will produce a new spirit that just might be more at peace with itself than any which have come before.

References
and Bibliography

Beck, A. T. *Love is Never Enough* (Penguin, 1988)

Benjamin, J. *The Bonds of Love*: Psychoanalysis, Feminism, and the Problem of Domination (Virago, 1990)

Block, J. H. and Gjerde, P. F. *Journal of Personality and Social Psychology* **60**, 726–738 (1991)

Broverman, I. K. et al. 'Sex Role stereotypes and Clinical Judgment of Mental Health' *Journal of Consulting and Clinical Psychology* **34**, 1–7 (1970)

Clulow, C. and Mattinson, J. *Marriage Inside Out: Understanding Problems of Intimacy* (Penguin, 1989)

Daldrup, R. J. and Gust, D. *Freedom from Anger* (Pocket Books, 1990)

Fincham, F. D. and Bradbury, T. N. 'Marital Satisfaction, Depression and Attributions: A Longitudinal Analysis' *Journal of Personality and Social Psychology* **64**, 442–452 (1993)

Fiske, S. 'Controlling Other People: The Impact of Power on Stereotypicing' *American Psychologist* **48**, 621–629 (1993)

Forward, S. *Men Who Hate Women and the Women Who Love Them* (Bantam Books, 1986)

Franz, C. E., McLelland, D. C. and Weinberger, J. 'Childhood Antecedents of Conventional Social Accomplishment in Mid-life Adults: A thirty-six year prospective study' (1991)

French, M. *The War Against Women* (Hamish Hamilton, 1992)

Gibran, K. *The Prophet* (Penguin, 1926)

Gottman, J. M. and Krokoff, L. J. 'Marital Interaction and Satisfaction: A Longitudinal View' *Journal of Consulting and Clinical Psychology* **57**, 47–52 (1989)

Kayser, K. *When Love Dies: The Process of Marital Disaffection* (Guildford Press, 1993)

Keen, Sam *Fire in the Belly: On Being a Man* (Piatkus, 1992)

Kimmel, M. S. *Changing Men: New Directions in Research on Men and Masculinity* (Sage Publications, 1987)

Kupers, T. A. *Revisioning Men's Lives: Gender, Intimacy and Power* (Guildford Press, 1993)

Lederer, W. J. and Jackson, D. D. *The Mirages of Marriage* (New York, Norton, 1968)

Lederer, W. *The Fear of Women* (New York, Grune & Stratton, 1968)

Margolin, G. 'Building Marital Trust and Treating Sexual Problems' in A. S. Gurman (ed.) *The Casebook of Marital Therapy* (Guildford Press, 1985)

Morgan, F. *A Misogynist's Source Book* (Jonathan Cape, 1989)

Nicholson, John *Men and Women: How Different Are They?* (Oxford University Press, 1993)

Norwood, R. *Women Who Love Too Much* (Arrow, 1986)

Phillips, A. *The Trouble With Boys: Parenting the Men of the Future* (Pandora, 1993)

Rusbult, C. E. 'Responses to Dissatisfaction in Close Relationships: The Exit-voice-loyalty-neglect Model' in D. Perlman and S. Duck (eds.) *Intimate relationships: Development, Dynamics, and Deterioration* (Newbury Park, Sage, 1987)

Scholtenberg, John *Refusing to be a Man* (Fontana, 1990)

Segal, L. 'Sensual Uncertainty, or Why the Clitoris is Not Enough' in S. Cartledge and J. Ryan (eds.) *Sex & Love* (Women's Press, 1983)

Segal, L. *Slow Motion: Changing Masculinities, Changing Men* (Virago, 1990)

Stafford, D. and Hodgkinson, L. *Codependency: How to Break Free and Live Your Own Life* (Piatkus, 1991)

Tannen, D. *That's Not What I Meant!* (Virago, 1992)

Tannen, D. *You Just Don't Understand: Women and Men in Conversation* (Virago, 1992)

Thompson, K. (ed.) *Views From the Male World* (Aquarian Press, 1992)

Thorne, B. *Gender Play: Girls and Boys in School* (Buckingham, Open University Press, 1993)

Tysoe, M. *Love Isn't Quite Enough* (Fontana, 1992)

Rachel Swift
Women's Pleasure £4.99

Q: Who should read this book?
A: Every woman in the world
    (And every woman's man!)

If you've never had an orgasm – this book will tell you how.

If you only have an orgasm sometimes – this book will double your score. (And, if you're a man – this book will help you become the sort of man a woman wants in her bed . . .)

'Her advice is simple, friendly and explicit and has worked wonders'   THE DAILY MIRROR

'A sizzling book'   SUNDAY WORLD

'A sex manual which makes Jackie Collins' novels look tame'   THE DAILY RECORD

'The nicest sex book I have ever read'   Celia Brayfield, SUNDAY EXPRESS

'Her frankness and humour makes the discussion compelling'   NEW ZEALAND DOCTOR

Rachel Swift
Fabulous Figures £9.99

Absolutely everything you need to know about dieting . . . that no one dared to tell you.

Rachel Swift, author of the international bestseller *Women's Pleasure or How to have an Orgasm . . . as often as you want* now turns her incisive pen to dieting and the fabulous figures all women (and men) dream about. This is the most surprising book about your body that you'll ever read.

Controversial, humorous and often shocking, *Fabulous Figures or How to be Utterly Uniquely Gorgeous* is essential reading for all women who have ever had even a passing thought about their figures.

All Pan Books are available at your local bookshop or newsagent, or can be ordered direct from the publisher. Indicate the number of copies required and fill in the form below.

Send to: Pan C. S. Dept
               Macmillan Distribution Ltd
               Houndmills Basingstoke RG21 2XS

or phone: 0256 29242, quoting title, author and Credit Card number.

Please enclose a remittance* to the value of the cover price plus £1.00 for the first book plus 50p per copy for each additional book ordered.

*Payment may be made in sterling by UK personal cheque, postal order, sterling draft or international money order, made payable to Pan Books Ltd.

Alternatively by Barclaycard/Access/Amex/Diners

Card No.

Expiry Date

_____
Signature

Applicable only in the UK and BFPO addresses.

While every effort is made to keep prices low, it is sometimes necessary to increase prices at short notice. Pan Books reserve the right to show on covers and charge new retail prices which may differ from those advertised in the text or elsewhere.

NAME AND ADDRESS IN BLOCK LETTERS PLEASE

. . . .

Name _____

Address _____

_____

_____

6/92